SOFTWARE SYSTEM DEVELOPMENT
A gentle introduction

SECOND EDITION

THE McGRAW-HILL
INTERNATIONAL SERIES IN SOFTWARE ENGINEERING

Consulting Editor

Professor D. Ince
The Open University

Titles in this Series

Further titles in this series are listed at the back of the book

SOFTWARE SYSTEM DEVELOPMENT
A gentle introduction

Second Edition

Carol Britton
Principal Lecturer
University of Hertfordshire

Jill Doake
Senior Lecturer
Anglia Polytechnic University

The McGraw-Hill Companies

London · New York · St Louis · San Francisco · Auckland
Bogotá · Caracas · Lisbon · Madrid · Mexico · Milan
Montreal · New Delhi · Panama · Paris · San Juan
São Paulo · Singapore · Sydney · Tokyo · Toronto

Published by
McGraw-Hill Publishing Company
Shoppenhangers Road, Maidenhead, Berkshire, SL6 2QL, England
Telephone 01628 23432
Fax 01628 770224

British Library Cataloguing in Publication Data
Britton, Carol
  Software systems development: a gentle introduction. – 2nd ed.
  1. Computer software – Development 2. System design
  I. Title II. Doake, Jill
  005.1

ISBN 0–07–709224–4

Library of Congress Cataloging-in-Publication Data
Britton, Carol,
Software system development : a gentle introduction / Carol Britton,
Jill Doake. – 2nd ed.
    p.   cm. – (The McGraw-Hill international series in software engineering)
Includes bibliographical references.
ISBN 0–07–709224–4
1. Computer software – Development.   2. System Design.
I. Doake, Jill.   II. Title.   III. Series.
QA76.76.D47B75   1996
005.1–dc20   96–9028   CIP

McGraw-Hill

A Division of The *McGraw-Hill* Companies

12345 BL 99876

Typeset by Computape (Pickering) Ltd, North Yorkshire
and printed and bound in Great Britain by the University Press, Cambridge

Printed on permanent paper in compliance with ISO Standard 9706

For
Christopher Doake
and
Oliver Britton

CONTENTS

PREFACE TO THE FIRST EDITION

Why yet another book on software system development? In our teaching we have found many useful books on individual topics, but no one volume which covers the whole subject at a level suitable for our students. We hope that this book will be helpful as a course text for two main groups: those studying system development at HND level and students of related subjects such as business studies, management and accountancy. The book is also designed for use as pre-reading on degree and conversion MSc courses in Computer Science. Finally, we have tried to present the material in such a way that the book can be read by clients who are considering installing or upgrading a computer system and want to understand the development process.

The book follows the development of a system from the initial idea through to the completed software product. It is designed to be worked through from start to finish, but for those who are interested in particular topics, it can be used as a reference manual since each chapter can be read in isolation. In this case it is advisable to read the introductory material on the Just a Line system in Chapter 1.

No technical knowledge is assumed; where computer terminology is used, this is explained in the glossary at the back of the book. As this book is written for newcomers to software system development, we aim to present an overall view of the subject. Some topics are discussed at an introductory level only, with suggestions for further reading at the end of each chapter. A full biography with comments can be found at the back of the book.

We would like to thank members of the Computer Science departments at the University of Hertfordshire and Anglia Polytechnic University: the staff for ideas and encouragement and the students for acting as willing guinea pigs. In particular, a major debt of gratitude is due to Juliet Brown for all the teaching material that she has so generously put at our disposal. On a more personal level, this book would never have been finished without the encouragement and support of our husbands. Finally, our children: they remained unmoved and mildly and amused by the whole process, but we are grateful to them for enabling us to keep a sense of perspective and not allowing the book to take over!

Carol Britton
Jill Doake

PREFACE TO THE SECOND EDITION

The whole area of software system development is changing rapidly. New methods and techniques to support the development process appear almost weekly and advanced technologies, such as multimedia and the Internet, are now household words. In spite of this, we feel that much of the basic material in the first edition of the book is still relevant, in particular the importance of sound engineering principles and techniques in the development of software systems.

One of our main aims, in this as in the first edition, has been to make the material accessible to beginners in system development and to non-computer specialists. Increasing numbers of people today are coming into contact with computer systems and need to know something about how such systems are developed. We hope that this book is simple enough to give these readers a clear introduction to the topic and interesting enough to make them wish to follow up our suggestions for further reading.

There are several changes in the new edition: the main ones are a new chapter on requirements capture, the division of the chapter on structured techniques into three separate chapters and an extended section on object orientation. We have also made numerous smaller changes throughout the main text, the bibliography and the glossary in order to bring the book up to date. In addition we have added more exercises, particularly in Chapters 4 and 5.

Once again, there are many people whom we would like to thank for their help and support, in particular Amanda Derrick, Mike Herman and Sara Jones at the University of Hertfordshire and Jo Stanley at Anglia Polytechnic University. We are also grateful to the users of the first edition and to the anonymous reviewers who made helpful and constructive comments. Finally, a big thank you is due to our families for putting up with another round of the book—one day they might even be tempted to read it.

Carol Britton
Jill Doake

LIST OF TRADEMARKS

Apple Macintosh Apple Computer Inc.
Automate Learmouth & Burchett Management Systems Plc.
dbaseIII Ashton-Tate Corporation
Eiffel Interactive Software Engineering Inc.
Excelerator Index Technology Corporation
Formalizer Logica UK Ltd.
IBM PC International Business Machines Corporation
MacWrite II Apple Macintosh
IEF Texas Instruments
IEW KnowledgeWare Inc.
Information Engineering James Martin Associates
JSD Michael Jackson
Lotus 1-2-3 Lotus Development Corporation
MacWrite II Apple Macintosh
Microsoft Excel Microsoft Corporation
Microsoft Office Microsoft Corporation
Multiplan Microsoft Corporation
MS–DOS Microsoft Corporation
Netscape Navigator Netscape Communications Corporation
SSADM Central Computer & Telecommunications Agency
Smalltalk ParcPlace Systems
Software Through Pictures Interactive Development Environment
Symphony Lotus Development Corporation
Teamwork Cadre Technologies, Inc.
UNIX AT & T
Windows 95 Microsoft Corporation
Word Microsoft Corporation
WordStar MicroPro International
Yourdon Yourdon Inc.

INTRODUCTION

This chapter serves as a route map for the rest of the book. In it we introduce the Just a Line case study, which is used for examples and exercises throughout the book. We then give an overview of the system development process, from the client's first tentative statement of the problem to delivery of the software system. We include a general description of what is meant by the word 'system' and a specific definition of the way it is used in this book. A summary is given outlining the contents of each chapter in the book. Finally, we include an interview with Harry and Sue of the Just a Line Company which gives further details about the problems and what they hope a software system can do for them.

1.1 INTRODUCTION TO THE JUST A LINE CASE STUDY

In the autumn of 1987 Harry Preston went up to university to study Psychology. Looking back, he was never really sure why—except that he was offered a place and it seemed like a good idea at the time. His three years at university were very busy ones, spent mainly on the rugby pitch, in bed or in the pub. While these activities were certainly character building, they did little to enhance his store of knowledge of psychology, the sum total of which lamentably failed to impress the examiners in his final year exams. He went down in 1990 with a third class degree, which worried him not a bit—though it caused his mother considerable social discomfort.

Harry's time at university was not entirely wasted. In the pub one evening he met Sue, a student at a local teacher training college, and was luckily still sober enough to ask her out the following night. They were married in the summer of 1990 and set up home in a tiny and very run-down Victorian terrace house in a Hertfordshire village. The only cloud on the horizon was that employers did not seem to be particularly impressed by Harry's work record—or lack of it. After six months of Harry's fruitless searching for a job Sue realized that drastic action was needed. She gave up her teaching post at the local school, withdrew all their savings from the building society and set up their own company, Just a Line, specializing in designing personalized postcards and selling them by mail order.

It is now six years on and the venture has proved to be a great success. Just a Line postcards range from 'Classic' (plain while with the customer's address printed discreetly across the top) to 'The Real You', which are personalized card and envelope sets with a design from the Just a Line range on the back of the card. Card designs are selected from the company list, which includes such items as old masters, botanical studies and famous quotations. Sue has the organizing ability to run the company and Harry has proved to have a distinct flair for picking popular lines—his 'Endangered Flora of the Hedgerows' and 'What the Butler Saw' ranges proved real winners. Harry and Sue moved two years ago into another run-down cottage, but larger this time and with two outhouses in the garden. These they have turned into a store-cum-shop with a view to developing the local side of their operations.

However, mail order remains the bulk of their business. At present, most of this is done by phone, which is time-consuming and inefficient, especially if the shop happens to be busy. The Prestons have a list of card types and prices which is updated regularly, but have not yet got round to organizing a proper mailing list of regular and potential customers. The card list is given to anyone who asks for a copy and is displayed in strategic positions locally, such as libraries and village halls. The company advertises weekly in the local paper and in the national press two or three times before Christmas. This has proved increasingly worth while, with the result that large retailers such as John Lewis and W. H. Smith are beginning to show an interest in selling a selection of the postcards.

While delighted with this development, the Prestons realize that a move into this type of market will have a considerable effect on the way they run the company. Their present rather casual methods of ordering, stock control and accounting will need to be tightened up and a more professional approach will have to be taken overall.

Since they are keen to make the most of the new marketing opportunities, Harry and Sue decide that the necessary reorganization will be greatly helped by introducing a computer into at least part of the organization. They consult a local firm of system developers who specialize in the computerization of small businesses, and agree that one of their staff will investigate the possibility of developing a computer system for Just a Line.

The rest of this book uses the Just a Line case study to illustrate the work of a software system developer.

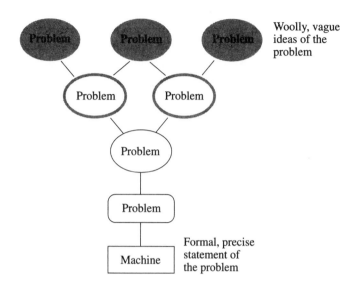

Figure 1.1 A view of the development process

1.2 DEVELOPING SYSTEMS

System development is a gradual progression from the client's initial vague ideas about the problem, via a series of transitional stages to a completely formal statement, expressed in a programming language, which can be executed on a machine. A diagram of the whole process can be seen in Fig 1.1. At each stage the problem is expressed in an appropriate modelling technique, notation or language.

Traditionally, system developers have worked within the context of a frame-work or methodology which provides an agreed structure for the development process. Normally, an organization will adopt a specific method of approach to developing a project which they may refer to as the system or project life cycle, methodology or project plan. This framework provides a standard method of approach to the system developer's work which is specified and documented before work starts. The same framework or methodology will generally be used for all projects developed within the organization.

However, it is increasingly being realized that different applications require different approaches. The approach used for a particular piece of software should be the one most suitable for the type of system being developed, the client, the developers and the techniques they have at their disposal. System developers are becoming aware that it is impossible for one single development methodology to prescribe how to tackle the great variety of tasks and situations encountered. The diversity of applications undertaken means that there cannot be a universal ideal way of developing systems. Rather than forcing a rigid methodology to fit unsuitable applications, system developers are beginning to realize that it may be more appropriate to have a tool-box process. For each a new application, a suitable selection of techniques, skills and approaches may be selected.

1.3   WHAT IS A SYSTEM?

It is beyond the scope of this book to embark on a detailed discussion of system theory; the interested reader will find a fuller account in Yourdon (1989). However, it will be useful at this stage to have a working definition of the word system. If we look at some examples of systems:

- Solar system
- Digestive system
- Public transport system
- Central heating system
- Computer system

we might arrive at the tentative definition: a system is a set of objects or elements which are viewed as a whole. On its own, this is inadequate for our purposes because we are concerned only with systems that are man-made, and therefore under human control, and that have a purpose—otherwise the system cannot be designed by a system developer. This rules out the solar system (no known purpose) and the digestive system (not under human control). An improved definition therefore would be: a system is a set of objects or elements which are viewed as a whole and designed to achieve a purpose.

Another essential feature in our view of systems is that the elements of a system have a relationship to one another, they work together in some way. A heap of stones, for example, although it may be man-made and have the purpose of marking the top of a hill, does not qualify as a system because the elements do not have a significant relationship to one another. If you take one stone from the pile, it does not matter much to the others. In a system this would matter. If you remove the train service from the public transport system, it puts pressure on the other services—it affects them. If you remove the boiler from the central heating system, the system will not work. For our purposes, therefore, the definition of a system we need is: a system is an interrelated set of objects or elements which are viewed as a whole and designed to achieve a purpose.

We must add to this definition that a system has a boundary. The system in question lies inside the boundary; outside the boundary is the environment with which the system interacts. Sometimes the boundary of a system is clear and obvious. If we view a person as a system the boundary is clear—normally one person is clearly separate from another and from the environment; similarly with a car. In computer systems, however, it is usually hard to define the boundary; it is dictated by which elements we choose to think of as being within the system, and which as being part of the environment. The normal rule is that inside the system are things the system is designed to control; outside the boundary are things the system is not designed to control. The boundary may be set because we cannot design-in control: in a central heating system the weather must be considered to be outside the boundary as we cannot control it. The boundary may also be set because we choose not to include certain elements. This choice may be dictated by:

- Money constraints. We may find it will cost too much to computerize more than a limited set of system functions.
- Time constraints. The more functions we computerize the longer it will take.
- Resources available. We may, for example, have to work on existing machines with limited storage space and computing power.
- Cost effectiveness. Sometimes very limited benefits are gained from expensive computerization.

The environment is defined as being the surrounding conditions, outside the boundary, which affect the system and are affected by it but not controlled by it. We might define the weather conditions as being part of the environment of a central heating system.

When we talk about a system we understand by this term that it is a set of objects or elements which are viewed as a whole and designed to achieve a purpose; it has a boundary within which it lies and outside of which is the environment. The purpose or objectives of the system are important to define; different users will want different things from the system. From the outset, the system developer must be clear about the purpose of the system as this is what will define the design. The boundary in computer systems is often hard to define; the system designer and user together must decide what is to be included in the system.

When we refer to a *system* in this book we base our understanding on the above description, but more specifically we interpret the word as comprising the software, documentation, method of operation, hardware, users and operators which together make up the software system.

1.4 CONTENTS OF THE BOOK

In this book, although traditional frameworks and methodologies are discussed, we concentrate on the most widely used modelling tools and techniques and examine alternative approaches to the development process. Issues relevant to the later stages of system development and project management are also covered. Chapter 2 outlines the main stages in the traditional approach to developing systems and relates these to the concept of a methodology. Chapter 3 discusses requirements capture. In Chapters 4, 5 and 6 traditional modelling techniques are introduced and illustrated with examples from the Just a Line case study. More recent tools, techniques and approaches: prototyping, CASE tools, formal notations and object orientation are discussed in Chapter 7. Once modelling has been completed and implementation issues have been considered, many new factors become relevant; these are discussed in Chapter 8. Chapter 9 covers the final stages of development and what happens after delivery of the system. Finally, Chapter 10 provides an introduction to simple project management techniques.

EXERCISES AND TOPICS FOR DISCUSSION

1.1 Discuss whether each of the following is a system according to the definition given in this chapter:

- An egg
- A television
- A business organization
- A painting
- A computer

For each of the above that you consider to be a system, discuss where the system boundary lies.

1.2 What are the systems that have the most influence on your life?

1.3 There are many different models of the systems life cycle. Look at some books on systems development and compare the different versions of the life cycle that you find in them. Make a short list of the most common life cycle models.

1.4 Imagine that you have been asked to design an information system for your local area. Discuss the factors that will influence your choice of boundary for the system.

REFERENCES AND FURTHER READING

Carter, R., Martin, J., Mayblin, B. and Munday, M. (1988) *Systems, Management and Change—A Graphic Guide*, Paul Chapman in association with The Open University

Edwards, P. (1993) *Systems Analysis and Design*, McGraw-Hill, Watsonville, Calif.

Skidmore, S. (1994) *Introducing Systems Analysis*, 2nd edn, NCC Blackwell, Manchester.

Yeates, D., Shields, M. and Helmy, D. (1994) *Systems Analysis and Design*, Pitman, London.

Yourdon, E. (1989) *Modern Structured Analysis*, Prentice-Hall, Englewood Cliffs. N.J.

2

FRAMEWORKS AND APPROACHES

Traditionally, the development of a system is divided into several main stages. The progression of a system through these stages is known as the system life cycle. In this chapter we discuss the reasons for splitting up the system development in this way and the general nature and content of the stages.

There is no single generally accepted life cycle. Various methodologies have evolved which do precisely define the stages into which the development process should be split and the exact sequence of tasks to be performed at each stage. A methodology gives a recipe for the development of systems. We introduce the concept of a methodology and discuss the advantages and disadvantages of using one.

2.1 THE SYSTEM LIFE CYCLE

The rapid increase in the power, speed and capacity of computers over the last four decades has encouraged software developers to attempt to develop ever more ambitious systems. First attempts, in the sixties and early seventies, to develop large and complex systems were discouraging: typically, systems were delivered years late, over budget, were unreliable, difficult to maintain and did not do what was required. These problems were so prevalent that this time came to be known as the *software crisis*. It was realized that solving big problems needed new methods—not scaled-up versions of techniques used for solving small problems. The system life cycle (Fig. 2.1) was an attempt to establish a structured approach to systems analysis and design; system developers started to introduce rigour into their method of producing software. They aimed to be able to deliver their product with the same stamp of reliability as more established professions, such as civil engineering or architecture, could deliver theirs.

The system life cycle divided the development of a system into stages. It specified the general nature of the activities involved at each stage, the

Problem definition

Feasibility study

Analysis

System design

Detailed design

Implementation

Maintenance

Figure 2.1 Stages in a typical system life cycle

sequence in which these activities should be ordered and the output or deliverables from each stage. There were several advantages to this approach to system development. The activities involved at each stage were defined, documented and agreed. This helped when training new staff, and among established staff it meant that a consistent approach to system development was achieved. Communication between teams of system developers was also improved by adopting an agreed approach. For managers, the advantage was that each stage could be used as a milestone. Managers could put a date to that milestone and use it to monitor the development of the project. Having the activities involved at each stage specified beforehand brought tremendous advantages in terms of estimating the timescale for the project, costing and controlling the system development (see Chapter 10).

Computer science is a young discipline which is still evolving. It has never agreed on a single right way to develop a system and, given the enormous diversity in the types of system it tackles, it probably never will. However, most structured system development approaches do partition the development process into a more or less agreed sequence of stages. The client's requirements are investigated, expressed and agreed in logical terms before decisions about the implementation are made. This means that the system is initially designed in terms of what it must do—for example record orders and keep track of changes of address—before deciding how—for example use a network of PCs and a database package. At the logical stage, the design is deliberately expressed in non-technical terms so that it can be understood and checked by the client. Once the logical design is agreed, the physical design can be tackled; at this stage the system developer proposes the hardware and software that will meet the client requirements. When this design is agreed the system can be implemented.

Stages in the system life cycle

As previously stated, there is no one definitive system life cycle: the stages in a typical life cycle are shown in Fig. 2.1. The output or product of each stage in the life cycle is known as its deliverable. In the early stages, the deliverables will be reports or documents describing first the existing and then the new system. At the end of each stage in the life cycle there is normally a review meeting with the client to examine the deliverables of that stage for correctness and to make a decision about whether or not to continue with the project. Deliverables produced at the end of one stage normally serve as working documents for the next stage until, in the final stages, the deliverable is the system itself. Deliverables also form part of the documentation of the system.

The content of each stage—the steps and activities involved—will vary from one practitioner to the next. If a standard methodology (see below) is used, precise details are given as to what should be done and what techniques should be used. A rough guide to the nature of each stage in the life cycle is outlined below.

Problem definition

The problem definition provides an initial description of the problem area by means of a written statement of the client's current problem and the objectives of the new system. It is normally produced after an initial meeting with the client, and it documents the system developer's understanding of the situation at that stage. The problem definition must be agreed with the client before progressing to the next stage. It provides a firm foundation for the rest of the project, ensuring that the right problem is being tackled. It normally takes the form of a report, divided into sections. Typically, the following points will be outlined:

- The problem, as stated by the client and interpreted by the developer
- The objectives of the new system
- The scope and size of the project—which areas are to be considered, who will be involved
- Preliminary ideas, from both the client and the developer, on how the system might be developed
- Recommended action for the next stage in the development of the system

Figure 2.2 shows an initial problem definition for the Just a Line system. The problem definition forms the basis of the problems and requirements list (see Chapter 9) which records all problems and requirements mentioned by clients in interviews, or which are subsequently discovered during analysis of the system.

PROBLEM DEFINITION—Just a Line

Problems

- Taking orders by telephone: difficult, time consuming and error prone as customers normally do not have list of card designs or prices. This will get worse as business increases.
- Lack of an efficient marketing strategy.
- Only one supplier who may let the company down.
- Haphazard stock control.

Objectives

- To ensure that customer orders are processed efficiently.
- To ensure that ordering is made easier for customers.
- To improve company advertising and marketing.
- To improve stock control to provide accurate information about current stocks, current stock requirements, identification of fast/slow moving lines and to ensure that at all times there are adequate supplies in stock, of all lines.
- To facilitate future expansion of the business.

Scope

The project will encompass the following areas of the business:

- Order processing
- Sales organization and administration
- Marketing
- Invoicing
- Stock control

The project will not encompass general accounting, payroll, personnel.

Preliminary Ideas

1. Improve the current manual system

   - Use stock control cards with calculated reorder levels and updated stock levels.
   - Compile a mailing list and circulate regularly with typed stock list, price list and order form.
   - Review mailing list regularly to include new customers and remove 'dead' customers.
   - Employ extra staff in key areas, e.g. for driving delivery van, secretarial work.

2. Use of computer

   - Computer(s) may be used to achieve the improvements listed above more efficiently.
   - If more than one computer is required, consider networking.
   - Consider time sharing, using bureau facilities or the equipment of a neighbouring business.

Recommended Action

Produce a feasibility study report to:

1. Investigate and produce recommendations for improved manual systems in each of the areas highlighted by this report.
2. Investigate and produce recommendations for the introduction of computer-based systems for all the areas highlighted by this report.
3. Research the costs and benefits for each proposed system, manual or computerized.

Figure 2.2 Problem definition for Just a Line

The process of discovering and agreeing with the client exactly what the problems are and what the new system is to do is known as requirements capture. In many ways this is the most crucial stage of developing a system: if the developer has got the wrong idea of what the client wants, then all subsequent work on the system is a complete waste of time. Chapter 3 describes some current requirements capture techniques and discusses the principal issues relating to this topic.

Feasibility study

The feasibility study investigates whether there is a practical solution to the problem outlined in the initial problem definition. At this stage there has been very little financial investment in the new project. The feasibility study is a precautionary survey, its purpose being to do just enough preliminary work to establish that the problem is one that can appropriately be tackled by a system development team. If this proves not to be the case, then the project can be abandoned at this stage before any great commitment of funds has been made.

In particular, the feasibility study examines the technical, financial and organizational feasibility of the project:

- Can it be done?
- Can we afford it?
- Will the proposed new system fit in with existing procedures?

The feasibility study will determine the criteria for a successful system and propose and evaluate several alternative solutions. The economic feasibility is of paramount importance and a careful cost–benefit analysis is done for each of the proposed solutions—financial benefits must demonstrably outweigh the costs. Alternative solutions may be assessed in terms of initial financial outlay only, the time it takes to recoup the investment or the long term profitability. Consideration will also be given to what will happen if no new system is developed. Other criteria for success should be specifically listed and may include tangible results—for example 'all orders must be processed within 24 hours' or 'increase by 75 per cent the number of customers using an order form'. Some criteria may be less tangible—for example 'the system must be "pleasant to use"'.

The feasibility study is effectively a high-level superficial run through the rest of the system life cycle, and will involve doing some of the work of all of the subsequent stages, possibly even some implementation. It will certainly involve more exploration of the client requirements and will suggest some ways of implementing the system—that is some alternative solutions with the developer's comments and recommendations.

At the end of this stage a feasibility study report is presented by the system developer to the client and a decision is made whether or not to proceed. The feasibility study report will vary according to the client organization and the system, but will usually contain sections on scope, client objectives, performance requirements, interfacing systems, impact on the organization and other systems, costs, benefits, risks and the consequences of not developing the system. Figure 2.3 shows one possible structure for a feasibility study report.

This used to be a crucial stage in all systems. Feasibility studies often involved a great deal of work and could last several months, with a very real chance of a recommendation at the end of this stage not to proceed with the development of the system. However, as experience of producing systems has accumulated, with advances in hardware and software, improvements in design techniques and advances in technical support for system developers, the feasibility study is not the great milestone that it used to be, and is often omitted or done in a very sketchy fashion.

Analysis

This stage is divided into several sections.

Fact finding The analysis begins with a period of fact finding during which the system developed gradually builds up a detailed picture of the client's current problems and his or her needs and wishes for the new system. This is a continuation of the process of requirements capture that began with the problem definition. Requirements capture is described fully in Chapter 3.

Current physical model Facts will rarely emerge in a neatly ordered fashion. It is much more usual for system developers to discover that they have a mass of detailed, incomprehensible and probably conflicting information. The next job is to sort out what has been discovered and document it in a way that will help organize the material. This must then be discussed with the clients to check that the system developer has correctly understood what was said in the interview, fill in any gaps and resolve any apparent conflicts. The modelling techniques discussed in Chapters 4, 5 and 6 are designed to help the system developer do this. It may be useful to begin by documenting how the system functions currently. In the Just a Line system this will include such details as:

- Orders come in by telephone.
- If Sue wants to check she has enough cards in stock to fill an order, she looks in the store.
- Orders are completed in triplicate and filed in the three-drawer filing cabinet.

Feasibility Study Report

1. Introduction. Project history and background, reference to any preliminary work on the project, agreed terms of reference, problem definition.

2. Definition of boundaries and scope of project. The existing system is described, using such techniques as data flow diagrams and ER models (see Chapters 4 and 5). The boundaries and scope of the investigation are clearly identified. Only high-level overviews of the system are used at this stage; the models will be fleshed out with detail during the analysis stage.

3. Requirements. The new system usually has to do everything the old one does plus solve existing problems and meet new client requirements. All requirements, those carried forward from the existing system and known new requirements, should be identified. This section should include performance requirements for the new system and the specific 'criteria for success' mentioned above. Any constraints should also be listed; for example that the new system must run on existing hardware, interface with existing systems or use specific software.

4. Alternative solutions considered. Usually several possible solutions, several ways of meeting the requirements specified, are outlined in the feasibility study report. The alternatives proposed may have different hardware, software, automation boundaries. They will therefore have different costs, benefits and development timescales. The technical, economic and operational feasibility of each solution will be evaluated. A rough implementation schedule for each solution will be included.

5. Recommendations. Normally the analyst presenting the report will be expected to recommend one of the proposed solutions. Material will be presented to support this recommendation; normally a detailed cost–benefit analysis will be the most important part of the supporting material.

6. Project plan. A fairly detailed development schedule should be produced for the recommended solution. Estimated costs for each stage should be included.

7. Conclusions and recommendations. A clear, concise summary of the report, the conclusions and recommendations will be given. This may be the only part of the report read by a busy manager, so summarize all important issues including main requirements, alternatives considered and rejected, the recommended solution, costs and timescales.

Figure 2.3 Structure for a feasibility study report

Sometimes a system developer will not attempt to document these physical details. Whether or not it is a useful thing to do will depend on the circumstances. If the system developer is tackling a complicated system with many existing interrelated procedures, or if there are many different users with many different and apparently conflicting versions of how the existing system works, or if the developer feels it is particularly important to get right the detailed workings of the existing system, then it is sensible to document such details. Often, the users will respond well to this type of model of the system (see below) because it depicts the system as it currently works, showing physical details they recognize and can relate to.

This model is referred to as the current physical model. Producing a current physical model is extra work and, moreover, some developers feel that if too much attention is paid to how the system currently functions, the new design will be constrained by this view of the system—the developer will be accustomed to seeing the system in one way and will be unable to come up with a radically new and more appropriate design.

Current logical model From the detail of how the existing system works, the developer must extract exactly what the existing system does, as the new system usually must do everything the existing system does plus solve current problems and meet additional client requirements. This second model of the system is known as the current logical model; it confines itself to documenting basic system events—for example that orders come in and are recorded—and omits the physical detail about how the order comes in (by telephone) or how it is recorded (stored in a filing cabinet). The logical events—orders coming in and being recorded—will almost certainly be perpetuated in the new system, which is why the developer needs to record them in the current logical model. The physical details—certainly the fact that orders are recorded in a filing cabinet—we would expect to change if a computerized system is introduced. Therefore, these can be safely dropped from the logical model.

Sometimes a developer will start with the current logical model and omit the current physical model. Sometimes there is no existing system to model and the developer must start at the next stage—the required logical model.

Required logical model The analysis stage moves from the logic of the current system—what the existing system does—to the logic of the required or new system. It aims to specify what must be done to solve the problems and meet the requirements specified in the problem definition and the feasibility study. However, at this stage, analysis must be done without making decisions about how the new system is to function—the design at this stage is implementation independent and can be implemented in several different ways. This is discussed further in Chapter 8. Experience has shown that if implementation decisions are made too soon, the design of the new system can be unnecessarily constrained by the limitations of the hardware or software selected. For example, if the developer decides at an early stage that the system will be implemented using a commercial database package, this may preclude the opportunity to use a file design that would have been more suitable. If the developer is committed from the start to a certain type of computer, this may mean that it is impossible to use a particular item of software that would have been ideal for the system. Sometimes there is no choice in the matter, it may be necessary to use existing client hardware, but if there is a free choice, decisions about implementation issues should not be made at this stage.

The deliverable from this stage is the specification of requirements, a logical model of the required system which states what the system is to do, but says nothing about how the system is to be implemented. The model usually includes data flow diagrams (see Chapter 4) of the required system, a supporting data dictionary, process definitions, a data model and entity life histories of the required system. It may also include preliminary discussions on sizing, performance requirements, security and the user interface.

System design

Once analysis is complete, the next step is to determine how in general the problem is to be solved. The deliverables of the system design stage will be outlines of several different technical solutions which will meet the requirements specified in the previous stage. These alternative solutions usually include:

- A very cheap solution which does the job and no more.
- A medium price solution which does the job well and is convenient for the user; it will probably have additional features the client did not request but which the system developer knows from experience will be needed.
- A high cost solution—everything the client could ever need, but at a price!

Different solutions may have different:

- *System boundaries*. The proposed systems might affect, though not necessarily computerize, different parts of the organization's functions. In Just a Line, one solution might include the accounting functions while another leaves them unchanged.
- *Automation boundaries*. One proposed solution might leave some functions to operate manually, while another computerizes them. In Just a Line a supplier purchase order could be automatically generated when stocks fall low. Alternatively, the new system could simply generate, on request, a weekly list of items that were low in stock, or supplier ordering could remain manual.
- *Hardware*. One solution might propose the use of a minicomputer with several terminals and a laser printer. A cheaper solution might recommend the use of a network of personal computers (PCs) and a dot matrix printer (see Chapter 8).
- *Software*. A traditional programming language like COBOL or Pascal could be used, or an integrated package like SmartWare 11. (Selecting software is discussed in Chapter 8.)
- *Design strategies*. The system developer might propose the development of a system using a traditional life cycle approach or using prototyping (see Chapter 7).

- *User interface*. The design of the user interface will be determined by the type of person using the system. Someone who is not used to computers and who uses the system only occasionally will need more help than someone who has been trained to use computers and sits at a screen all day (see Chapter 8).
- *Costs*. All of the factors discussed above will affect the cost of the system.

Detailed design

By this stage one of the solutions proposed in the previous stage will have been chosen. The new system is now specified in detail—the implementation-independent design of the analysis stage is converted to a design which includes specific hardware and software. This is often referred to as the technical design specification and may include:

- Program design and specification
- Specification of the user interface
- Specification of the layout of reports and other system outputs
- File and record specifications
- Hardware specifications, including costs
- Implementation schedule

Implementation

During this stage the system is physically built: the program code is written and tested, and supporting documentation (see Chapter 9) is produced. The deliverables from this stage of the life cycle include:

- Program listings, test plans and supporting documentation
- Hardware on which the system will run
- Manual or operating procedures
- Manual of clerical procedures
- User manual

The system must then be installed at the clients' site on their equipment and the changeover from the old to the new system supervised (see Chapter 9). This will involve training users and ensuring that the data from the old system is successfully taken on by the new system. There is often a hand-holding period before the new system is formally handed over to the client. Installation is sometimes listed as a separate stage in the life cycle. After installation, the system development team will only be involved in maintaining and modifying the system.

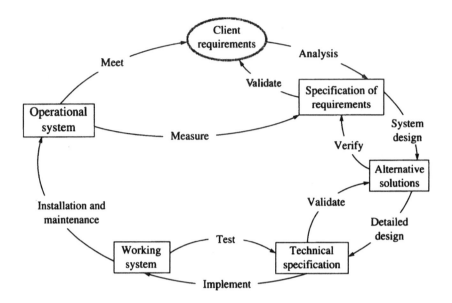

Figure 2.4 Simplified system life cycle

Maintenance

The maintenance stage starts as soon as the system is formally handed over to the client. The term 'maintenance' is often used as a euphemism for finding and correcting errors which were not detected before the system was handed over. True maintenance is modifying the system to meet evolving client requirements. In either case, the system developer must start again at the beginning of the cycle by ascertaining the client requirements. Figure 2.4 models a simplified system life cycle as a completed circle, starting and ending with client requirements. Note also the backward-pointing arrows at each stage which indicate the iterative nature of system development. At each stage the system development team must check back to the requirements specified in the previous stage and re-do the work if necessary.

2.2 METHODOLOGIES

A software development methodology, or structured method, is usually based on a life cycle model of system development and has a number of development phases with a set of steps and rules for each phase. Whereas a life cycle coarsely partitions the development of a system into stages, a methodology takes a life cycle and further divides each of the stages into a number of steps. A methodology will prescribe in great detail what tasks are involved in each step, the nature of each task, the order in which the tasks need to be done, what documents are produced at each stage and what documents are required as input to each stage. In fact, it provides a detailed plan for producing a system.

Why do we need a methodology?

Comparisons are often made between the stages involved in designing and building software and other artefacts such as houses or bridges. Relatively speaking, methodologies for developing software have not been around for very long. However, they embody knowledge and wisdom gained by system developers through trial and error over a number of decades. For example, it is now generally accepted that one of the first and most important tasks in system development is to find out exactly what the new system is required to do. This may involve a detailed and time-consuming study of the existing system. Experience has shown that failure to do this successfully is what causes the type of errors that are hardest to find and most expensive to correct. Most methodologies incorporate this experience by prescribing a set of tasks designed to ensure that client requirements are successfully captured. Non-technical models are drawn that can be discussed with the client, to check that the requirements have been understood.

Building a system involves constructing many different models of the system (see Section 4.1 on modelling). Each model is only a partial description of the system. To understand the whole system, we have to understand how the models relate to and complement each other. A methodology provides a framework, an agreed structure, in which these models can be related to each other.

A methodology provides inexperienced system developers with a recipe to follow. Some methodologies are specifically designed for this purpose. Each step along the development process is prescribed, as are the ingredients, i.e. the required documents for this step and the nature of the output from this step.

Building a system, especially a large and complex system, is a long and complicated process during which a great number of tasks have to be done. Many of the tasks are interdependent; often, large teams of developers will be involved and their work will need to be co-ordinated. Using a methodology helps with the management of the whole project by breaking down the development process into small tasks, specifying the order in which they should be done and the interdependencies of the tasks. This helps with planning, scheduling and monitoring the progress of the system.

Different methodologies

There are many different methodologies, incorporating many different views on how to go about building a system. Different methodologies are suitable for developing different types of systems. Examples of methodologies used for developing real-time systems are those of Yourdon and Hatley and Pirbhai, while methodologies used for developing information systems include SSADM (Structured Systems Analysis and Design Method), JSD and Information Engineering (James Martin). Different methodologies place emphasis on different aspects of system development. Some concentrate on the flow of data through the system, modelled using data flow diagrams; others consider the structuring and interrelationships of the stored data in the system, modelled using entity relationship diagrams, to be of primary importance.

Methodologies are constantly changing to accommodate new technological advances and new ideas in system development. For example, the development of fourth-generation languages (4GLs) and CASE tools, together with a change in client attitudes to system design, has led to the development of radically different approaches to software development. These are discussed in Chapter 7.

There are still many practitioners who firmly believe that the way to produce perfect software consistently is to find the right methodology and make sure the developers stick to it. However, there is a growing body of system developers who believe that to follow blindly a rigid methodology is not appropriate, given the diversity of systems tackled today. They advocate instead a tool-box approach. A craftsman asked to design and build a table will select certain tools for the job and will go about the task in a certain way. If asked to make a picture frame, the craftsman will select some of the same tools and some different ones. The process of constructing the frame is also different in many ways from that of building the table. The system developer, it is believed, should be armed with a tool-box of techniques which might be helpful for developing systems. For each new application appropriate techniques should be used in an appropriate way. Sometimes, an entity–relationship model may be an appropriate starting point, while at other times a data flow diagram may be useful; sometimes both may be used. However, the choice of techniques should be determined by the nature of the problem, not predetermined by a methodology.

SUMMARY

The system life cycle approach was developed in response to the software problems of the sixties and seventies. It partitioned the development of a system into predetermined stages, each of which had to be completed and agreed with the client before progressing to the next stage. The particular contribution this brought to improving the quality of the delivered system was in concentrating more attention on capturing client requirements. It also allowed much more effective project management. Progressing from the coarse partitioning of the life cycle, methodologies refine each of the stages into a prescribed series of activities with precisely defined inputs and outputs. Using a methodology for system development has tremendous advantages in terms of improved communication between clients, system developers and project managers. However, using a single methodology to tackle very different types of system can prove to be an inflexible and inappropriate approach to system development.

EXERCISES AND TOPICS FOR DISCUSSION

2.1 The development of large and complex systems requires a new approach, not a scaled-up version of the techniques used to develop small systems. Discuss.

2.2 List the documents you would expect to examine during the fact-finding stage of the Just a Line system. You will find it helpful to read the interview with Sue and Harry at the end of Chapter 3.

2.3 Once we have discovered the perfect methodology, perfect systems will be developed every time. Discuss.

2.4 Draw a chart which summarizes the stages of the life cycle and the deliverables at each stage.

2.5 Large stores such as John Lewis and W. H. Smith have shown an interest in the Just a Line cards. Amend the problem definition in Fig. 2.2 to show the extra problems this may bring and how the system may solve them.

REFERENCES AND FURTHER READING

Goodland, M. (1995) *SSADM Version 4: A Practical Approach*, McGraw-Hill, London.

Skidmore, S. (1994) *Introducing Systems Analysis*, 2nd edn, NCC Blackwell, Manchester.

Sommerville, I. (1995) *Software Engineering*. 5th edn, Addison-Wesley, Wokingham.

3

REQUIREMENTS CAPTURE

The first task for a system developer in any development project is to find out as much as possible about the client organization and its problems. There are many ways of doing this, such as observing the company at work and studying relevant documents, but often the most effective way is to talk directly to the clients. In this chapter we include an interview with Harry and Sue of the Just a Line Company which gives further details about their problems and what they hope a software system can do for them.

3.1 BACKGROUND

Anecdotal evidence suggests that errors in requirements may account for approximately 50 per cent of the total cost of debugging a software system, yet it is only relatively recently that serious research has been carried out on the subject of requirements capture. In general, traditional system development methodologies, most of which are underpinned by a standard life cycle model, merely pay lip-service to the problems of identifying, describing and validating the client's requirements for the system.

Chapter 2 describes the initial problem definition of a system. In the past this was agreed and signed off by the client, who would then frequently have little more to do with the development process until delivery and installation of the final system. Needless to say, this method of development often led to unsatisfactory systems and unhappy clients. Today, requirements capture is recognized as a crucial stage in the development of software. Each year more and more requirements methods become available, often as expensive commercial products, involving computer-based tools, training programmes and extensive documentation. However, since research into requirements capture is still in its early stages, we have, as yet, little reliable information about the relative effectiveness of the various methods.

3.2   WHAT ARE REQUIREMENTS?

The problem of definition

One of the main problems in this area is that there is no consensus of opinion as to what is meant by the term 'requirements capture'. Some developers and writers talk about requirements, others about constraints, while some make a distinction between system requirements and software requirements. In addition to the expression 'requirements capture', which seems to imply that the requirements are out there somewhere waiting to be bagged, there are several other common ways of describing this process. These include 'requirements elicitation' (which suggests that requirements can be drawn out by talking to clients and users), 'requirements specification' (which emphasizes the task of describing, rather than identifying the requirements) and 'requirements engineering' (which implies that the requirements are somehow built or engineered during the development process).

For the purposes of this chapter we shall assume that 'system requirements' refers to the client's needs and wishes, whereas 'software requirements' covers constraints put on the system development, such as hardware, software and design methods. When capturing system requirements the developer works with clients and users (in the case of Just a Line, this means Harry and Sue), identifying their needs, wishes and available resources, and must produce documents that can be understood by them as well as by computer professionals. When capturing software requirements the developer works from the system requirements documents, producing software requirements that must be understood by software designers and programmers. We shall also assume that the expression 'requirements capture' covers the three phases of elicitation (identifying requirements), specification (describing them in an appropriate language or notation) and validation (checking with the client that the description accurately records his or her needs and wishes).

Evolving requirements

Modern approaches to requirements capture differ significantly from traditional methodologies in that they do not assume that a requirements specification document is agreed by the client and then remains cast in stone for the duration of the software development project. System developers today are fully aware that requirements are dynamic and evolve constantly during development of a software system. Organizations themselves are constantly changing; although the basic business, such as selling cards for Just a Line, will remain the same, the company's scope and objectives will change. Moreover, development of the software system itself has an effect on the organization; in-depth discussions about the company and its problems often lead to fresh ideas and to new ways of working which will, in turn, have an effect on the original system requirements. In the Just a Line interview, which you will find at the end of this chapter, Sue admits to 'an overall feeling of being disorganized'. It is likely that close examination of current working procedures during development of the new software system will make both Harry and Sue aware of where these can be improved and this will have an effect on their original list of requirements.

Function and non-functional requirements

In the past requirements capture meant defining functional requirements: what the system was to do, what its inputs and outputs were and how these were linked. Correct functional requirements are still considered essential for successful software development today, but in recent years developers have also come to realize the importance of non-functional requirements. These can be defined as the attributes of the system as it performs its job and can be divided into non-functional requirements of the system and non-functional requirements arising from external sources.

Non-functional requirements of the system will include:

- Usability. Does the system attract or put off its intended users? Is the right level of help provided? Are options clearly displayed and easy to follow? Does the system fit in with the user's preferred way of working?
- Performance. Does the system respond quickly enough for the user's needs? Can it cope efficiently with the required volume of transactions? What will happen in the case where the volume of data exceeds the specified capacity of the system?
- Reliability. Can the client have confidence that the system will behave consistently as expected?
- Security. How easy is it for non-authorized users to access the system and read or modify confidential data?

Non-functional requirements that arise from external sources include methods of operation, such as the client's existing procedures, physical constraints, such as the layout of the accommodation available, and international quality control standards, such as ISO/9001.

3.3   THE PROCESS OF REQUIREMENTS CAPTURE

Requirements elicitation

Requirements capture begins with the task of finding out as much as possible about the clients' organization, their current problems and what they would like the new system to do for them. This is deceptively simple, since it involves sifting through large amounts of information and deciding what exactly is relevant. It is also extremely difficult for the system developer to be sure that he or she has a complete and accurate understanding of what the clients want. Good communication skills, both oral and written, are essential for requirements elicitation, since nearly all methods of fact-finding depend on communication with clients and users. Requirements elicitation covers several different types of activity, such as observation of the users at work, a study of relevant documents and user questionnaires, but the most effective way of getting information is simply to talk to the people involved in the system.

A useful interview is one that has been prepared thoroughly. Both the developer and the interviewee should be clear about the purpose of the interview and what they each want to get out of it. The developer should have established relevant details about the interviewee, such as his or her background, position in the organization, length of time with the company and special skills, such as level of computer expertise. It is part of the developer's job to put the interviewee at ease, particularly if the interview takes place away from the interviewee's place of work. It is worth spending some time chatting to the interviewee in general terms and very important to listen carefully to what he or she has to say, even if it does not appear to be directly relevant. The ability to listen attentively and identify important and relevant information is one of the essential skills for a system developer during requirements capture. Although direct questions are needed to control the interview, a lot of information can also be discovered by smiling, nodding encouragingly and making the interviewee feel that what he or she is saying is important. The developer should direct the interview, but must not dominate it.

At the end of this chapter you will find the first interview between the system developer and Harry and Sue of Just a Line. In any conversation of this type we can find several different kinds of information. Some of these are listed below:

- Information which is already structured in lists or forms.
- Information about company procedures; how certain tasks are carried out at present.
- Measurements such as the number of customers or the average size of an order.
- Problems that the client has identified in the current system.
- Definite requirements for the new system.
- Information that is not stated directly, but where there are definite 'vibes'. An example of this might be where the clients complain that they are always rushed when the supplier's order comes in, whereas what is actually happening is that the supplier always delivers late.

As you read the interview with Harry and Sue, try to identify examples of the different kinds of information that tell the system developer about Just a Line.

Apart from interviews with clients and users, the most useful form of requirements elicitation is often a questionnaire. This is particularly effective when a small, well-defined amount of information is needed from a large number of people, especially if they are widely scattered. It could be used, for example, in the Just a Line case study to find out what the company's customers think about the Just a Line method of ordering cards.

As with interviews, it is essential to prepare questionnaires thoroughly, including testing on a small sample of people to ensure that the questionnaire is easy to understand, simple to fill in and that it will produce useful results. It is the responsibility of the system developer to make sure that people who fill in the questionnaire are aware of its purpose and how their answers will be used. A variety of question types may be used, including multiple choice, short answer and extended answer questions, but the main priority must be to ensure that all questions are as clear and straightforward as possible. If a question does not contain enough information, the person filling in the questionnaire will not understand what is required, but if it contains too much information, nobody will bother to read it.

Figure 3.1 shows an extract from a questionnaire on Just a Line's ordering methods. The purpose of the questionnaire is to help the system developer find out what Just a Line's customers think about the way ordering of cards is handled at present and to elicit ideas from them on how the process might be improved.

Requirements specification

Whereas requirements elicitation involves an expansion of the developer's knowledge about the problem domain and the client's wishes, requirements specification involves sifting through the information to filter out the important and relevant issues and record them in an appropriate form. This may be narrative English, diagrams or a mixture of the two. The techniques described in Chapters 4, 5 and 6 are a commonly used form of recording requirements. Alternatively, in certain safety-critical or security-critical systems, it may be appropriate to describe requirements using a formal, mathematical language, such as those described in Chapter 7. One of the most effective ways of recording requirements is rapid prototyping, where the developer builds an unpolished version of all or part of the system. Clients and users can then get a feel for what the new system will be able to do and what it will look like. Rapid prototyping allows clients to see how their requirements translate into a computer system; it is particularly useful when requirements are uncertain. You will find a discussion of prototyping in Chapter 7 of this book.

Just a Line Ordering Service—Customer Survey

We are intending to move to a new computerized ordering system for our cards in the near future. It would be a great help to us if you could spare a few minutes to give us your opinions of our current ordering system and any suggestions you have for improving it. Please answer the questions below and return the form to us in the enclosed pre-paid envelope.

1. Have you ever bought cards from Just a Line?

    Yes u   go to question 2

    No u   go to question 5

2. How many times have you bought cards from Just a Line?

    Once only u

    2–5 times u

    6 times or more u

3. Have you experienced any problems with the Just a Line ordering system?

    Yes u   please explain briefly below

    No u

    _____

    _____

4. For each of the statements (a)–(e) shown below, circle the number that is closest to your own view, where 1 means that you agree strongly with the statement and 5 means that you strongly disagree.

    (a) The current system works well.   1   2   3   4   5

    (b) The staff are always friendly and helpful.   1   2   3   4   5

    (c) It is easy to choose and order cards.   1   2   3   4   5

    (d) I would like to see more information about   1   2   3   4   5
    my order.

    (e) I feel that a computerized ordering system would   1   2   3   4   5
    be more efficient.

5. Please note below any other comments you have on the current system.

    _____

    _____

    _____

6. Please note below any suggestions for the new system.

    _____

    _____

    _____

Your name: _____

Your address: _____

Thank you for completing this questionnaire.

Figure 3.1 Just a Line ordering service—customer survey

Whatever language or method is chosen for the specification of requirements, certain information must be provided and the requirements specification itself must have certain qualities. For each separate requirement the following information should be included:

- The source of the requirement.
- Who will be affected by the requirement.
- The priority of the requirement; how essential is it?
- The benefits that arise from fulfilment of the requirement.
- A full description of the requirement.
- A list of related requirements and how they are linked.
- Alternatives to the requirement, if any.
- If the new requirement involves a change to a previous one, then this must be fully documented, together with the reasons for the change and the effects it will have on other system requirements.

Much has been written recently about the qualities of the requirements specification. One of the most useful sources is the IEEE Recommended Practice for Software Requirements Specifications from the IEEE Standard 830–1993. The Standard describes qualities that are essential for a good requirements specification document, including correctness, consistency and understandability. Many of these qualities are simply common sense, but the Standard is useful as a check-list.

Requirements validation

Although it is a time-consuming process to check that a requirements specification has all the qualities listed above, it is technically feasible for the system developer to feel satisfied that the requirements specification document is actually of the desired quality. What is much more difficult to ascertain is whether the requirements expressed in the specification are really what the client wants and needs. The situation is further complicated by the fact that the client may not know what he or she wants, or that what is wanted may be completely different from what is needed. The process of checking that the requirements as specified are a true representation of the client's needs and wishes is known as validation.

Validation of requirements is essential from the earliest stages of requirements capture. During interviews with clients and users there should be constant feedback to ensure that the developer has fully understood what is being said. This is also useful in that it helps the interviewee to feel that what he or she is saying is helpful and relevant. Initial validation is also carried out by taking notes during the interview and later producing a written summary for the interviewee. The developer should always ask permission to take notes and be prepared to show the interviewee what is in them. The written summary should be produced shortly after the interview, so that the interviewee remembers what was said, but has had time to think about it and can check that the developer has understood the important points.

Different methods of requirements elicitation can be used in conjunction to validate requirements. This may be carried out by comparing answers on a particular topic from a questionnaire with comments on the same topic that have been obtained during interviews. A client's account of certain business procedures may be checked by observation of how the procedures are carried out in practice.

Other techniques may also be introduced to aid the validation process. These techniques include animation of a requirements specification that has been written using a formal notation. Formal notations and their use in modelling systems are discussed in Chapter 7. For the purposes of require-ments validation a formal specification of a process can sometimes be animated to produce a graphical representation of the process in action. The technique of prototyping, also discussed in Chapter 7, is useful at all the stages of requirements capture. When used for validation, a prototype allows the client and users to get some feeling for how their ideas of what they want will work once implemented in a computer system. The structured modelling techniques, described in Chapters 4, 5 and 6, are designed to be user-friendly and to facilitate validation. Since the client's original requirements are generally expressed in natural language, one of the most effective methods of validating the requirements specification is simply to talk through it with the client and users. Although it is never possible to prove conclusively that a requirements specification describes exactly what the client wants and needs, it is essential that both the system developer and the client are happy that the requirements as stated have been thoroughly validated. The validation process can be seen as the application of quality assurance as applied to the requirements specifica-tion, leading to a well-founded belief on all sides that the specification is an accurate description of the system requirements.

3.4   INTERVIEW WITH SUE AND HARRY FROM JUST A LINE

HARRY: Now, how about a drink?

SYSTEM DEVELOPER (SD):   Well ... er, I don't think so, thanks, as it's only half past five.

SUE: A cup of tea perhaps. I'll put the kettle on and we can tell you a bit about the company.

SD: Yes, I've heard a lot of good things about your cards, and I was wondering if you could show me some samples later on. I'm very interested to hear how you got the idea for the business.

SUE: Of course we'd love to show you the cards and we're always keen to get comments on possible new lines.

SD: Well, just to put you in the picture about this meeting—what I'd like to do is get a good idea of the company and what you'd like from a computer system. I'd like to cover what you do, how you work, what you see as your current problems and how you think a system could help. Is that OK with you?

HARRY: Fine, Sue will be quite happy to talk Just a Line all night.

SD: Right, perhaps you could start by describing the main jobs you have to do to run Just a Line. What about the first contact with the customers, for example?

SUE: Well, we meet them when we take the orders, or speak to them at least, if it's a phone order—it usually is. That's a real pain. Most of the customers are so chatty, they ask all about what we do and what we stock, and we have to explain all about the different sorts of cards and designs and all that. We try to persuade them to come into the shop to see for themselves, but they don't always want to. Then we get on to the personalized bit and we have to talk them through all the various typefaces and colours and what have you. People are always so friendly and interested and they usually end up ordering quite a few cards, but it's terribly awkward to deal with it all over the phone.

SD: What happens when they ask you detailed questions? Do you have all the information in your heads, or do you have to go and look things up all the time? And perhaps you can tell me how you keep information about card designs, prices, etc.

SUE: We've got a list of the card designs we offer on a regular basis—there's a copy stuck on the wall by the phone. We can usually remember what the design or picture is like by the name, so we just describe it to them as best we can.

HARRY: There've been one or two disasters though—remember that old girl who ordered a hundred 'Garden of Paradise' with her name and phone number on the back? She was absolutely livid when she found Adam and Eve stark naked in the middle of the picture! I should think it would have livened up her social life no end, sending out those cards, but she didn't seem to see it that way.

SD: Now, what about the prices? Is that a separate list?

SUE: Yes, we keep that by the phone as well, but it gets updated more often than the design list—in fact here's an old one; you can keep it.

SD: I see. I suppose this is how you hold information about suppliers, too. I see it's got their name and address on it, as well.

SUE: Yes. Well, at the moment there's only one supplier. We're thinking about using a different one who does recycled paper. We're very keen on that. But we may be able to persuade our present supplier to sell it as well, which would be a lot simpler than dealing with two suppliers. Anyway, eventually the customers tell us what they want to order and we take it down, in triplicate, on our order forms using carbon paper.

SD: Why three copies?

SUE: The top two copies go out with the order. The customer keeps one as a delivery note, the other comes back with the customer's payment. We keep the third one until the signed copy comes back with the payment. Everything's cash on delivery at the moment, although we realize we're going to have to start thinking about credit accounts and that sort of thing.

SD: What about pricing? Do you work out the cost when you take the order?

SUE: Sometimes, because customers want to know how much it's going to cost. But quite a lot of people just leave it to me to work out the cost later. That's better really.

SD: Then what happens?

SUE: To the orders? Well, they go in the order file—our whole filing system is just one big filing cabinet with three drawers and orders go in the top drawer. They go in the drawer in the order we receive them, unless there's a very urgent one. We generally tell the customers to allow a maximum of 28 days before they get the cards.

SD: Then, when the cards are ready, you deliver them?

SUE: Yes, if it's local—or else we use the post.

SD: Well, I've got a reasonably good picture of how you handle orders. We can always come back to it. What about stock? How do you organize that?

SUE: We usually reorder about once a month. Our current supplier delivers free if we can order more than £300 worth of stuff. At first we couldn't always afford to make that saving, but things are going reasonably well now, so we usually manage to. It's complicated. We can't just order one particular line if we've got a run on it, but we usually manage to organize a large enough order each month. Fortunately, we can get what we order delivered within a week. When it's obvious we're getting low on a few lines, I check to see if we can order enough to get the free delivery. We swore we'd never run into debt with the supplier, and so far we've managed to keep that.

SD: How do you actually decide what to order?

SUE: It's a bit hit and miss sometimes. I look in the store where we keep all the cards and see what's getting low, particularly with popular lines. Then I have a look through the orders and make an estimate of what we need. The idea is to order so that everything runs down at about the same rate. I've pretty well got the hang of it by now.

SD: What happens if you do run out of something and can't meet a customer's order within the 28 days?

SUE: We just tell the customers we haven't got what they want at the moment. They usually don't mind as long as we tell them when they order.

If we find out later, then we phone them if we've got a number. They're mostly very nice about it. I get Harry to tell them, he's much better at that sort of thing than I am and he can often persuade them to order something else instead. We always try to remember to say everything is 'subject to availability' when they place the order, but it's easy to forget.

SD: So, you send out orders to your suppliers a bit irregularly, but roughly once a month. What happens when the stuff arrives? How do you pay?

SUE: They send an invoice with the goods. We check everything's there and sign for it. Then they invoice us. Then we pay them.

SD: What is it you sign, when they deliver?

SUE: It's the bottom copy of their invoice.

SD: You have to record customer payments, too, of course?

SUE: Yes. When we get a payment we take our copy of the order out of the top drawer of the filing cabinet and put it in the second drawer. We call that one 'past orders'. We make a note of the payment in our cash book. Harry usually banks the money weekly, or daily if a lot has come in.

SD: Cash book? What else goes in there?

SUE: Everything, I'm afraid! We record all the money going in and out. So, as well as customer payments, we record payments we make to our supplier, and all our running expenses, like petrol, stamps, phone calls, and so on.

SD: Well, I think I've got some idea about how you run the outfit, now. What I'd like to do is go away and sort it all out a bit in my mind, then come back to you and check I've got things right. Are there any other problems you feel we haven't covered?

SUE: Not really, it's just an overall feeling of being disorganized. That worries me, especially now that some of the big stores seem to be interested in the cards. I do think we've got a good product to sell and I don't want to mess it all up by seeming to be unprofessional.

SD: Well, that's just the sort of problem we deal with. I'll be in touch again soon and I'm sure we'll be able to get you organized. Now could I have a look at the cards? I'm really keen to see them after all you've told me.

HARRY: Great, that's terrific. And what about that drink?

EXERCISES AND TOPICS FOR DISCUSSION

3.1 Find an example from the Just a Line interview of each of the different types of information listed in the chapter in the section on requirements elicitation.

3.2 What other questions could the system developer usefully have asked Harry and Sue?

3.3 In what ways could the system developer improve the management of the interview with Harry and Sue?

3.4 You have been asked to develop an information system for your local area. Design a questionnaire that will help you to find out what sort of information people feel should be included in the system.

REFERENCES AND FURTHER READING

Davis, A. M. (1993) *Software Requirements: Objects, Functions and States*, Prentice-Hall, Englewood Cliffs, N.J.

Institute of Electrical and Electronics Engineers, Inc. (1994) *IEEE Recommended Practice for Software Requirements Specifications*, New York.

Loucopoulos, P. and Karakostas, V. (1995) *System Requirements Engineering*, McGraw-Hill, London.

Yeates, D., Shields, M. and Helmy, D. (1994) *Systems Analysis and Design*, Pitman, London.

4

PROCESS MODELLING

In Chapters 4, 5 and 6 we discuss a range of modelling techniques used by most structured system development methodologies in the analysis stage of system development. The techniques introduced are data flow diagrams, data dictionary, process definitions, data modelling and entity life histories. Examples are given of each technique and part of the Just a Line system is modelled using each technique in turn to give a complete picture.

Each technique provides its own view of the system and concentrates on this view while ignoring other aspects. These perspectives are explained and illustrated. The order in which the techniques are discussed here is: process modelling, data modelling and finally entity life histories. This order was dictated by personal preference; readers who prefer to tackle data modelling before data flow diagrams may read the chapters in that order. Entity life histories, however, use information provided by both the data model and the data flow diagrams. Chapter 6 should therefore be read after the other two.

This chapter begins with a discussion of modelling in general and why it is used in system development and then discusses process modelling. A process model consists of a set of data flow diagrams and their supporting documentation: a data dictionary and process specification. The section on data flow diagrams—Sec. 4.2— is divided into two parts. Part 1 gives an overview of the technique, its rules, purpose and notation. This section includes the concept of levelled data flow diagrams but avoids detailed discussion of the differences between physical and logical models. Exercises 4.1 to 4.8 test the reader's understanding of the ideas introduced here. Part 2 discusses the difference between physical and logical data flow diagrams. Exercises 4.9 to 4.14 relate to this part. Beginners may omit the second part of the section.

4.1 MODELLING

Introduction

Modelling is used extensively in structured system development. For this reason it is important to understand what system developers mean by the term. A model of a system represents a part of the real world. The model differs from reality in that it concentrates on certain aspects while ignoring others—it is an abstraction. Modelling is the process of abstracting and organizing significant features of part of the real world, or how we would like it to be. A useful model will represent only those features of reality that are useful for the current purpose. Each model says something about the subject, but not everything. Different types of models illustrate different things.

The system developer is not alone in using modelling in this way. An architect, for example, is modelling when he or she draws a rough sketch of a house to show a client approximately what the house will look like. This model is different to, and serves a different purpose from, a scaled drawing of the same house which might be drawn to show planners how it will fit in with its surroundings. Both of these models, however, are two-dimensional and drawn with pen and paper. When the design is at a more advanced stage, the architect might construct a three-dimensional model of the house out of wood and glue to give the client a clearer understanding of the design, of how the house will look from all angles and how the rooms relate to each other. Plans will also have to be drawn to serve as working documents for the builders and site engineers—blueprints drawn to scale with precise measurements of widths, depths, materials and loadings specified. Each model is a partial representation of the house the architect is designing; each model says something about the building, but not everything. Each is used for a particular purpose and makes a different contribution to the development of the building.

Using models for communication

It is no accident that structured system development has introduced the extensive use of modelling, particularly graphical modelling. Earlier attempts to produce documents expressing the client requirements of the system— known variously as the *requirements* or *functional specification*—were conspicuously unsuccessful. This document was typically an enormously thick and indigestible text with little or no use of graphics to leaven the lump. Clients were supposed to 'agree' and sign it. Frequently, it was unread both by the clients, who therefore failed to pick up any errors, and by the programmers, who eventually had to translate it into a piece of software.

Most, but not all, of the models used by system developers today make use of graphics. A graphic representation of the system has several advantages over a narrative document. Diagrams tend to be more readily understood by both clients and system developers. Diagrams can express ideas more concisely which makes the size of the documentation less daunting.

System developers use models in the analysis stage for various purposes. Experience has demonstrated the benefits of modelling to be:

- Models impose structure on the jumble of facts and opinions gathered while discussing the system with the client. They are used both to record facts and to sort them into some kind of order.
- The system developer models the system as he or she currently understands it. Discussion of these models with the other people involved, including the client, will identify misunderstandings. Having a model on which to centre discussions makes this process easier.
- During the construction of the models the system developer becomes aware of questions that need to be asked, details that have been left out and contradictions in his or her understanding of the system. Producing the model highlights the shortcomings; discussing the model with clients will help to resolve them.
- The same modelling techniques are used to describe the existing system and the new, required system. Clients may find some effort is required to understand the modelling techniques, but the effort will be worth while as the understanding gained can be applied to models at all stages of system development.
- Once modelling of the new system is complete, the system developer can test the model and check it for consistency and completeness. It can be evaluated informally and provide a fairly good idea at an early stage in the development of a system whether or not it can satisfy the specified client requirements. This sort of checking would be almost impossible to do using a purely narrative document because of its unwieldy nature.

Using models to tackle complexity

Models help the system developer to communicate with the client and help the client to understand the new system. They are also useful to the system developer when tackling the complexity of large systems. Computer scientists have commonly used two main intellectual techniques to cope with complexity:

- *Decomposition*—dividing the problem into 'brain-sized' chunks
- *Abstraction*—concentrating on the most important elements while ignoring currently irrelevant details

The models used in structured system development make use of both these techniques. The first, decomposition, takes a divide and conquer approach. A large and complex problem will be made up of lots of smaller problems. The developer will keep splitting the problem into smaller and smaller sub-problems, until a brain-sized problem is left, i.e. one that is small enough to be held in the developer's head.

The second technique, abstraction, allows a developer to concentrate on one aspect of a problem at a time. In designing a house, the architect can safely ignore, for example, consideration of the precise type of brick to be used, when deciding how many bedrooms the house will have. In the same way, the system developer can safely ignore consideration of precisely how much disk space the system will require, when deciding what the user interface will look like.

The modelling techniques used in structured system development support the developer's need to concentrate on one aspect of the problem at a time. In the following sections we discuss the particular perspective of each modelling technique. Decomposition and abstraction both help the system developer to reduce the size of the problem to be thought about at any one time. To model large and complex systems therefore, a system developer needs:

- Different kinds of models to highlight different parts of the system, i.e. to model it from different perspectives
- Modelling techniques with the ability to partition a problem, to allow him or her to concentrate on a sub-section, independently from the rest of the problem

We will see that the modelling techniques used in structured system development support both abstraction and decomposition. They support the developer's need to concentrate on one aspect of the problem at a time in that each technique had its own view of the system—its own perspective on the problem. The developer's need to decompose the problem is supported, in particular, by the use of data flow diagrams (see Sec. 4.2) which can be used to split up the problem using top-down functional decomposition. We will see that some of the modelling techniques used in structured system development allow us to view the problem at different levels. They offer us the ability to have both a general overview of the problem and to view, selectively, parts of the problem in detail.

Different perspectives

Most structured methodologies use some of all of the following modelling techniques during analysis. As with the architect's models, each is used for a particular purpose. Each model has its own view or perspective of the system—it concentrates on certain aspects and ignores others. Combining these views gives the whole picture. The list below illustrates the perspective offered by each of the techniques discussed in this chapter.

Modelling technique	Perspective
Data flow diagram	Flow of data or information through the system
Process definition	Detailed textual descriptions of processes identified in the data flow diagrams
Data dictionary	Detail about the system data, e.g. contents of data flows and data stores
Data model	Identification of data objects in the system, their structure and the relationships between them
Entity life history	Examination of how data change over time

Each of these modelling techniques is explained in detail below.

Different stages

During the analysis of a system the same technique may be used to model the system at different stages. Like the architect's models, the models in the early stages of system design are non-technical. Later on in the project development a more precise version of these early sketches may be used as the basis for a technical design. A data flow diagram, for example, may be sketched during the feasibility study and then used to describe the existing system and to describe the required system. In this form it is a non-technical diagram and can be discussed with the client. Eventually, the data flow diagram may provide the basis for the design of the system structure and program specifications. Similarly, a data model may be drawn of both the existing and required system and eventually used as the basis for file design.

Documentation of system models

Each of the modelling techniques listed above views the system from a different perspective. Each model can be used on its own, but can only be fully understood when its part in the overall framework is appreciated. The models refer to each other and must be carefully cross-referenced. In the sections that follow we explain how the models relate to each other, but is useful to have a guide to the structure of the documentation of the models. Different methodologies organize the documentation differently, particularly in regard to the contents of the data dictionary. The diagram in Fig. 4.1 shows one possible arrangement.

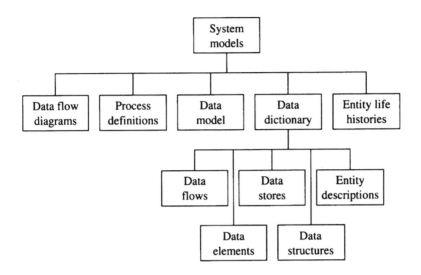

Figure 4.1 Structure of modelling techniques

4.2 DATA FLOW DIAGRAMS: PART 1

Introduction

Most structured methodologies use data flow diagrams (DFDs) as one of their modelling techniques. Like other modelling techniques, data flow diagrams use decomposition and abstraction to limit the amount of detail tackled at any one time. They use abstraction in that they attempt to model only certain limited aspects of the system, leaving other aspects to be modelled using other techniques. They use decomposition in that they partition the system in a top-down manner, allowing us to concentrate on one part of the problem at a time.

Data flow diagrams identify the *system boundary* and *external entities* (see below) and the *data* or *information flows* into and out of the system. They chart the progress of the data through the system and through the *processes* that affect them. Data flow diagrams are, fundamentally, process based. They concern themselves with the question: *What does the system 'do' to the data: how does it process the data?* This process-oriented view of a system may be contrasted with the object-oriented view discussed in Chapter 7. Data flow diagrams are useful because they provide a graphic overview of what the system does in a manner that is easy to understand. However, they deliberately leave many questions unanswered. Many aspects of the system are modelled

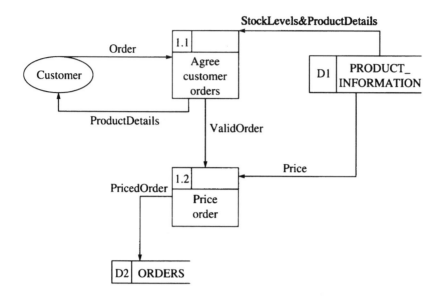

Figure 4.2 Fragment of a data flow diagram showing processes to agree and price orders. Customers are given information about the products stocked and send in orders. Stock levels are examined to check that the order can be met; if so, the order is deemed to be 'valid' and is priced and filed.

using the complementary techniques of: data dictionary, data modelling, process definitions and entity life histories.

How do data flow diagrams work?

Data flow diagrams aim to be immediately accessible to layman and specialist alike. The best way to understand them is to look at examples. Figure 4.2 shows a fragment of a data flow diagram modelling part of the Just a Line system.

This figure illustrates the four basic elements that data flow diagrams use to model the system:

- Data flows
- Processes
- Data stores
- External entities

Data flows Data flow diagrams model the flow of information or data through the system. In Fig. 4.2 a customer's order is modelled as a data flow labelled **Order** going from a customer into the system. The list of products and prices given to customers is modelled as a data flow from the system to the customer, labelled **ProductDetails**. Data flows are modelled as a directed arrow with a unique label which briefly describes the content. Usually a data flow represents a group or packet of data items. When something significant happens to a data flow its label should reflect this. In Fig. 4.2 for example, before orders are agreed, stock levels are checked to see that the order can be met. Once this check has been made an **Order** becomes a **ValidOrder**; the label of the data flow changes to reflect the new status of the order.

Processes A process models what happens to the data; it transforms incoming data flows into outgoing data flows, i.e. it processes the data. Typically, a process will have one or more data inputs and produce one or more data outputs. Processes are shown on the data flow diagram as rectangles (see Fig. 4.2) and labelled with a brief description of their function, e.g. **Agree customer orders**, **Price order**. Each process has a unique reference number, in the top left-hand corner of the process box. The top right-hand corner of the box is used to document (optionally) the location of a process—where it takes place. Names such as **Personnel** and **Accounts** appear here. Normally, the location of a process is only documented on a diagram describing how an existing system works, i.e. a current physical data flow diagram (see below). Sometimes this corner is used to identify the person normally associated with this process— who does this job.

Data stores A data store represents permanent data which is used by the system and must therefore be held in the system if it is to function correctly. Data stores are shown on the data flow diagram as open-ended rectangles with a label reflecting their content. In Fig. 4.2 there are two data stores. **PRODUCT_INFORMATION** and **ORDERS**. Stock levels are recorded in the data store **PRODUCT_INFORMATION** and examined before an order is agreed. **PRODUCT_INFORMATION** is also used to store descriptions of the Just a Line product range and product prices. The second data store, **ORDERS**, is used to store priced orders until they are ready to be made up and delivered.

External entities External entities are people, organizations or other systems— anything outside the system boundary that sends data into the system or receives data from it. They are not considered to be part of the system but are external to it. In Fig. 4.2 the customer is modelled as an external entity who receives information about products—**ProductDetail**—and sends in **Orders**. External entities are represented on the data flow diagram as ellipses with an appropriate label. Sometimes external entities are referred to as *sources* and *sinks*; an external entity either supplies data to the system, which makes it a source, and/or receives output from the system, which makes it a sink. External entities are drawn

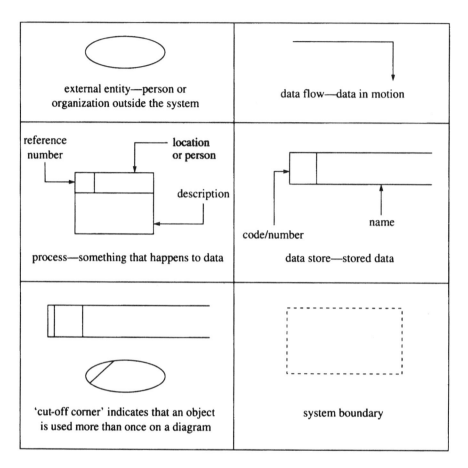

Figure 4.3 Notation for data flow diagrams

outside the system boundary. The system boundary is represented on a data flow diagram by a dotted line and should be shown on all diagrams. It is not drawn on Fig. 4.2 only because this is a partial data flow diagram, used for illustrative purposes (the complete diagram appears later in Fig. 4.6).

Data flow diagram notation

Several different notations exist for expressing data flow diagrams—there is no definitive standard. However, it is only the shape of the symbols that vary, not the underlying logic. The notation used in this text follows one of the most commonly used set of conventions (see Fig. 4.3). All varieties of notation use the four basic elements identified above—data flows, processes, data stores and external entities.

In this text we have adopted a standardized notation for labelling. Labels for data flows are written in lower case; where a label consists of more than one word, the words are run together with no spaces but with a capital letter at the start of each new word, e.g. customer name becomes **CustomerName**. Labels for data stores are written in upper case; where there is more than one word, the words are joined by the underscore symbol, e.g. **PRODUCT_ INFORMATION**.

Levelled data flow diagrams

Data flow diagrams clearly and graphically represent the flow of data through a system. However, even a small system may have several hundred processes— the data flow diagram could cover a wall. To overcome this problem, levelled data flow diagrams are used. The idea of levelling is to allow us to view the system at different levels of detail—to offer a general overview of the system and selective viewing in progressively greater detail. This is a familiar technique; we use maps in the same way. Maps of different scales allow us to view the whole world at one time or one country in more detail—to see the finer detail of one particular region we can use a large-scale map of the area; street plans are used to home in on the detailed layout of a town.

Context diagram (level 0) The top-level diagram, level 0, is known as the context diagram. It models the whole system as a single process box whose sides represent the boundary of the system. It identifies all external entities and related input and output flows. By defining the boundary of the system, the context diagram delineates the domain of study so as to define those functions or areas of activity that are to be included and those that are to be excluded. Figure 4.4 shows the context diagram of the current Just a Line system. The diagram identifies **Customer** and **Supplier** as external entities. **Customers** receive information about the Just a Line products— **ProductDetails**, **Invoices** and **DeliveryNotes**; they supply Sue and Harry—the Just a Line system—with **Orders** and **Payments**. Sue and Harry send orders to the **Supplier** for more ·stock—**StockOrder**—and the **Supplier** sends them a **SupplierInvoice**. Sue and Harry confirm delivery—**ConfirmationOfDelivery**— and send a **SupplierPayment**.

Expanding processes The level 1 data flow diagram in Fig. 4.5 gives an overview of the whole system, identifying the major system processes and data flows between them. The single process on the context diagram is expanded to partition the system into its main constituent parts, each part being an identifiable function or group of functions. The Just a Line system has been split into three main areas of activity: activities concerned with handling customer orders, activities concerned with ordering from the supplier and

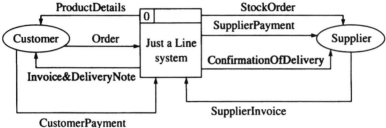

Figure 4.4 Context diagram for Just a Line

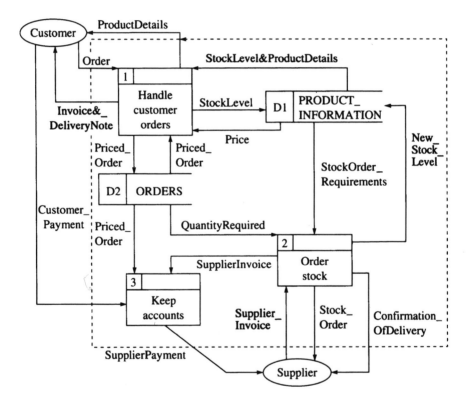

Figure 4.5 Just a Line: level 1 diagram of the current system

activities concerned with keeping the accounts. There three areas are logically distinct.

The external entities need only be shown on the context diagram; they may be shown at lower levels if this adds to the clarity of the diagram there. External entities are shown here at levels 0 and 1, but not at level 2.

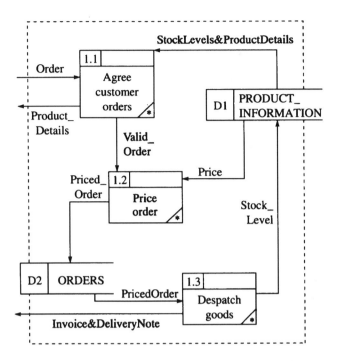

Figure 4.6 Just a Line: level 2 expansion of process 1 in Fig. 4.5

Each of the level 1 processes can in turn be expanded or decomposed into a level 2 data flow diagram to reveal more detail (see Fig. 4.6 which expands process 1. 'Handle customer orders'). At this stage it is shown that processing a customer order involves three stages:

- Accepting (and writing down) the order provided that there are sufficient stocks to meet it
- Pricing the order and filing it
- Making up the order and dispatching it with the invoice and delivery note.

There are three further points of interest:

- On this diagram the data stores are shown crossing the boundary. This indicates that these data stores have already appeared on a higher-level diagram. In this situation it is also permissible to show the data stores completely outside the boundary.
- Just as the outline of the single process box on the context diagram becomes the boundary of the level 1 diagram, the boundary of each lower-level data

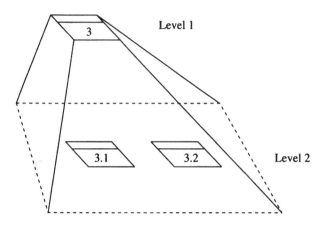

Figure 4.7 Relationship of process 3 level 1 to its sub-processes at level 2

flow diagram is provided by the frame of the higher-level process it expands (see Fig. 4.7).

- The asterisk in the bottom right-hand corner (see Fig. 4.6) signifies that this is a bottom-level process, i.e. one that is not further decomposed. This is a useful notation because it indicates that there will be a process definition (see Sec. 4.5) for this process.

Processes can continue to expand in this way until the required level of detail is reached. Not all processes have to be decomposed to the same level. A simple process may not be decomposed further than level 1; a more complex process may be expanded to several levels.

When has the required level of detail been reached? As with many other aspects of modelling this is something that comes with experience. A simple rule of thumb is that decomposition should continue until each process has no more than one input data flow and one output data flow. A precise description of what happens in each of the bottom-level processes is given in the process definitions.

Numbering On the level 1 diagram processes are numbered 1, 2, 3 ... (see Fig. 4.5). If a process at any level is decomposed, the sub-process numbers are prefixed with the number of the process they decompose. For example, if process 3 at level 1 is decomposed, the processes at level 2 will be numbered 3.1, 3.2 (see Fig. 4.7). Each process therefore has a unique number which is used for cross-referencing between the various models of the system. For example, a process will be referred to by this number when described in its corresponding process description. A detailed data dictionary may also refer to process numbers. It is tempting to make the process numbers represent the order in which the processing is done. However, this temptation should be resisted because the numbering is for reference purposes only. In order to avoid cramming too much information into one diagram, data flow diagrams make no attempt to model the processing sequence.

Labelling

The labels on the data flow diagram are as important as the numbers. Data flow diagrams see the system from the point of view of the data moving through it—this should be reflected in the choice of descriptions for processes and names used to label data flows:

- Process labels should be short sentences describing what the process does, e.g. **Price order** and **Order stock**. Normally they contain an active verb.
- Data flows should be labelled with nouns representing the data items flowing along them, e.g. **Order** and **CustomerPayment**. If you are tempted to label a flow with an active verb, e.g. **Display the price**, it probably means you are trying to make a data flow do the work of a process. Data stores should be similarly labelled to indicate the type of data stored in them. Each data store has a unique reference number. To distinguish them from processes, data stores are often numbered D1, D2, etc., or M1, M2 for manual data stores (see below). The prefix D is used where no reference is made to how the data store is implemented.
- Labels should carry as much meaning as possible, but should be short, to avoid cluttering the data flow diagram. Data flows and the contents of the data stores should be documented in a data dictionary (see later in the chapter).

Conventions of data flow diagrams

At a first glance, data flow diagrams look as if they were drawn and labelled very informally, but when used correctly the diagrams have a precise meaning. The technique of drawing data flow diagrams is underpinned by a set of 'syntax' rules or conventions, which give them rigour and allow them to take their place in the total picture of the system as provided by the combined set of structured modelling techniques. If these rules are not adhered to, the diagrams are almost meaningless. A system developer should regard these rules with the same degree of attention as a programmer whose syntax will be checked by a compiler. In fact, if a CASE tool is used (see Chapter 7) it will not allow diagrams to flout the rules.

Balancing rules The balancing rules require that the data flows entering or leaving a parent diagram must be equivalent to those on the child diagram.

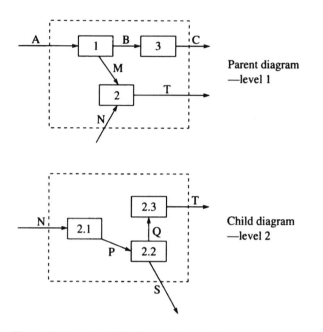

Figure 4.8 Parent and child diagrams do not balance

The context diagram of the Just a Line system (Fig. 4.4) has exactly the same data flows as those crossing the boundary of its child diagram, the level 1 data flow diagram (Fig. 4.5). New flows may not be arbitrarily introduced at lower, more detailed, levels. In Fig. 4.8 the balancing rule has been broken twice:

- A flow S has appeared crossing the boundary at level 2 which was not on the level 1 diagram.
- The flow M appears on the parent diagram but not on the child diagram.

The flows P and Q are introduced in the child diagram, but as these are internal to the child diagram they do not infringe the balancing rule.

Modelling data stores   In the interests of keeping clutter on the data flow diagrams to a minimum, data stores which are local to a process need not be drawn until the process is expanded in a lower-level diagram. For example, in the parent diagram in Fig. 4.8, no data stores are modelled. The decomposition of process 3 (Fig. 4.9) reveals a data store local to process 3.

At level 1 the data store D1 is not used by any process except process 3, i.e. it is not shared by the processes at level 1. At level 2 the data store is used by more than one process and therefore must appear in the diagram.

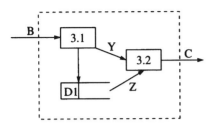

Figure 4.9 Decomposition of process 3 from level 1 in Fig. 4.8 revealing a local data store

Level 1

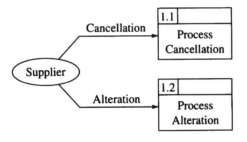

Level 2

Figure 4.10 Decomposing a data flow

Expanding data flows   The balancing rule prohibits the uncontrolled introduction of data flows at lower levels. However, if all the lower-level flows are to appear on the context and level 1 diagrams, the diagrams could get very cluttered. To avoid this, it is permissible to bundle together several lower-level flows under a unifying label. The top-level diagrams can use this convenient bundle which can be unravelled (or decomposed) as required at the lower levels. Figure 4.10 shows the data flow **Amendment** at level 1 which decomposes at level 2 into two separate flows, **Cancellation** and **Alteration**.

Decomposition of data flows must be documented in the data dictionary:

Amendment = Cancellation + Alteration

Data dictionary notation is described in Sec. 4.4.

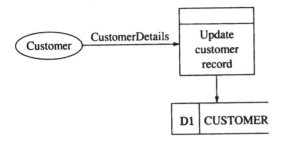

Figure 4.11 Unlabelled flow

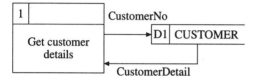

Figure 4.12 The search key **CustomerNo** should not appear on the diagram

Flows to and from data stores   All flows should be labelled except when a flow to or from a data store consists of exactly the same items of data as are in the data store. Figure 4.11 shows a fragment of data flow diagram where the data store **CUSTOMER**, containing customer details, is updated by an unlabelled flow whose content is the same as that of the data store.

Conventionally, a flow into a data store means that the data store is being updated in some way. Search keys used to extract data are not modelled on data flow diagrams. For example, in Fig. 4.12 the flow **CustomerNo** should not appear. The justification, again, is that the diagrams must be kept as uncluttered as possible.

Modelling deletion of a record from a data store

Sometimes we need, specifically, to model the deletion of a record from a data store, e.g. an old stock record from the stock file or a customer record from the customer file. This can be modelled as shown in Fig. 4.13. However, for the sake of keeping a diagram uncluttered, deletion of records is often assumed as part of a general update process (see Fig. 4.14).

Different stages

Data flow diagrams can be used to model the system at different stages of development. They can be used to model both the existing and the new

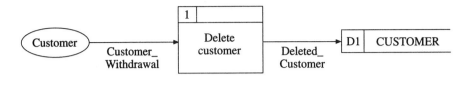

Figure 4.13 Modelling record deletion 1

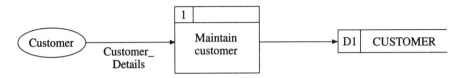

Figure 4.14 Modelling record deletion 2

systems. A data flow diagram of an existing system can focus on the mechanics of the current operation of the system, i.e. *how* the existing system works; this model is known as the current physical data flow diagram (CPDFD). Alternatively, a data flow diagram of the existing system can focus on the logic of the system—*what* the existing system does, without reference to how it does it; this is known as the current logical data flow diagram (CLDFD). In the same way, data flow diagrams of the new (required) system can focus on either the logic (what it will do) or the implementation (how it will work).

Figure 4.15 summarizes the stages a data flow diagram can model. If all stages are modelled the order will be CPDFD, then CLDFD, then RLDFD and finally RPDFD. However, a system developer may not find it necessary or desirable to model all of the stages. There may be no current system, in which case the RLDFD will be the starting point. If the current system is complex and used by many people, accounts of how it works may be different and even contradictory. In this case a CPDFD may be useful for the system developer both to sort out his or her own ideas and as a focus for discussions with the clients to resolve conflicts. Some system developers prefer not to draw CPDFDs as they feel it prevents them from producing a radically different (and better) design—once they have modelled the system one way it is hard to rethink the basic structure. A detailed discussion of the differences between physical and logical data flow diagrams is given in Sec. 4.3.

Limitations of data flow diagrams

Data flow diagrams are deliberately limited in the information they show. They make no attempt to model the following features:

	Physical system	Logical system
Current system	CPDFD current physical *How* the existing system works	CLDFD current logical *What* the existing system does
Required system	RPDFD required physical *How* the requirements are to be implemented	RLDFD required logical *What* the required system will do

Figure 4.15 Stages where a data flow diagram may be used

- The sequence in which processes occur
- The time intervals at which processes occur
- Detail about the structure of data flows or data stores (what does an **Order** consist of, what data is stored in **PRODUCT_INFORMATION**?)
- How often a process is repeated
- Conditions governing the occurrence of certain events (e.g., if the card design is in stock, then the order is accepted)

If all this information were recorded on data flow diagrams they would become too cluttered to be useful.

Checking data flow diagrams

We can never prove that a data flow diagram is correct—we can never know for certain that we have drawn what really exists or what the clients really want. However, data flow diagrams can be checked for internal completeness and consistency. The basic points to check are listed below:

- Does each process receive all the data it requires? A process that prices orders (Fig. 4.6) will need the relevant prices as well as details of what has been ordered.
- Does any data store have only data flows coming out and nothing going in? Data must be updated somewhere: suppliers change their products

and prices, customers change their addresses. The system must allow for this.

- Does any data store appear to have only incoming data which is never used, i.e. no data flow out of the data store? Is this correct?
- Are the data flow diagrams consistent across levels, i.e. have the balancing rules (see Balancing rules, page 47 been infringed?)
- Do all the external entities appear on the context diagram? Are any introduced at lower levels?
- If a named bundle of flows is decomposed at a lower level, is this documented in the data dictionary?
- Are all flows labelled? Are the labels documented in the data dictionary?
- Do all the flows on the diagram represent genuine flows of data? Do any of them represent flow of control? If the diagram reads 'after process A you do process B' it is showing flow of control. The numbers on the process boxes are for reference only; they do not represent the order in which the processes should be done. The directed arrows represent data flows only, they do not show which process should be done next.

Points of style to check:

- Data flows can be drawn between two processes, between a process and an external entity and between a process and a data store. Data flows cannot be drawn between two external entities, between an external entity and a data store or between two data stores.
- Do not let any data flow cross another flow on the diagram. To avoid this, draw duplicate external entities or data stores and mark them with a cut-off corner, as shown in Fig. 4.3.

A summary of the 'syntax' rules for data flow diagrams is given in Fig. 4.16.

4.3   DATA FLOW DIAGRAMS: PART 2

Logical and physical data flow diagrams

A physical data flow diagram models how the system does or will operate. Current physical data flow diagrams of an existing system describe the system in the user's terms—symbols on the diagram correspond to physical objects the user can recognize. Data flows may represent identifiable bits of paper; a data store may represent an identifiable ledger book or filing cabinet. In the Just a Line system, the data stores should represent objects mentioned in the interview: the card store, the filing cabinet, the price list and the design list (see

1. Label all flows except where a flow going into or coming out of a data store consists of exactly the same data items as the data store.

2. A data flow into a data store implies data are going into that data store, i.e. it is being updated in some way. Search keys used to extract data are not modelled.

3. Every data flow diagram must have a boundary marked on it.

4. Data flow labels must be unique—a flow label must change if the content of the data flow changes or if significant processing is done to it.

5. A flow cannot be made to model an action—the flow label is just a name for the bits of data that the flow contains, e.g. 'Order' is a legal name; 'send order' is not.

6. Each process must have a unique reference number.

7. Each data store must have a unique number and name.

8. All diagrams must be labelled, e.g. Just a Line: Context diagram.

9. Duplicated external entities and data stores must have 'cut-off corners'.

10. Do not allow data flows to cross—use duplicate external entities or data stores.

11. No external entities or I/O flows (flows to and from external entities) can be introduced in lower-level diagrams—they must all be introduced in the context diagram. Flows may be 'bundled' at higher levels and decomposed in lower-level diagrams.

12. With levelled data flow diagrams the boundary at any given level is the perimeter of the process box it decomposes. Flows must balance between levels.

13. If a data store is shared between two processes at any given level, it must be modelled. If, at a given level, a data store is internal to a process (i.e. only used by that process) it need not be modelled.

14. If a flow ever occurs, it is modelled. The data flow diagram should not attempt to model the conditions under which a flow occurs.

15. Data flows can take place between two processes, an external entity and a process, a data store and a process, but not between external entities and data stores, data stores and data stores, or between two external entities (except in SSADM version 4).

16. Triggers of events are not modelled.

17. Sequence and timing of flows and processes relative to each other are not modelled on a data flow diagram—the data flow diagram has nothing to say about the order in which flows or processes occur.

18. Data flows may not be split into two different flows.

Figure 4.16 'Syntax' rules for data flow diagrams

Fig. 4.17). The data flows **SupplierInvoice** and **Priced Order** correspond to identifiable documents. The diagram records other relevant physical details, e.g. that orders come in *by telephone*, that orders are filled *in triplicate* and a *signed copy* of the supplier invoice is returned to the supplier as confirmation of delivery. A physical data flow diagram may specify who does a particular

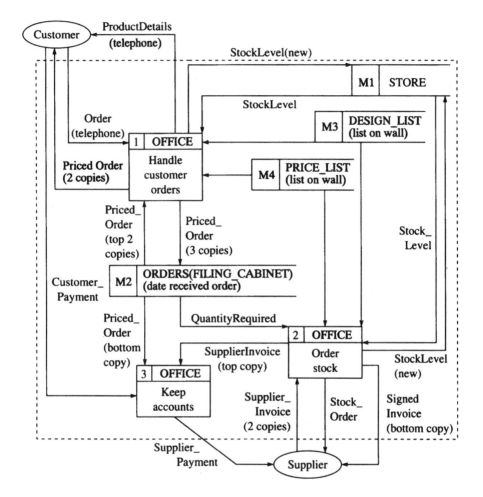

Figure 4.17 Just a Line: level 1 CPDFD

Figure 4.18 Modelling material flow

Current Physical DFDs:

1. Show how the existing system works in implementation terms, i.e. show physical details about how the system currently works:

   - Indicate who does a particular job.
   - Indicate where a particular job is done; if it is relevant indicate when it is done.
   - Indicate how a flow is communicated (by telephone, post, internal mail, visual display).
   - Indicate how data are stored (in a loose leaf file, on a white board, in someone's head, in a filing cabinet, in a shoe box).
   - Indicate the sequence in which data are stored (date order, customer name order).
   - Indicate the nature of the document (signed copy of invoice, annotated price list).
   - Model material flows.

2. Model the system in the users terms, i.e. on the data flow diagram describe elements of the system in terms that the user recognizes:

   - Describe data stores using the user's descriptions even if these are obscure to an outsider. If the user calls a list of products his bible, have a data store labelling 'bible' on the diagram.
   - Label data flows in terms that the user will identify with: if they know a form as the 'pink order', or the 'LC1', use these terms on your diagram.
   - Users often describe a system in terms of its functionality, i.e. in terms of the different jobs that are done. Your diagram should reflect their view of the system—their view of the way it breaks down into separate jobs. This may dicatate the entire decomposition of the diagram.

3. Model the system exactly how it is without any attempt to make it look more logical or improve it in any way:

   - As you draw and document the current physical system, you may become aware of several anomalies such as data stored being stored in more than one place, jobs being done in an inefficient sequence, etc.
   - Improvements can be incorporated in the current logical model; a good current physical model shows things exactly as they are, warts and all.

Figure 4.19 Main characteristics of current physical DFDs

job or where it is done; it may also record the order in which data is stored in a data store. Current physical DFDs show the 'what, how, who, when and where' of a system (Robinson and Prior, 1995).

Sometimes it is useful to model material—or physical resource—flows rather than just data flows. We might want a diagram which emphasizes the movement of physical objects of interest. This is done using broad arrows as shown in Fig. 4.18. The main characteristics of current physical data flow diagrams are summarized in Fig. 4.19.

A required physical data flow diagram (RPDFD) describes how the new system will work and may indicate such things as which parts of the system will be automated and which will remain manual, what physical devices will be used, and what input and output forms or reports will be used.

To move from current physical to current logical DFD:

1. Get rid of references to physical implementation:
   - Remove references to 'who', 'when', 'where' and 'how' a job is done or data are stored.
   - Get rid of material or resource flows and concentrate on the associated flow of data or information only.
   - Rename data stores and data flows so that the name reflects the content; this is the time to get rid of idiosyncratic user names or very physical names.
   - Remove processes that are required purely to support the current implementation, e.g. those that reflect the way someone does their job at the moment but which could be done otherwise.

2. Make minor 'improvements' in logic of stored data:
   - If several data stores in the current implementation store essentially the same data, these could be combined.
   - If a single data store in the current implementation stores data about several things which are logically distinct, consider creating several separate data stores.
   - Remove any data stores that are only used as an implementation dependent time delay between processes. For example, if Sue kept orders in a shoe box until she had time to price them, the shoe box might appear on the current physical DFD but would disappear in the current logical DFD.

Figure 4.20 Moving from current physical to current logical DFD

In contrast, logical data flow diagrams reflect *what* a system does or will do. They separate the essential functionality of the system (what it does) from the implementation detail (how it does it). This separation of concerns is an essential step for the system developer as the new system usually has to do everything that the existing system does, plus meet the new requirements and solve any current problems. What the existing system does, therefore, will filter through to the new system, although how it does it will almost certainly change in the new implementation. The current logical DFD retains 'what' happens and removes the 'how', 'who', 'when' and 'where'. Figure 4.20 summarizes the steps from the physical to logical DFD.

Comparison of current physical DFD and current logical DFD for Just a Line

The difference between logical and physical data flow diagrams can be illustrated from the Just a Line case study by comparing Figs. 4.17 and 4.21.

- On the current physical DFD it is recorded that orders come in 'by telephone', that there are 'two copies' of the **SupplierInvoice** and 'three copies' of the **PricedOrder**; there are references to the 'top copy' of the

SupplierInvoice and the 'bottom copy' of the **PricedOrder**. These details about the current implementation are omitted from the logical DFD.

- The current physical DFD records that all three processes are done in the office. This information about how the current system is implemented is discarded in the current logical DFD.
- The data stores on the current physical DFD represent actual physical things in the current system: the **STORE** where the supplies of cards are stored and the **DESIGN_LIST** and **PRICE_LIST** which refer to the two lists pinned up near the telephone—Sue mentions both lists in the interview (see Chapter 3). The current logical DFD extracts the information that will be used in the new system, i.e. the supplier's name and address, product code and prices from the **PRICE_LIST**, the product description from the **DESIGN_LIST** and the amount in stock from the **STORE**. This data is combined in a new data store **PRODUCT_INFORMATION**. The new system will certainly need to store this information although in a different form from the way it is recorded in the current system. The relevant information is therefore recorded in the current logical DFD but the old method of storing it (in the **STORE** and on the **DESIGN_LIST** and **PRICE_LIST**) is discarded.
- Information about the order in which data is stored in the current system is discarded, i.e. that orders are stored in the order in which they are received.
- The data stores on the current logical DFD have a reference number beginning with D rather than M—they no longer refer to manual data stores.
- The two copies of **PricedOrder** sent to the customer with his or her order are renamed **Invoice&DeliveryNote** on the current logical DFD. This tells us more about their function and less about which physical bits of paper are sent.
- The only other thing that is different is that the bottom copy of the **SupplierInvoice**, which is signed and returned to the **Supplier**, becomes **ConfirmationOfDelivery** on the current logical DFD. This tells us more about its function and less about how it is done physically.

Required logical DFDs

The new system must, usually, do everything that the old did *plus* solve any identified problems and meet any new requirements; these will be outlined in the Problem Definition and Problems and Requirements List. The simplest approach to developing the required logical DFDs is to combine the current logical DFDs with the problems and requirements list, i.e. add the requirements for the new system to the current logical DFD.

Another approach to developing the required logical model is to do the data modelling first so that the data stores that appear on the required logical

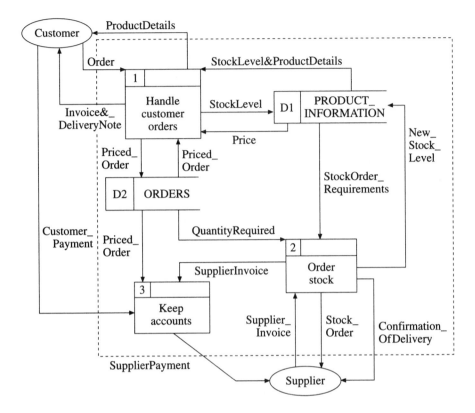

Figure 4.21 Just a Line: level 1 CLDFD

DFDs are the entities on the E–R diagram. Others start by identifying all the system outputs (from the current logical DFDs plus the problems and requirements list), drawing the outputs on the required logical DFD, documenting them in the data dictionary and working backwards. If we have to produce an itemized bill, where do we store the data we need to print on the bill and, working back from there, where does that data come into the system?

Another school of thought requires us to find all the bottom-level processes on the CLDFD with their inputs, outputs and data stores, list them in a completely unstructured way or even draw them on a huge sheet of paper, sort out which processes 'go together' and structure them into a levelled set of DFDs. This is a bottom-up approach which is designed to help the designer get completely away from a decomposition of the new system which is based on the decomposition of the current physical system.

We will adopt the first approach and combine the current logical DFDs with the requirements for the new system as specified in the problems and requirements list.

Just a Line—requirements for the new system

The new system for Just a Line must incorporate several new requirements. The system developer will already have listed most of these in the problem definition (see Chapter 2). The list will certainly be added to during the investigation of the current system—users will raise problems which for various reasons they did not mention earlier (perhaps they did not think of them or considered them too insignificant). System developers, from past experience, will spot features they think should be incorporated in the new system.

The list of requirements includes some points not mentioned in the original interview and which we can assume were mentioned at supplementary interviews. Harry has decided that he does not want the accounting side of the system computerized at this stage. He feels that he has a nice simple system in place and does not want to change it. This has been agreed with the system developer, who feels that if Harry changes his mind later it will be simple to buy an accounting package and incorporate that into the computerized part of the system. Sue, on reflection, has also stipulated that there is a part of the system she does not want computerized at this stage. She feels that it would be more effort than it is worth to keep track of stock levels on the computer and fully automate the stock control. She thinks it will be simpler to continue more or less as she is doing at the moment, but with the addition of a list of items currently ordered on pending customer orders. The list is to be produced by the computer to help her with supplier ordering. An extract from the problems and requirements list is given below.

Just a Line—requirements list

- The system must produce a personalized combined price list and order form to be sent out to existing customers. A non-personalized version of the same form will be distributed for publicity purposes.
- The system must know when a customer last ordered, to avoid mailing customers who have not ordered within the past year.
- The system must check whether a customer order is valid by checking that the card design ordered is one that is stocked. Checking that there is enough of that particular design in stock to meet the order will remain a manual process. The computerized system must keep a record of pending customer orders (not yet made up or delivered).
- When the orders are made up the system must produce invoices to go with the goods.
- The process of preparing a supplier order will remain manual but the system must be able to list products and quantities on the current batch of pending customer orders, to facilitate supplier ordering.

Sue and Harry feel that the combined price list/order form will solve most of their current problems with ordering. Customers will either send in the order form, or if they still telephone in the order, at least they will have a price list in front of them which will avoid the tedious process of reading over the telephone the list of items available. Pricing orders and producing the invoices will be automated. While the main stock control and ordering from suppliers is still manual, Sue will be helped when ordering by the list of items required by current pending customer orders. These requirements are modelled in the level 1 required logical data flow diagram for the Just a Line system, shown in Fig. 4.22.

Notice that **Accounts** and **StockOrdering**, which appeared as processes on the data flow diagrams of the current system, are now shown as external entities. As the clients have requested that these functions remain unaltered, they are considered to be outside the current domain of interest and therefore external to the system. However, they still interface with the system as they receive system outputs. The system will keep a file of information about products which will include descriptions of products stocked and their prices. This file must be kept up to date. However, the system will not attempt to keep track of current stock levels.

The system will also maintain a file of customers to facilitate the production of the price list/order form, and a file of current and past orders.

Summary

Data flow diagrams model the flow of data through the system. Data flow diagrams are used to describe the system at different stages of development. They are mostly used in the analysis stage to describe the current physical system, the current logical system and the required system. They can also be used to model the system during the feasibility study and to show the automation boundary when modelling the required physical system. Data flow diagrams are used to force structure and coherence on the mass of facts gathered during the fact-finding stage of analysis. They give a semi-technical, pictorial representation of the system which will form the basis of good communication with the client. In the process of drawing the data flow diagrams and discussing them with the client, inconsistencies, omissions and misunderstandings may be observed and corrected.

Data flow diagrams partition the system by identifying the major processes. Each major process may in turn be partitioned. In this way the system can be viewed as a whole, or selectively in detail.

Data flow diagrams deliberately make no attempt to show the order or frequency of events, nor the circumstances under which a flow will occur. These and many other features of the system are modelled elsewhere.

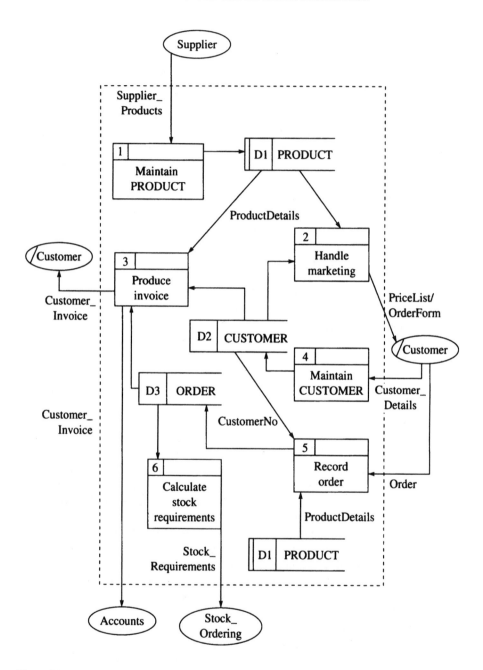

Figure 4.22 Just a Line: level 1 RLDFD

4.4 DATA DICTIONARY

Purpose

Data flow diagrams give us an overall picture of what the system does and of the movement of data through the system. To keep the picture clear and uncluttered they deliberately do not give us any detailed description of the data. Data flows and data stores have simple names that give us some idea of their content; processes are given a short description which tells us roughly what they do. This level of detail is sufficient for the purposes of the data flow diagram, but it only gives a partial description of the system. For a more complete understanding, the system developer and the client need detailed descriptions of all the labels used in the data flow diagrams. This is the type of detail recorded in the data dictionary. Descriptions will be required, for example:

- When capturing all the information given on documents input to the existing system, such as order forms
- When designing output documents such as reports, mail shots and invoices
- When describing repositories of data in the existing system or designing files for the new system

In all of these cases and many others, a complete detailed description of the data is needed.

A data dictionary can be recorded manually, on paper, or it can be automated, often as part of a CASE tool (see Chapter 7). This section describes a notation and approach suitable for a manually recorded data dictionary. The precise content and layout of the data dictionary varies from one methodology to another. The data dictionary technique described here is suitable for describing a small system. A different technique, suitable for larger and more complex systems, is described in Gane and Sarson (1979).

Value of the data dictionary

Whether automated or manual, the data dictionary is an invaluable tool. Data dictionary descriptions are used at the analysis, specification and design stages of system development. The amount of detail required changes as the project progresses; normally it is inappropriate to attempt to describe the data with too much low-level detail in the early stages. The data dictionary provides an unambiguous and concise way of recording *data about data*. It forms a central store of data which supports the information given in other models of the system, not only the data flow diagrams but also the entity–relationship diagram, the process definitions and the entity life histories. One of the advantages of this is that these models of the system can use short simple labels to describe data objects. The models are kept uncluttered and readable with no loss of precision as the labels are cross-referenced to the data dictionary. Another advantage of using a data dictionary common to all system models is that it encourages consistency between the models; if the same name is used in two models it means the same. Wherever the reader of the model requires more detail about a label, it can be looked up in the data dictionary. For example, the current logical data flow diagram in Fig. 4.5 uses simple labels for the data flows **Order, StockLevel** and **PricedOrder**. The data stores are labelled **ORDERS** and **PRODUCT_INFORMATION**. Each of these labels will have an entry in the data dictionary where a full description will be given. To ensure that all labels are properly documented, the data dictionary should be built up as the data flow diagrams are created.

A well-maintained data dictionary avoids ambiguity about the terminology used on a project and ensures that everyone working on the project is using terminology consistently. The data dictionary also resolves problems of *aliases* where different people or departments use different names for the same data item. Both names will be entered in the data dictionary and shown to be equivalent.

Notation

There are several notations for recording data dictionaries. The one summarized in Fig. 4.23 is simple, but capable of describing the basic configurations in which data items can occur.

A label on a data flow or data store usually names a *data group* which consists of more than one *data element* or *attribute*. For example, the data flow labelled **CustomerDetails** in Fig. 4.24 describes a *data group*. This data group might consist of a title, initials, an address, and a telephone number e.g. Mr A. H. Green, 14 Ferry Road, Littleburgh, Tel. 012 345 6789. This could be described in the data dictionary as:

CustomerDetails = Title + {Initial} + Surname + CustomerAddress + (CustomerPhone)

The notation must accurately document the way these attributes are combined, i.e. it must express:

- The *sequence* in which attributes occur
- Attributes or groups of attributes which *repeat*
- Attributes that are *optional*
- That one of several possible attributes must be *selected*
- A *possible set of values* for an attribute
- *Comments* about the entries in the dictionary

Function	*Symbol*	*Description*
definition	=	consists of
sequence	+	attributes are joined by +
repetition	{ }	repeated attributes enclosed in braces { }
optionality	( )	optional attributes enclosed in parenthesis ( )
selection	[ ]	selection is indicated by enclosing the alternative attributes in square brackets [ ] separated by a vertical bar, e.g. ["Y" I "N"]
separate	I	separates alternatives in [ ]
value	" "	values are given in "..."
comment	*...*	comments between asterisks

Figure 4.23 Notation for data dictionary

Figure 4.24 Fragment of a data flow diagram to record customer details

In the data dictionary description of **CustomerDetails** the parentheses, ( ), indicate that the telephone number is optional—not all customers have telephones. The braces, { }, indicate that there may be one or more initials. If, as analysis proceeds, it is discovered that some customers give their forenames in full, while others only give their initials, the entry in the data dictionary can be updated to reflect this by using square brackets:

CustomerDetails = Title + [{ForeName} I {Initial}] + Surname + CustomerAddress + (CustomerPhone)

The square brackets, [ ], indicate a selection while the vertical bar, I separates the alternatives. If it is discovered that customers do not always give their title the entry can indicate this by using parenthesis:

CustomerDetails = (Title) + [{ForeName} | {Initial}] + Surname + CustomerAddress + (CustomerPhone)

We may wish to describe the possible *values* of **Title** with an entry in the data dictionary:

Title = ["Mr" | "Mrs" | "Miss"]

Describing documents

Figure 4.25 shows an order form currently used in the Just a Line system. When a customer phones in an order (or comes into the shop to place an order), the details of the order are recorded, in triplicate, on this form. The order form is represented in several places on the current physical data flow diagram (Fig. 4.17); it has different labels according to what state it is at and how much information has been recorded on it. Initially, it corresponds to the flow labelled Order, and is used to record the details of the customer's order before it is priced. In the data dictionary, assuming details of pricing are added at a later stage, the details of the order might be described by the entry:

Order = (Title) + [{ForeName} | {Initial}] + Surname + CustomerAddress + (CustomerPhone) + (DeliveryAddress) + DateRequired + {ProductDescription + PacketSize + NumberOfPackets}

This description is rather long, difficult to read and difficult to reproduce without introducing transcription errors. **Order** can be described more elegantly as:

Order = OrderHeader + {OrderLine}

OrderHeader = CustomerDetails + (DeliveryAddress) + DateRequired

CustomerDetails = (Title) + [{ForeName} | {Initial}] + Surname + CustomerAddress + (CustomerPhone)

OrderLine = ProductDescription + PacketSize + NumberOfPackets

This description means that an **Order** consists of an **OrderHeader** and one or more **OrderLines**. Notice that in one respect the data dictionary can be used like a normal English dictionary; terms that are used in the description of one entry may themselves be entries in the dictionary. Thus, **OrderHeader** is used

Just a Line

ORDER FORM

Mr/Mrs/Miss ______________________________

Address ______________________________

Delivery Address ______________________________

Date Required ______________ Telephone ______________

Description	Packet Size	No. Packets	Price	£	p

Total Cost		
Delivery Charge		
Amount Owing		

Figure 4.25 Just a Line: order form

to describe **Order** and can also be looked up in the data dictionary. **Order-Header** is an example of a *data structure*, a group of data attributes referred to by a label. Notice how this data structure is used again in the description of **PricedOrder** (below). Data structures are used for convenience in the data dictionary in that a long string of attributes can be replaced with a label that describes them. This technique keeps descriptions concise and more readable, avoids repetition of long strings of attributes and helps to prevent transcription errors creeping in.

Once the prices have been added to the order form it becomes a **PricedOrder**. The corresponding entry in the data dictionary reads:

PricedOrder = OrderHeader + {PricedOrderLine} + TotalCost +
(DeliveryCharge *if total cost <£30*) + AmountOwing

PricedOrderLine = OrderLine + CostPerPacket + CostOfLine

Notice the economical use of the already defined data structures **OrderHeader** and **OrderLine**.

All the essential information recorded on the order form currently used in the Just a Line system has been captured in this data dictionary description. The information content of the order form has been abstracted from the physical document on which it is recorded. The process of describing the order form in data dictionary notation results in the separation of *what* the system records from *how* it records it. The information content of the order form, *what* the system records, will be carried forward to the current logical data dictionary.

What is an appropriate level of detail?

The amount of detail appropriate for a data dictionary depends on how the data dictionary will be used. A data dictionary for a current system, for example, will normally go into less detail than a data dictionary built at the detailed design stage. If the data dictionary is to be used simply to document the system developer's understanding of current processing and to support discussions with the client, a label like **DateOfOrder** will be self-explanatory; no more detail is required. At the detailed design stage, however, the system developer is thinking ahead to the detail required in a computerized system. Decisions have to be made that were unnecessary earlier—decisions, for example, about input and output formats for dates and how they are going to be represented internally. Will the system, for instance, use '20/10/199x' as input format and '20th October 199x' as output format? Will dates be stored internally as three integers or a string of eight numeric characters? Decisions must be made about the format or 'picture' of each data element and about its permissible range of values. This information will be required when input documents or screens are being designed and when input validation checks are designed, and will be recorded in the data dictionary.

Just a Line: current logical data dictionary

A data dictionary to support the current logical data flow diagrams in Figs. 4.4, 4.5 and 4.6 of the Just a Line system is listed below:

ConfirmationOfDelivery = SupplierInvoice + JustaLineSignature

CustomerDetails = Title + [{ForeName}|{Initial}] + Surname + CustomerAddress + (CustomerPhone)

CustomerPayment = PricedOrder + CustomerSignature + Payment

DeliveryNote = PricedOrder

Invoice	= PricedOrder
Order	= Orderheader + {OrderLine}
OrderHeader	= CustomerDetails + (DeliveryAddress) + DateRequired
OrderLine	= ProductDescription + PacketSize + NumberOfPackets
ORDERS	= {PriceOrder}
Price	= ProductDescription + PacketSize + CostPerPacket *in the current system Price must contain the same information as ProductDetails*
PricedOrder	= OrderHeader + {PricedOrderLine} + TotalCost + (DeliveryCharge *if total cost < £30*) + AmountOwing
PricedOrderLine	= OrderLine + CostPerPacket + CostOfLine
PricedStockOrderLine	= StockOrderLine + CostPerUnit + CostOfLine
ProductDetails	= ProductDescription + PacketSize + CostPerPacket
PRODUCT_INFORMATION	= {ProduceInformation} *i.e. currently the design list, the price list and the contents of the store*
ProductInformation	= SupplierName + SupplierAddress + {ProductCode + ProductDescription + PacketSize + CostPerPacket}
QuantityRequired	= *quantity of product required to fill outstanding orders*
StockLevel	= ProductDescription + QuantityOnHand *number of packets left in the store*
StockOrder	= SupplierName + SupplierAddress + {StockOrderLine}
StockOrderLine	= {ProductCode + ProductDescription + PacketSize + NumberOfPackets}
SupplierInvoice	= SupplierName + SupplierAddress + {PricedStockOrderLine} + TotalCostOfGoods + (SupplierDeliveryCharge) + TotalAmountOwing

StockOrderRequirements = SupplierName + SupplierAddress +
{StockOrderLine}

SupplierPayment = SupplierInvoice + Payment

Notice the following points:

- The notational convention used here is the same as that used for labelling data flow diagrams—labels for data flows, elements and structures are written in lower case. Where a label consists of more than one word, the words are run together with no spaces but with a capital letter at the start of each word. Names of data stores are written in capital letters; where there is more than one word, the words are joined by the underscore character,
- This data dictionary is short and uncomplicated. It is therefore sufficiently structured if kept simply in alphabetic order.
- Order, PricedOrder, Invoice and DeliveryNote refer to the same piece of paper at different stages in the system.

Contents of data dictionary

A simple data dictionary can be kept as an alphabetic list, as above. A more sophisticated data dictionary may have separate sections for data elements, data structures, data flows, data stores and entity descriptions (see Chapter 5).

Data elements Data elements are the *primitives* of the data dictionary. Examples in the description of the Just a Line order form are **DateRequired**, **CostPerPacket** and **ProductDescription**. These are the smallest data items used in the system and are not further decomposed. A full description of a data element in the later stages of system development will include a description, information about the format (or picture) of the data element, the range of permissible values, aliases and an indication of where the data element is used.

Data structures, data stores and data flows Data structures are combinations of data elements of other data structures—all of which are defined elsewhere in the data dictionary. A data structure is a named (labelled) list of data elements. Data flows and data stores are data structures. A data structure may correspond to a data flow or a data store on a data flow diagram, but it does not have to. It allows us simply and unambiguously to describe a long sequence of data elements. This is particularly useful when the list of elements is used repeatedly.

Summary

A data dictionary provides a central store of data about data. It allows the system developer to describe data flows and stores by simple names, keeping the data flow diagrams readable and uncluttered. A data dictionary solves many communication problems—everyone working on the same project knows the exact meaning of the words and terms used. It also resolves the problems of aliases where different users use different names for the same thing. The data dictionary is also used to record data about the data model, the process definitions and the entity life histories.

4.5 PROCESS DEFINITIONS

What are process definitions?

Process definitions form part of the supporting documentation for data flow diagrams. The data dictionary describes in detail the data flows and data stores on the data flow diagrams; the process definitions describe in detail what is happening in the process boxes on the data flow diagram. Only the bottom-level processes on each data flow diagram are described—any process box that is decomposed at a lower level does not have a corresponding process definition. High-level process boxes simply serve as structuring devices; they bundle together lower-level processes to provide a convenient overview of the system. The action takes place in the lowest-level processes only; therefore these are the only processes that need to be described. Nothing happens in the higher-level processes over and above what happens in the lowest-level processes. Bottom-level processes may be marked by an asterisk in the bottom right-hand corner of the process box on the DFD (see Fig. 4.6).

Why are process definitions useful?

Before structured techniques were used to develop systems, developers described the functionality of the existing and the new systems in a natural language, such as English. These descriptions often proved to be ambiguous, incomplete and inconsistent. Process definitions try to avoid this by using more precise techniques to describe what the system does. They are used to support the data flow diagrams for the following reasons:

- The labels on data flow diagram processes are too brief to give sufficient information.
- Nouns used in process definitions are defined in the data dictionary—this helps to avoid ambiguity and ensure consistency.

- Process definitions use descriptive techniques which avoid the ambiguity inherent in natural language descriptions; these include structured English, decision tables and decision trees.

Structured English

Structured English is a limited and structured sub-set of natural language, with a syntax similar to a block-structured programming language. The following set of constructs is suggested:

- A sequence construct—statement 1 is executed before statement 2

  1. Add A to Total
  2. Divide Total by Count

- Two decision constructs, for example:

  IF ... THEN ... ELSE construct
  CASE construct, for deciding between more than two alternatives

- One or two repetition constructs, for example:

  WHILE ... DO
  REPEAT ... UNTIL

Guidelines for writing structured English

- Develop a consistent style. Once you have selected a set of constructs (such as the above) stick to these; do not introduce new ones.
- Use layout conventions to help reveal structure and meaning; be consistent in using layout conventions
- Use the data dictionary. Refer to nouns by their data dictionary names.

Just a Line example

In a supplementary interview, Sue told the system developer how they decided whether or not a customer was entitled to free delivery of their order. This is how Sue described the process:

'To be entitled to free delivery, customers must place an order worth £30 and live within a five mile radius or have been with us for more than a year. If customers do not live locally we post the cards.'

This description has the drawbacks of many natural language descriptions in that it is:

- *Ambiguous.* Does it mean '£30 and (live within five miles or one year's custom)' or '(£30 and live within five miles) or one year's custom'?
- *Imprecise.* What is a 'five mile radius'? Is it five miles as the crow flies or five miles on the mileometer? What does 'local' mean?
- *Incomplete.* We assume it is '£30 or more. In this case that seems to be obvious, but we should not have to make any assumptions.

Structured English The system developer rewrote Sue's description in structured English, avoiding the pitfalls of the natural language description:

```
if not local Customer (*lives outside 20 miles radius*)
        charge P&P
else (*local customer*)
        if TotalCost (* of Order*) < £30 then
            set DeliveryCharge
        else if TotalCost (* of Order*) > = £30 then
            if Distance < = 5 miles then
                no DeliveryCharge
            else (*Distance > 5 miles*) then
                if CustomerTradeRecord > = 1 year then
                    no DeliveryCharge
                else (*CustomerTradeRecord < 1 year*)
                    set DeliveryCharge
```

The comments are made between an opening parenthesis and asterisk and a closing parenthesis and asterisk, (* ... *). Capitalized nouns must all be defined in the data dictionary.

Additions to the data dictionary The Just a Line current logical data dictionary must be updated to record the nouns used in the above structured English description:

> CustomerTradeRecord
> DeliveryCharge
> Distance
> P&P
> TotalCost

As the nouns are being used to describe the current system it is sufficient to describe them with an informal comment:

> CustomerTradeRecord   = *DeliveryDate of first order*
>
> DeliveryCharge   = *calculated at a flat rate of xxp per mile*

Distance	= *number of miles on mileometer*
P&P	= *package and posting; cost of postal stamps plus flat rate of xxp for package*
TotalCost	= *total cost of order before adding delivery or postal charges*

Decision trees

System developers use two other techniques for expressing process definitions—decision trees and decision tables. The free delivery process is expressed as a decision tree in Fig. 4.26. The decision tree expresses the logic of the process clearly and graphically and is a useful technique for communication with a client. Descriptions of complicated decision-making processes in structured English can be hard to follow.

Decision tables

Where a decision process involves a complicated combination of conditions and actions it is more appropriate to use a decision table. The general format of a decision table is shown in Fig. 4.27. A decision table is created by listing all the relevant conditions in the top left-hand quarter of the decision table and all the relevant actions in the bottom left-hand quarter of the decision table. The top right-hand corner of the table tabulates, in separate columns, all possible combinations of conditions. Each column, recording a possible combination of conditions, is called a *rule*. Below each rule, in the bottom right-hand corner of the table, the appropriate action is specified.

The conditions that affect the free delivery process are:

- TotalCost (* Order *) < £30
- Local (* Customer*).
- Distance more than 5 miles
- CustomerTradeRecord < 1 year

The possible actions are:

- Charge for delivery
- Charge P&P
- No charge

The rules dictating which combination of conditions result in which actions are shown in Fig. 4.28.

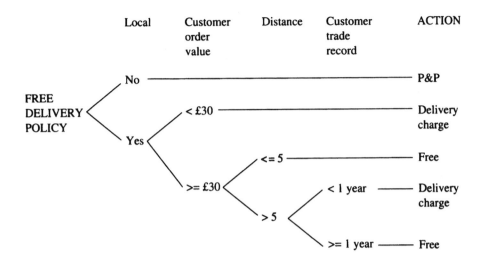

Figure 4.26 Free delivery process as a decision tree

	RULES			
CONDITIONS	1	2	3	4
List of conditions				
ACTIONS				
List of actions				

Figure 4.27 Decision table structure

Summary

Process definitions describe what happens in the bottom-level process boxes of a set of data flow diagrams. Natural language descriptions can be ambiguous, incomplete and inconsistent. Process definitions are normally expressed in structured English or by a decision table or a decision tree. Decision tables are

RULES

CONDITIONS	1	2	3	4	5
Local (*Customer*)	N	Y	Y	Y	Y
TotalCost (*Order*) < £30	–	Y	N	N	N
Distance > 5 miles	–	–	N	Y	Y
CustomerTradeRecord < 1 year	–	–	–	Y	N
Charge for delivery		X		X	
Charge P&P	X				
No Charge			X		X

Figure 4.28 Free delivery process as a decision table

useful for describing complex processes with many interdependent conditions and many possible actions. Decision trees have the advantage of immediate at-a-glance clarity but can be inflexible. Structured English is very flexible, makes use of the data dictionary and is much favoured by those with a programming background as it leads naturally, through pseudocode, to many high-level programming languages.

EXERCISES AND TOPICS FOR DISCUSSION

Data flow diagrams: Part 1

4.1 Study the level 2 current logical data flow diagram of the Just a Line system in Fig. 4.6. Check that it is consistent with the level 1 diagram in Fig. 4.5—is the balancing rule infringed?

4.2 In Fig. 4.8 the parent and child diagrams do not balance. Redraw the child diagram so that the flows balance with the parent diagram.

4.3 Read the case study below:

The management of the Underground train service have requested an automatic ticket machine to function as outlined below. The user of the machine asks for a destination and ticket type (e.g. single, return or day return) and the machine displays the price. When enough money has been put in, the machine issues a date-stamped ticket containing the issuing station, the destination, ticket type and price. If appropriate, the machine also gives change. The machine records the number of tickets issued for each destination and the number of tickets of each type for each day. Once a week these statistics are transferred to the main computer.

(a) Draw the context diagram of the automatic ticket machine case study.
(b) Draw a level 1 CLDFD of the automatic ticket machine case study.

4.4 **Capital Taxis system.** Capital Taxis is a firm that provides transport for passengers based in London and the South East. Organization of these journeys is handled centrally from Capital's control centre near Marble Arch.

When a call is received in the control centre the receptionist writes down the call details on a pre-printed form. The pick-up address is identified from a map-book, together with the map reference coordinates. On completion of the call the form is placed in a central collection point with other call forms.

The distribution clerk collects the call forms from the central collection point and, from the details on the forms, decides which division should deal with it (the control centre is divided into four divisions—North, South, East and West). The clerk also tries to pick out any duplicate calls at this point. The call form is passed to the relevant division where an assistant examines it together with location and availability information on the taxis in the division. The journey is allocated to the taxi which is nearest the pick-up address and is currently free.

(a) Draw a context diagram of the current system at Capital Taxis.
(b) Draw a level 1 current physical data flow diagram of the system at Capital Taxis.

4.5 **Department store credit system.** A large department store has an arrangement whereby regular customers can pay for purchases using a store credit card. When customers wish to buy something in the store, they present their credit card to the assistant. The card is then passed through a machine to check that the credit holder has sufficient credit. The sale is then authorized or refused by the company.

If the sale is authorized, the transaction is carried out using a two-part voucher. This records details of the customer and the transactions. The customer signs the voucher and then keeps one copy. The assistant puts the other copy of the voucher in the till. At the end of each day all vouchers are collected and sent to the accounts department.

Each credit card holder receives a monthly statement showing the details of payments and purchases since the last statement, any interest due, the total amount owing and the minimum amount which must be sent to the company. This is calculated as a percentage of the amount owing or £10, whichever is the greater. Records of customer transactions are archived and kept for at least five years.

(a) Draw a current physical context diagram of the system described above.
(b) Draw a level 1 current physical DFD of the system described above.

4.6 **Estate agent's system.** A potential buyer contacts the office and is given details that meet his requirements. He is then added to the mailing list and will be sent particulars of suitable properties as they come on to the market.

Sellers ask for a valuation and an agent is sent round to value the property. Valuing the property consists of making notes of the property details, measuring rooms and estimating the price the property could fetch. Afterwards the sellers are sent a standard letter outlining the service provided by the firm and quoting a price for the property. Property detail leaflets are typed from the valuation notes. Property details for the newspaper have to be ready by Monday at 4 p.m.

Buyers put in an offer on a house to the agent who conveys it to the seller. If the seller accepts the offer then the house is marked as 'under offer'. The agent does nothing further until the legal details are sorted through the solicitor.

(a) Draw a context diagram of the current physical system at the estate agent's office.
(b) Draw a level 1 data flow diagram of the current physical system at the estate agent's office.

4.7 **X-ray system**: an exercise in drawing levelled data flow diagrams

1. **Overview.** A hospital X-ray clinic does X-rays by appointment. A patient is given an X-ray request form by his GP. The patient calls at the clinic to make an appointment and receives an appointment card.
2. When the appointment falls due, and patient reports to the clinic. He is X-rayed, and a report is prepared, one copy of which goes to the GP.
3. When the appointment falls due the patient reports to the clinic, the appointment is checked by the clinic receptionist and the X-ray request retrieved. A history request slip is sent to the filing room so that the patient's reports and X-rays can be extracted and sent to Radiography. The X-ray is taken and clipped to any patient history. This information is passed to the consultant, who produces a new

report. One copy is filed with the X-rays and old reports; another copy is sent to the GP.

4. **Checking understanding.** The analyst now feels he has a reasonable understanding of the system. To check, he 'walks through' the level 2 DFD with the people responsible for each stage. The consultant's secretary tells him: 'When the new report is ready, I clip it to the past X-rays and reports and return the updated history to the filing room, who copy it, file one copy and send the other copy to the GP.'

Using the information given in paragraphs 1 and 2:
(a) Draw a context diagram for the system at the X-ray clinic.
(b) Draw a level 1 diagram for the system at the X-ray clinic.
Using the extra information given in paragraph 3:
(c) Expand your level 1 diagram as appropriate to produce a level 2 diagram.

Using the information given by the consultant's secretary in paragraph 4:
(d) Revise your level 2 diagram to take account of the new information.
(e) Expand your level 2 diagram as appropriate to produce a level 3 diagram.

4.8 **Milk delivery system.** The level 2 data flow diagram in Fig. 4.29 contains several 'syntax' errors. These errors should be apparent without further information about the system. List the errors. A correct version of this diagram is shown in Exercise 4.14, Fig. 4.32.

Data flow diagrams: Part 2

4.9 Convert the level 2 current logical data flow diagram in Fig. 4.6 to a current physical data flow diagram (CPDFD) by including the physical details supplied in the interview about the Just a Line system in Chapter 1 and which are incorporated into the level 1 CPDFD in Fig. 4.17.

4.10 The interview in Chapter 1 is intentionally brief. Drawing the current physical data flow diagram in answer to Exercise 4.9 should reveal some gaps in the picture of the Just a Line system. Make a list of questions you would ask at a supplementary interview.

4.11 Study the CLDFD for the Just a Line System in Fig. 4.5. Write a brief description of what happens in the system for Harry and Sue based on this diagram.

4.12 Use the information supplied in the Just a Line interview (Chapter 3) to expand the process **Order Stock** in the current logical data flow diagram in Fig. 4.5 to a level 2 diagram.

4.13 Discuss the relative merits of using physical or logical data flow diagrams to model a current system. What factors would influence your decision?

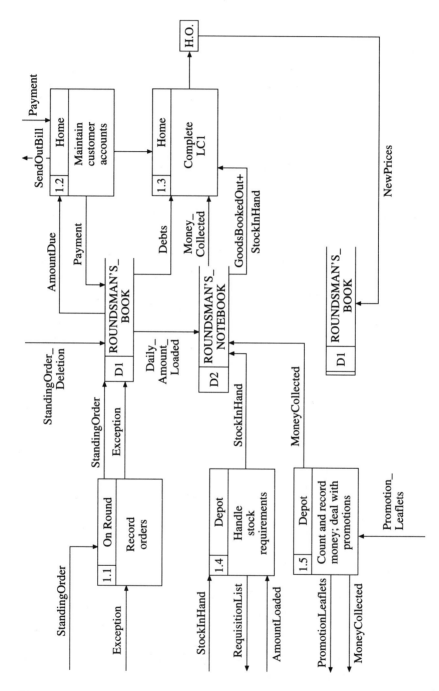

Figure 4.29 Milk delivery; level 2 CPDFD (with errors)

4.14 **Milk delivery system.** Cowdenbeath is a branch of Buttercup Dairies which is a nationwide chain. Staff at Cowdenbeath include the branch manager, Ian Renshaw, two clerks, one storeman and 21 roundsmen (milkmen).

Each round is made up of regular customers who have standing orders for milk and other products. Customers can change their standing orders as they wish—they can order an extra pint or cancel their order for a week while they are away on holiday. In the dairy these variations are known as exception orders. Customer's standing orders, exceptions and account details are recorded in the roundsman's book.

On return to the depot each roundsman gives the storeman a requisition list—his order for the next day. The requisition list is derived from the standing orders, any known exceptions (e.g. holidays) and left-over stock. Goods are booked out to the roundsmen each morning and recorded in the storeman's book.

A customer's weekly bill is calculated from his or her standing order and exception orders for that week. The roundsmen deliver the bills on Thursdays and collect the money on Fridays. When they get back to the depot, the roundsmen count the money and hand it over to one of the clerks who records it in a cash book. Each roundsman keeps a notebook in which they record the amount booked out to them by the storeman, any stock left over at the end of the day and the amount of money handed over to the clerk.

At the end of each week all the roundsmen have to complete an LC1. This is a form which shows the current financial state of their round. The LC1 is given to the clerk who then checks it against the storeman's book and against the cash book. At the end of the month Ian Renshaw has to send the checked LC1s to Head Office.

From time to time Head Office organize promotions on certain goods, in order to boost flagging milk sales. Leaflets about the goods on promotion are distributed to regular customers.

Examine the levelled set of current physical data flow diagrams of the milk delivery system (Figs 4.30 to 4.32). Draw a level 2 current logical data flow diagram of the milk delivery system.

Data Dictionary

4.15 In the Just a Line case study, check that all the data flows and data stores on the current logical data flow diagrams are defined in the data dictionary. Do the same with the required logical data flow diagram.

4.16 Using the information given in the interview with Sue and Harry, and information recorded in the current logical data dictionary of the Just a Line system, write data dictionary descriptions of the data stores:

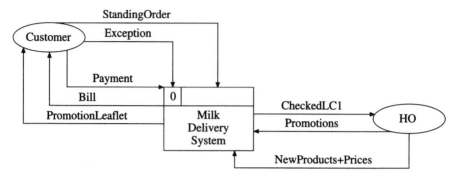

Figure 4.30 Milk delivery: context CPDFD

STORE
DESIGN_LIST
PRICE_LIST

shown on the current physical data flow diagram in Fig. 4.17.

4.17 Update the data dictionary to support the data flow diagram you produced as an answer to Exercise 4.12.

4.18 Write a data dictionary to support the data flow diagram of the automatic ticket machine system case study, Exercise 4.3.

4.19 The document in Fig. 4.33 is an example of a customer's monthly statement from the department store credit system described in Exercise 4.5. Describe this document in data dictionary notation.

4.20 Using the case study notes and current physical DFDs of the milk delivery system specified in Exercise 4.14, write data dictionary descriptions for the flows StandingOrder, Exception and ROUNDSMAN'S_BOOK.

Process definition

4.21 Under what circumstances would you choose to write a process definition using:

(a) Structured English
(b) Decision table
(c) Decision tree

4.22 Use a decision table to describe the appropriate action for a driver approaching traffic lights in each of the possible combinations of red, amber and green.

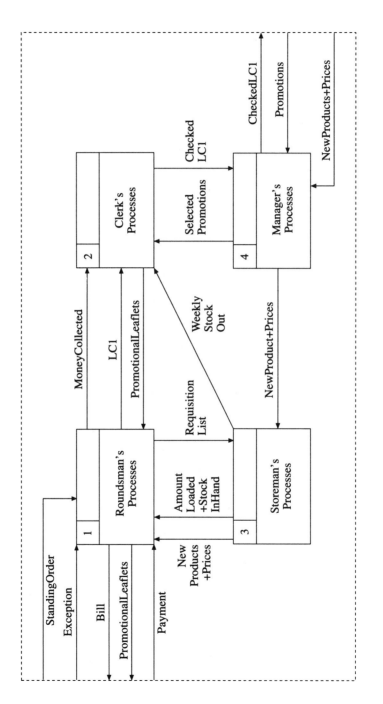

Figure 4.31 Milk delivery system: level 1 CPDFD

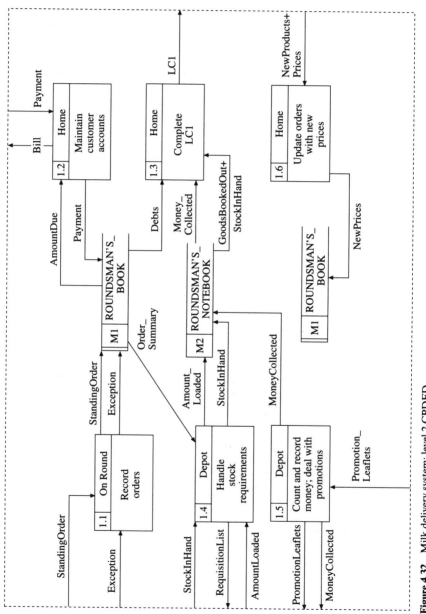

Figure 4.32 Milk delivery system: level 2 CPDFD

Joshua Prichards :	Joshua Prichard & Sons Ltd, Customers' Accounts, PO Box 12, Cambridge, England, CB1 1PT. Telephone (01223) 654321	Statement of Account
Statement No. 1737	**Card No.** B37787	**Statement Date** 31/12/95

Mrs V. I. Paterson,
8, Walden Road,
Saffron Walden,
Essex.

Date	Department/Reference		Debit	Credit
3/12/95	L /124814	A	£23.95	
7/12/95	D /143712	A	£21.45	
15/12/95	A /141497	A	£7.99	
17/12/95	TC2189	A		£7.99

			Payment Due £45.40	**Credit Balance**

Figure 4.33 Monthly customer statement

4.23 The following is a description of the procedure for determining carpet-fitting charges for carpets bought from Paradise Goods Ltd:

For the purpose of determining delivery charges, customers are divided into two categories, those who are account holders and those who are not. If an account holder buys a carpet costing less than £1000, the fitting charge to be added to the cost of the carpet is £1.25 per square metre. However, if the carpet costs £1000 or more, the fitting charge is £0.75 per square metre. If a customer is not an account holder and the carpet cost is less than £1000, the fitting charge is £1.65 per square metre. For a carpet costing £1000 or more, however, the fitting charge is £1.15 per square metre.

(a) Draw a decision tree showing the process described above.

(b) Describe the same process using structured English.

4.24 Miss Take takes pride in dealing appropriately with all weather conditions. She follows a strict set of rules which ensure that she never lives up to her name. She never goes to work if it is raining in November. If she does go to work she takes an umbrella when it is raining and a coat when it is windy. She always wears a hat when she goes to work, unless it is windy. If it is windy in November she switches on her central heating.

Draw a decision table to show Miss Take's routine.

4.25 (a) Figure E4.3(b) in answers to Selected Exercises shows a level 1 data flow diagram describing an automatic ticket machine. Write a process definition in structured English for process 1: 'Calculate ticket price'.

(b) Write a process definition in structured English for process 2: 'Issue ticket'.

REFERENCES AND FURTHER READING

Crinnion, J. (1991) *Evolutionary Systems Development*, Pitman, London.

Gane, C. and Sarson, T. (1979) *Structured Systems Analysis*, Prentice-Hall, Sydney.

Goodland, M. (1995) *SSADM Version 4: A Practical Approach*, McGraw-Hill, London.

Robinson, B. and Prior, M. (1995) *Systems Analysis Techniques*, International Thomson Computer Press, London.

Yourdon, E. (1989) *Modern Structured Analysis*, Prentice-Hall, Englewood Cliffs, N.J.

DATA MODELLING

5.1 PRINCIPLES OF DATA MODELLING

Introduction

Earlier methodologies did not include, or paid limited attention to, data modelling. Increasingly, a data model is developed in parallel with the data flow diagram and given equal emphasis. Some methodologies do the data flow diagram before the data model, some do the data model first. Our own view is that the order is not significant, both are tools the developer should use where and when they will be helpful. The data flow diagram is concerned with the question, *What does the system do with the data?* The data model is concerned with the question, *What data does the system need to store and what is the most efficient way of organizing it?* Stored data requirements are not ignored by the data flow diagram; its data stores model the stored data. However, when designing data stores, the system developer is not attempting to find an efficient way of organizing the data, merely identifying the stored data items and grouping them in some way. In a data flow diagram of the current physical system the data stores correspond to identifiable physical repositories of data, e.g. ledger books, filing cabinets and reference manuals. A·data flow diagram of the current logical system abstracts the data from the current implementation and groups data that seem to be associated in some way, each group being represented by a data store. The basis for identifying a data group or entity in the data model is rather more rigorous and is discussed in the following sections.

Data modelling uses two separate techniques to achieve a satisfactory set of entities, entity–relationship (E–R) modelling and normalization. We discuss data modelling in three sections. The first section discusses issues common to E–R modelling and normalization, the second discusses E–R modelling and the third discusses normalization.

Purpose of data modelling

The data model sets out to capture all the data that the system needs to store and to organize the data into an efficient structure. It goes about this by pursuing four main objectives:

1. The *identification of the data objects or entities* in the system, their structure and the relationships between entities.
2. The construction of a model of the stored data requirements of the system which is *independent of specific processing requirements*.
3. The construction of a robust data model, i.e. of a *minimal* model of the data required to be stored by the system.
4. The construction of a *logical* model of the data, i.e. a model that is not concerned with *how* the data storage will be, or is currently, physically implemented.

Identification of entities Data modelling aims to identify the system entities, i.e. items about which the system needs to store data (e.g. customers, orders, products, etc.). Data modelling also shows the internal structure of these entities, i.e. describes the details stored about each entity (e.g. for each customer store the **CustomerName**, **CustomerAddress**, **CustomerPhone**, etc.). The system developer also uses the data model to show the relationships between entities, i.e. show any relationships between entities that are significant to the system (e.g. customers place orders therefore there is a significant relationship between them).

Process-independent model Whereas the data flow diagram concentrates on what *happens* to the system data, the data model concentrates on the properties of the data itself, *independently of the processing requirements* of the system. The data model aims to collect all the data that needs to be stored for the system to operate and to organize that data into a sound structure. The data needs to be organized in such a way that it will operate best in an information storage and retrieval system, i.e. in an insert, update and delete environment. The data model considers the data independently of the processing requirements because the stored data in a system is more stable than the processing requirements of a system. During the lifetime of a system the processing requirements will almost inevitably evolve as the system changes to meet a changing environment. For example, the system may be required to produce extra reports, include a new set of functions (perhaps the accounting functions) or do its calculations differently. However, the data does not tend to change significantly over the system life span. A correct data model provides a solid foundation on which to build the rest of the system.

Minimal model Data modelling was originally devised for database design. Database design stresses the importance of a process-independent approach to the organization of the stored data and the importance of allowing as little redundant data as is feasible—as far as is possible one item of data should be stored in one and only one place. If the same item of data is stored in more than one place, it is unnecessarily using up precious storage space and may result in the system having discrepancies between data that has been updated in one place but not in another. Another potential source of discrepancy is stored data that has been derived (i.e. calculated) from other data stored in the system. A robust data model is one that does not permit this sort of discrepancy.

Logical model Data modelling is not concerned with how the data is physically stored either in the current system or in the computer-based system being developed. The reason for this is that the most efficient way of organizing data on, for example, a card index in a manual system will almost certainly be very different from the most efficient way of storing data in a computer-based system. The data model aims to develop an efficient model of the data independently of how it is implemented.

Two techniques: E–R modelling and normalization

Data modelling uses two quite distinct techniques to achieve a satisfactory organization of the system's data: a top-down approach, which we refer to as E–R modelling, and a bottom-up approach, which we refer to as normalization. The successful data model uses both. Both aim to achieve the goals listed above. E–R modelling begins by looking for the data groups in the system. It starts with the questions, *Who or what do we need to store data about?* It provides a useful first attempt to organize the data but results in a data model which may be incomplete and may have redundant data. It can also be vague about relationships. However, this first data model can provide a sensible starting point for the second technique, normalization. Normalization starts *bottom-up*, by looking at the smallest individual items of data recorded by the system. Theoretically, this technique can take as its starting point the mass of disorganized data items collected during the fact-finding stages of analysis. Following a series of well-defined rules, normalization will structure these data items into a set of entities, forming a data model. The two data models are then reconciled. However, this is often impractical because of the volume of data items involved. It is more practical to take the entities identified during E–R modelling and normalize these.

Terminology and notation

Data modelling has its own terminology: It describes data in terms of *entities: occurrences* of entities, *attributes* of entities, *values* of entities, entity *keys* and *relationships* between entities.

Entities An entity is an object about which the system requires to hold data, such as CUSTOMER or PRODUCT. It is represented as a box on the E–R model diagram with the name of the entity inside, as in Fig. 5.1. In a computer-based system an entity will probably be implemented as a computer file.

CUSTOMER   **PRODUCT**

Figure 5.1 Representation of entities

An *occurrence* of an entity describes, for example, one *particular* customer or product. The entity itself represents a number of entity occurrences, all the customers or all the products in the system. In this book an entity is always referred to in block capitals (e.g. CUSTOMER) and an occurrence of that entity is referred to in lower case but begins with a capital letter (e.g. Customer).

The *attributes* of an entity are the data items or elements that make up that entity. For example, **CustomerName**, **CustomerAddress** and **CreditStatus** might be three attributes of the entity CUSTOMER. Entities often represent something in the real world, as is the case with the entity CUSTOMER. However, the attributes we record about a **Customer** are only those of significance to the system. The Just a Line system will not record, for example, a customer's taste in music or beer. These attributes might be of significance, respectively, in systems processing orders for records or dealing with off-license sales, but not one that deals with mail-order card sales. In a computer-based system attributes will be implemented as *fields* in a computer file.

The *value* of an attribute is the value of that attribute for a particular entity occurrence; for example, John Barrett might be the value of the attribute **CustomerName**.

Keys A key to an entity is an attribute or set of attributes whose values uniquely identify one occurrence of that entity, e.g. one **Customer** or one **Product**. If the system is to work, each occurrence of an entity (or each record of a computer-based implementation) must be distinguishable from the others. It must be possible to identify it and to extract the relevant stored details. To do this we need a distinguishing feature for that occurrence. Normally, this will be one of its attributes but sometimes a combination of more than one attribute has to be used. For example, in an entity STUDENT, a collection of **Students** may be distinguishable from each other by **Name**. However, if their **Name** does not uniquely identify each **Student**, then a combination of **Name** and **DateOfBirth** may work. Failing this, we could give each **Student** a unique **StudentNumber**. We would then be able to guarantee that, given the appropriate **StudentNumber**, we could extract the rest of the stored details about that **Student**—the value of the **StudentNumber** *determines* the value of the other data items in the entity. All keys that uniquely identify an occurrence of an entity are known as *candidate keys*. If a combination of **Name** and **DateOfBirth** can be relied on to uniquely identify each student, then this combination of attributes is one *candidate key*; **StudentNumber** is another candidate key. If **StudentNumber** is what we decide to use as the key for this entity, it becomes the *primary key*. In the Just a Line system, **CustomerNumber** might be used as the primary key to CUSTOMER if we design the customer numbers in such a way that no two **Customers** have the same **CustomerNumber**. In the data dictionary, entity primary keys are underlined.

To fulfill its function of uniquely identifying each instance of an entity, a primary key should have the following properties:

- A primary key must be unique for each instance (or occurrence) of an entity.
- A primary key must always have a value—it must never be allowed to have a null value, otherwise the possibility arises of several entity occurrences having the same primary key. As soon as an instance of an entity is created it must have a value assigned for its primary key, e.g. a new student must immediately be given a student number.
- Ideally a primary key should not contain an attribute that is liable to change; e.g. student name is not an ideal primary key, even when combined with date of birth, as it may change. The danger of using a key whose value may change can be illustrated from an early data processing system which used as a key to its customer file a combination of the sector, track and disk surface number of the disk location where each customer's details were stored. Of course when the disk had to be reorganized, all the customer keys had to be changed.
- System developers should maintain control over the primary keys. The disk example above illustrates this point. Another system team—developing a milk delivery system—suffered in the same way because they were persuaded to use their customers' telephone numbers as the primary key. The team did not realize that the telephone company might change the numbers or that there would be households like student flats where there might be several customers with the same telephone number.

Foreign keys An entity may contain as one of its attributes a data item which is the primary key of another entity. For example, Figure 5.2 shows an entity EMPLOYEE while Fig. 5.3 shows an entity DEPARTMENT. One of the attributes of the EMPLOYEE entity is **DeptNo** which is the primary key of the entity DEPARTMENT; this makes **DeptNo** a foreign key in the EMPLOYEE entity. Foreign keys act as links or navigation routes between related entities.

EmpNo	Name	StartDate	Scale	DeptNo	ExtNo	OfficeNo
143	M. Cobby	12/04/86	S1	42	2345	663
267	S. Bedbrook	01/06/82	GS2	42	4271	663
281	B. Watts	23/10/91	P3	21	9478	251
296	D. Hawkins	01/09/92	P2	16	4364	382
341	I. Oxford	07/10/89	GS2	33		337
367	A. Varty	10/09/70	D4	33	3216	338

Figure 5.2 Employee entity

DeptNo	DeptName	HeadOfDept
16	English	A. C. Taylor
21	French	G. F. A. Andrews
33	Computer Science	M. H. Martin
42	Maths	J. F. Smith

Figure 5.3 Department entity

Relationships A relationship is a link between two entities which is significant for the system. For example, a **Customer** places an **Order**—'places' describes a relationship between a **Customer** and an **Order**. This is a relationship in the real world and one that would be significant in an order-processing system. The relationship is represented by a line between the two entities concerned, as in Fig. 5.4.

It is important to capture all the significant relationships when designing information systems because they trace the access from one entity occurrence to another. If a relationship exists between CUSTOMER and ORDER, this implies that for each individual order we can trace the customer who placed

Figure 5.4 Representation of relationships

Figure 5.5 Named relationship

that order; for each occurrence of CUSTOMER (i.e. each customer in the system), we can trace all the associated occurrences of ORDER (i.e. all the orders they placed). Entities must be linked to reflect all significant real-life relationships so that when implemented on a computer-based system, all processing requirements, both now and in the future, can be satisfied. Sometimes it is useful to name the relationship between entities as in Fig. 5.5.

The degree of relationships The relationship between CUSTOMER and ORDER is one to many in that any one Customer places many (one or more) Orders and any one Order is placed by just one Customer. A relationship is indicated by a line between entities on the E–R diagram. The degree of the relationship is indicated by a crow's foot on the 'many' end of the line. Relationships between entities can be:

- One to one
- One to many
- Many to many
- Reflexive

Figure 5.6 gives an example of each type of relationship using E–R diagrams.
Occurrence diagrams (Fig. 5.7) can also be useful for explaining relationships. However, E–R diagrams are a more concise technique.

One to one Assume that a husband has one wife (at a time) and a wife has one husband. More formally, any occurrence of the entity HUSBAND (i.e. any Husband) is associated with only one occurrence of the entity WIFE (i.e. one Wife). Figure 5.7 illustrates with an occurrence diagram the nature of the one to one relationship between HUSBAND and WIFE. Figure 5.6 models the same relationship with an E–R diagram.

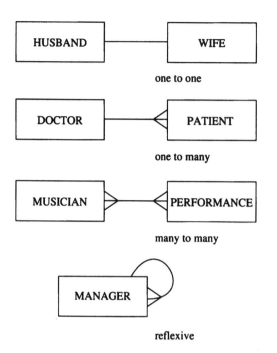

Figure 5.6 Degree of relationships: E–R diagram

One to many A doctor has many patients but the rules of the practice dictate that a patient is registered with only one doctor.

Many to many A musician plays in many concerts and a concert is performed by many musicians.

Reflexive An occurrence of an entity can have a relationship with another occurrence of the same entity. The diagram in Fig. 5.6 shows an example of a reflexive relationship. Any manager may manage several people who are themselves managers of others. A manager can therefore manage another manager. Similarly, a parent may be the parent of someone who is also a parent. A parent can therefore be a parent of a parent.

Optional and mandatory relationships A relationship between two entities can be mandatory or optional. A relationship is optional if, where a relationship exists between two entities, it is possible for an occurrence of one entity to exist without being associated with an occurrence of the other entity. The relationship between the entity MOTHER and the entity SON is mandatory for SON and optional for MOTHER—a Son cannot exist without having (at some stage) a Mother but a Mother does not have to have a Son. Optional relationships are shown by dotted lines and mandatory relationships by solid

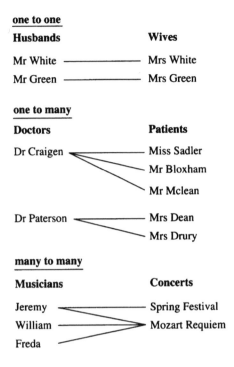

Figure 5.7 Degree of relationships, occurrence diagrams

lines, as in Fig. 5.8. A relationship between two entities is mandatory if every occurrence of one must participate in a relationship with an occurrence of the other. In Fig. 5.9 a mandatory relationship exists between STUDENT and COURSE—every Student must take at least one course and every course must be studied by at least one student.

The notation used here for drawing E–R models is one of several different notations that serve the same purpose. However, it is only the symbols in the various notations that are different, the underlying logic is the same. A summary of the notation used in this book is given in Fig. 5.10.

5.2 ENTITY–RELATIONSHIP MODELLING

Practical guidelines

We gave stated above the purpose of data modelling. These purposes are common to both the techniques of E–R modelling and normalization. In practical terms we achieve these purposes by building a data model with various well-defined characteristics, outlined below:

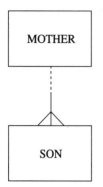

Figure 5.8 Optional relationship for MOTHER, mandatory relationship for SON

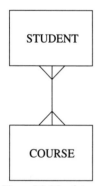

Figure 5.9 Mandatory relationship between STUDENT and COURSE

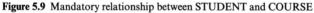

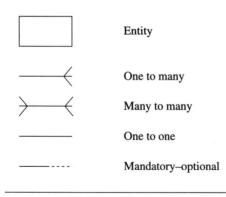

	Entity
	One to many
	Many to many
	One to one
	Mandatory–optional

Figure 5.10 Summary of notation for data modelling

1. The first is that data items should be put into logical groups, groups that 'go together'. For example, we might group together all the data relating to **Customer**—name, address, etc.—just as in a manual filing system we might have a card file of customers, each card having the details about one customer. Failure to group data items into groups that go together or are mutually dependent can cause unexpected problems. For example, in the current system at Just a Line there is no customer data held except on the orders. It follows that, as far as the system is concerned, a customer ceases to exist for any period that he or she does not have an order in the system. This does not matter much in the existing system, but the new system is required to send out mail shots to all customers. Without a permanent file of customers details this is impossible.

2. The second characteristic is that for each data group, or entity, there should be a key that uniquely identifies individual members of that entity. For example, a customer's name might uniquely identify an individual customer in a small system. In a larger system with more customers we might have to introduce a customer number to uniquely identify each customer.

3. The third characteristic of a good data model is that there should be no redundant data in the model. Data is deemed to be redundant in the following situations:

   (a) The data is never used by the system.
   (b) The same data items (e.g. **CustomerName**, **CustomerAddress**) are stored in more than one place in the system.
   (c) Data in one place can be derifed from data held in another place in the system (e.g. the total order price can be derived from the individual item prices and ordered quantities).

The first of these situations just wastes space. The other two can cause real problems. If a customer's address is stored in more than one place in the system, then if the customer changes address, we have to track down and update all copies of the address. If we miss some, we will have data in the system that is out of date.

If the system stores derived data, this both wastes space and can create situations where the system is storing data that is out of date and therefore incorrect. For example, a system might have customers with regular standing orders. If we decide to store with these orders the price of each item on the order and the total order price, we are almost certainly storing derived data. The total order price can be derived from the individual item prices on the order. The item prices themselves do not need to be stored with the order as they will almost certainly be stored with the rest of the data about the products. The danger is that if the product prices change, the prices stored with the order, and the total order price, will be out of date.

To summarize, when designing a data model we must:

- Put data items into logical groups that go together.
- Ensure that each data item needs to be stored, i.e. cannot be derived.
- Ensure that each data item is stored only once.
- Ensure that there is enough information to identify a particular instance of a data group (e.g. can we uniquely identify one particular customer record?).

E–R modelling and normalization are aiming at the same target but get there by different routes and with different degrees of success. E–R modelling starts by identifying, in a fairly arbitrary manner, the objects about which the system needs to store data. It then investigates the attributes of each entity and the relationships between the entities. These objects can then be *refined* using the informal rules outlined above. This is a top-down approach. Normalization uses a bottom-up approach that starts with the data items and applies a formal set of rules. These rules achieve the same effect as the informal approach used by E–R modelling.

How to build an E–R model

The steps in building an E–R model are outlined below and then illustrated with an example from the Just a Line case study

1. To build the E–R model we look at the system and identify data objects (entities) about which the system needs to store data.
2. For each entity, lists its attributes.
3. For each entity, check the attributes for completeness; using the practical guidelines outlined above, make any necessary improvements.
4. Investigate and record relationships. We need to be able to link entities so that all significant real-life relationships are captured.
5. Check the entity descriptions against the data dictionary descriptions of data stores, inputs and outputs, data flows, etc. Make sure that each process on the data flow diagram has available to it all the data it needs; i.e. we make sure we have captured all the data the system needs to function.

Before attempting to construct an E–R model for the Just a Line system it will be useful to recap the requirements for the new system, as these will to a large extent dictate the content of the model.

Requirements list for Just a Line

- The system must produce a personalized combined price list and order form, to be sent out to existing customers. A non-personalized version of the same form will be distributed for publicity purposes.

- The system must record when a customer last ordered, to avoid mailing customers who have not ordered within the past year.
- The system must check whether a customer order is valid, by checking that the card design ordered is one that is stocked. Checking that there is enough of that card design in stock to meet the order will remain a manual process. The computerized system must keep a record of outstanding customer orders.
- When the orders are made up the system must produce invoices to go with the goods.
- The process of preparing a supplier order will remain manual, but the system must be able to list products and quantities on the current batch of outstanding customer orders, to facilitate supplier ordering.

E–R model for Just a Line

We will do this using the stages identified above.

Identifying entities In the Just a Line system it seems a reasonable guess that we will want to store data about customers, their orders and about the products the system deals with. Our initial list of candidate entities therefore is:

CUSTOMER
ORDER
PRODUCT

The system will certainly need to store details about these three entities. At this stage the selection of entities seems to be done by plucking them out of the air rather than anything more technical. In fact, all we are trying to do is achieve a starting position to which we can apply more technical methods.

Attributes of Just a Line entities Decisions about the attributes for these entities need some thought. At this stage it may be worth checking the data flow diagram of the current system in Fig. 4.5. There are two data stores, **ORDERS** and **PRODUCT INFORMATION**. The data dictionary description of these data stores will be useful to us in the search for attributes for our entities.

Customer At the moment, the system stores no data about customers, except when an order is going through the system. We know the new system must send mail shots to customers and must keep track of when they last ordered, to avoid mailing those who have not ordered within the last year. A useful set of attributes, therefore, will be:

```
CUSTOMER  = CustomerName
            CustomerAddress   *needed for mailings*
            (CustomerPhone)   *optional because they might not
                              have one*
            LastOrderDate     *users require this to eliminate
                              customers who have not ordered
                              for 12 months*
```

Product The current system only has product information on a scribbled price list, supplemented by the supplier's design list. The new system will need information about products for printing the price list/order form, for checking customer orders for validity, for pricing orders, for producing customer invoices and for producing the list of items on outstanding customer orders that is required to help with supplier ordering. The attributes we need to store about products, therefore, might be:

```
PRODUCT = ProductDescription +
          PacketSize +        *number in a packet*
          CostPerPacket       *cost per packet*
```

Order If we examine the current order form (Fig. 4.25) and its data dictionary description, we can see that orders in the current system include the following attributes (the list is simplified to make the example clearer):

```
ORDER = CustomerName +
        (CustomerPhone) +
        CustomerAddress +
        DateRequired +
        {ProductDescription +
        PacketSize +
        NumberOfPackets}
```

This list of attributes will serve as our starting point. Now we need to see what can be done to improve this initial list.

Improving the E–R model Using the practical guidelines above we can tidy up our list of attributes.

Customer

- The item **LastOrderDate** in the entity **CUSTOMER** will be stored as **DateRequired** on the **Order**. This is therefore a derivable item and can be omitted.

- It is unlikely that **CustomerName** will always be sufficient to uniquely identify a customer. It will be safer to introduce a **CustomerNumber**. This gives us:

  CUSTOMER = CustomerNumber + CustomerName + CustomerAddress + (CustomerPhone)

Product Cards are sold in packets of different sizes, packets of 5, 10, 25, etc. It will simplify identification of products if we introduce an internal **ProductCode** so that we do not need to rely on **ProductDescription** alone to identify individual products. If the same card is sold in two or more **PacketSizes** then there will be a different **ProductCode** for each, so that the **ProductCode** identifies the card design and the number in the packet. This gives us:

  PRODUCT = ProductCode + ProductDescription + PacketSize + CostPerPacket

The current supplier also uses a product code which Sue uses when ordering. However, as the business might in the future decide to use more than one supplier (and each supplier would probably have a different set of product codes), it is not sensible to use the supplier's product codes. At the moment, Sue can look up the supplier's product codes and add them manually to the supplier order. If in future we want to automate this part of the system, it will be a simple process to add a look-up table to translate from the internal product code to the appropriate supplier product code.

ORDER   At the moment our tentative list of attributes for **ORDER** is:

  ORDER = CustomerName +
          (CustomerPhone) +
          CustomerAddress +
          DateRequired +
          {ProductDescription +
          PacketSize +
          NumberOfPackets}

   The first three items are already stored in **CUSTOMER**, and as we want to avoid storing redundant data they should not be repeated within **ORDER**. However, we do need to be able to link this order with the customer who placed it. Therefore, we can add **CustomerNumber** and omit **CustomerName**, **CustomerPhone** and **CustomerAddress**.

We need to be able to identify which products the customer has ordered. The safest way to do this is to include **ProductCode**, which uniquely identifies a product and the packet size. **ProductDescription** and **PacketSize** are stored in **PRODUCT** and can be derived by using ProductCode; they are therefore redundant here. This gives us:

CUSTOMER = CustomerNumber +
CustomerName +
CustomerAddress +
(CustomerPhone)

PRODUCT = ProductCode +
ProductDescription +
PacketSize +
CostPerPacket

ORDER = CustomerNumber +
DateRequired +
{ProductCode +
NumberOfPackets}

The corresponding E–R diagram is shown in Fig. 5.11.

Examine the relationships In Fig. 5.11 the relationship between **PRODUCT** and **ORDER** is modelled as many to many; one order may be for many products and one product may be on several orders. E–R modelling does not encourage many to many relationships. One reason for this is that there is often information associated with the relationship which cannot sensibly be attached to either of the participating entities.

To clarify this it is worth digressing to consider a different example. An organization might want to record information about employees and on-going projects. Employees can work on many projects and projects can be worked on by many employees. So we have a many to many relationship as in Fig. 5.12.

If the organization also wants to record the number of hours each employee works on each project, it is not obvious whether to keep this information in the **EMPLOYEE** entity or the **PROJECT** entity. If we record it in **EMPLOYEE** we will introduce redundancy into the model. What we will be trying to model can be recorded in tabular form, as in Fig. 5.13. However, E–R modelling assumes a flat file structure which would mean that this information would have to be recorded as in Fig. 5.14, with an employee's number, name and address being repeated once for each project he or she works on.

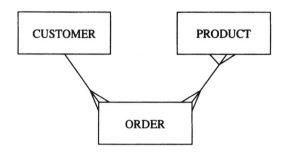

Figure 5.11 Just a Line—first cut E–R model

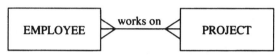

Figure 5.12 Many employees work on many projects

EmployeeNo	Name	Address	ProjectNo	HoursWorked
123	Smith J.	Hedgerley Close	4	23
			7	16
			3	3
456	Bloggs F.	West Road	6	1
			9	7

Figure 5.13 Hours worked per project, tabular form

EmployeeNo	Name	Address	ProjectNo	HoursWorked
123	Smith J.	Hedgerley Close	4	23
123	Smith J.	Hedgerley Close	7	16
123	Smith J.	Hedgerley Close	3	3

Figure 5.14 Flat file recording of hours worked

The same repetition would happen if the information about hours worked were added to the **PROJECT** entity. The information is associated with the relationship 'works on'. The situation is resolved if we introduce an extra *intersection* entity to represent the information associated with the relationship, thereby splitting the many to many relationship into two, one to many relationships (Fig. 5.15). The data will now be recorded as in Fig. 5.16.

Many to many relationships can cause problems, even if there is no information associated with the relationship. The organization in our example will probably want to be able to link employees to projects as in Fig. 5.17 so that, given an employee number, they can list the projects he or she is working on and, given a project number, they can list the employees working on it.

We have the same problem—of deciding whether to keep the relevant employee numbers with the **PROJECT** data or the project numbers with the **EMPLOYEE** data. Either way, we will be introducing redundancy of the sort illustrated in Fig. 5.14. The solution again is to introduce an intersection entity to record the allocation of employees to projects (Fig. 5.18). Another reason for not allowing many to many relationships is that many databases cannot implement them.

Returning to the Just a Line example, we can simplify the many to many relationship (Fig. 5.11) into two, one to many relationships, by introducing an intersection entity **ORDERLINE**. This gives us the diagram in Fig. 5.19, which can be read as follows:

- Any one Order may have many OrderLines.
- Any one OrderLine is on only one Order.
- Any one Product may appear on many OrderLines.
- Any one OrderLine is for only one Product.

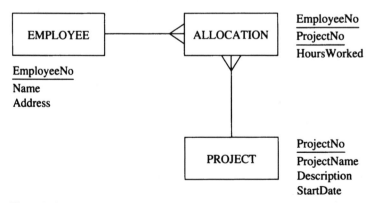

Figure 5.15 Intersection entity—ALLOCATION

Employee	Project	HoursWorked
123	4	23
123	7	16
123	3	3
456	6	1
456	9	7

Figure 5.16 Data recorded in intersection entity ALLOCATION

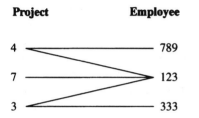

Figure 5.17 Occurrence diagram—Project/Employee

Employee	Project
123	4
123	7
123	3
456	6
456	9

Figure 5.18 Intersection entity, recrods allocation of employees to projects

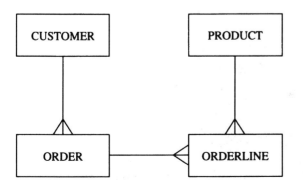

Figure 5.19 Simplified E–R model.

The attributes of **ORDER** and **ORDERLINE** are:

ORDER = CustomerNumber +
DateRequired

ORDERLINE = CustomerNumber +
DateRequired +
ProductCode +
NumberOfPackets

Keys for Just a Line We must define keys for each of our entities. So far we have decided that the key for **CUSTOMER** will be **CustomerNumber** and the key for **PRODUCT** will be **ProductCode**. For each order to be uniquely identifiable we could either introduce order numbers or make a decision that the **CustomerNumber** and **DateRequired**, taken together, will uniquely identify any order. For Just a Line it was decided that the latter would be sufficient; if a customer does send in a second order to be delivered on the same day, it is simply added to the end of the first. If we assume one **Product** per **OrderLine**, then each **OrderLine** can be identified by a combination of the attributes **CustomerNumber**, **DateRequired** and **ProductCode**.

Summary of attributes (key attributes are underlined)

CUSTOMER = <u>CustomerNumber</u> +
CustomerName +
CustomerAddress +
(CustomerPhone)

PRODUCT = <u>ProductCode</u> +
ProductDescription +
PacketSize +
CostPerPacket

ORDER = <u>CustomerNumber</u> +
<u>DateRequired</u>

ORDERLINE = <u>CustomerNumber</u> +
<u>DateRequired</u> +
<u>ProductCode</u> +
NumberOfPackets

The system documentation at this stage will include the E–R model (Fig. 5.19), supplemented by a description of the entities in the required logical data dictionary, as shown below.

Just a Line—required logical data dictionary (fragment)

CUSTOMER   = *entity*
                 {Customer}

Customer   = <u>CustomerNumber</u> + CustomerDetails

CustomerDetails = CustomerName + CustomerAddress +
                 (CustomerPhone)

ORDER   = *entity*
                 {Order}

Order   = <u>CustomerNumber + DateRequired</u>

ORDER_LINE   = *entity*
                 {OrderLine}

OrderLine   = <u>CustomerNumber + DateRequired + ProductCode</u> +
                 NumberOfPackets

PRODUCT   = *entity*
                 {Product}

Product   = <u>ProductCode</u> + ProductDescription + PacketSize +
                 CostPerPacket

What have we achieved by building the E–R model?

The E–R model and the associated data dictionary entries should have captured *all* the data required by the system (and *no* data in excess of these requirements) and the relationships between groups of data items. It is very likely at this stage that there is some redundancy in the model and that we are rather unsure about relationships between some of the more complicated entities. Normalization, which is discussed below, aims to resolve these problems. The process of creating this model and documenting it in the data dictionary forces us to study the system data in great detail. The model also provides a basis for useful discussion with the users.

5.3 NORMALIZATION

Introduction

We can summarize the aims of data modelling as:

- To capture all the system data
- To organize the data into logical groups
- To organize it in such a way that one item of data is held in one and only one place
- To map the relationships between data groups

E–R modelling sets out to achieve these objectives using a top-down approach and the informal application of a set of guidelines. Normalization provides an algorithm for reducing complex data structures to irreducible simple structures. It has been observed over the years that some data groupings behave better in an insert/update/delete situation. This observation has been formalized in a set of rules known as Codd's laws. The aim is to ensure that the data the system needs to store is organized into its minimal form; we are concerned during normalization with tidying up the data so that there is no data redundancy. We are also concerned during normalization with ensuring that the data is grouped logically. During normalization we rigorously apply these rules to the mass of data accumulated during the fact-finding stage of the analysis of the system. Once we have produced normalized entities, the process of normalization provides automatic mechanisms for mapping the relationships between entities.

Although normalization gives us a set of rules for determining whether we have grouped our data items correctly, it cannot, in itself, ensure that we have captured all the data the system may require, which is why it is useful to use a two-prong approach: E–R modelling and normalization.

Normal form

The phrase 'normal form', when applied to data, simply means a convenient form or structure into which the data can be organized—in this case the forms dictated by Codd. We shall concern ourselves with the first, second and third normal forms. In fact, several higher forms have been defined, but the higher normal forms are appropriate only if the system is to be implemented in a relational database. A data model normalized to the third normal form is useful, however we decide to implement, in that it will have removed data redundancy and grouped the data logically.

Determinancy and dependency

The concepts of dependency and determinancy are both important in the context of normalization. The terms express complementary concepts—if A determines B, then B is dependent on A. For example, in the patient appointment system (see Fig. 5.20), if every time we come across the patient name John Knowles we find that the associated patient number is 5632, then patient number determines patient name and, conversely, patient name is dependent on patient number.

Patient number	Patient name	Appointment date	Appointment time	Doctor
5632	John Knowles	12/3/96	9.30	Dr Paterson
2534	Jennifer Seath	12/3/96	9.40	Dr Dean
3216	Jill Crerar	12/3/96	9.40	Dr Thompson
5632	John Knowles	22/3/96	11.10	Dr Paterson
2555	Jane Hamilton	25/4/96	10.20	Dr Paterson
5632	John Knowles	25/4/96	10.40	Dr Paterson

Figure 5.20 Extract from a patient appointment system

An example of normalization

To illustrate the process of ensuring that data is in the first, then second, then third normal form, a simple example will be used. The situation we shall consider is the data recorded by a firm of civil engineers on their staff development course form, illustrated in Fig. 5.21. The staff development course form can be described in data dictionary notation as:

```
STAFF_DEVELOPMENT_COURSE = CourseCode +
                           CourseDescription +
                           {EmployeeNo +
                           Name +
                           Block +
                           RoomNo +
                           DateJoinedCourse +
                           AllocatedHours}
```

In line with recent company policy all staff are released for two hours a week to improve their foreign language skills. This form records data about foreign language courses, a particular course being identifiable by its **Course-Code** (which has therefore been underlined as a key). Several employees can

STAFF DEVELOPMENT COURSES					
COURSE CODE:			*FRLANGS*		
COURSE DESCRIPTION:			*Conversation*		
Employee Number	Name	Block	Room	Joined Course	Allocated Time (hours)
213	Jones H.N.	J	124	5/4/9x	24
164	Smith J.E.	H	603	1/5/9x	6
465	Baker K.P.	G	21	12/7/9x	12

Figure 5.21 Staff development courses form

be working on the same course, as they work at their own pace using the language laboratory. A total of six attributes is recorded about each employee, including their normal office location (block and room number), the date they joined this course and how many hours it is planned for them to work on it.

We can immediately see that this does not form a satisfactory entity. For example, if there is a separate entity **EMPLOYEE**, much of the information in **STAFF_DEVELOPMENT_COURSE** will be duplicated there. If there is not a separate entity **EMPLOYEE**, then all record of an **Employee** vanishes for any period when that person is not working on a particular course.

First normal form (1NF)

Definition. An entity is in 1NF if, and only if, it has an identifying key and there are no repeating attributes or groups of attributes.

Therefore, to get into 1NF we must remove repeating groups:

- The attributes that do not repeat are left as the original entity, now a 1NF entity.
- The repeating attributes are removed into a separate 1NF entity which has as its key the original key, and a key to the repeating group.

For our example, applying this rule gives the following two 1NF entities:

1. COURSE	2. EMP_ON_COURSE
CourseCode +	CourseCode +
Course Description	EmployeeNo +
	Name +
	Block +
	RoomNo +
	DateJoinedCourse +
	AllocatedHours

The problem of vanishing employees has not yet been solved; the second normal form will help us with this.

Second normal form (2NF)

Definition. An entity is in 2NF if, and only if, it is in 1NF and has no attributes which require only part of the key to identify them uniquely.

Therefore, to get into 2NF we remove part-key dependencies:

- Where a key has more than one attribute, check that each non-key attribute depends upon the whole key to determine it, and not just part of the key.
- For each sub-set of a key which identifies an attribute or set of attributes, create a new separate entity.

This sounds daunting, but all that is really happening is that the data is being split into logical groups of data items that go together.

In our example, **COURSE** is already in the second normal form. However, **EMP_ON_COURSE** is not, and requires some consideration. **CourseCode + EmployeeNo** form the key for this group of attributes. It is worth considering which of the remaining attributes in the group are dependent on the whole of this key.

Attribute	*Depends on*
Name	EmployeeNo
Block	EmployeeNo
RoomNo	EmployeeNo
but	
DateJoinedCourse	CourseCode + EmployeeNo
AllocatedHours	CourseCode + EmployeeNo

If you are in any doubt about this ask yourself 'Are employee's names affected when they join a course?'. The answer is obviously not. Therefore, **Name** is not dependent on **CourseCode**, only on **EmployeeNo**. We could imagine a situation where an employee's room number and block number change when he or she starts a course. However, in this case the room and block numbers refer to their permanent office numbers and are not affected when they start a course. The date in question is the date that one particular employee joined one particular course and therefore is dependent on both the employee number and the course code. The same is true of the number of hours an employee has been allocated to a particular course.

Putting the data into the second normal form has identified a new entity. **EMPLOYEE** giving us three 2NF entities:

1. COURSE	2. EMP_ON_COURSE	3. EMPLOYEE
CourseCode +	CourseCode +	EmployeeNo +
CourseDescription	EmployeeNo +	Name +
	DateJoinedCourse +	Block +
	AllocatedHours	RoomNo

This is better. We no longer lose employees who leave courses, but there is still a problem. Presumably, **Block** and **RoomNo** are related in some way; if one is updated, the other will be affected. This again is a question about the meaning of the data. In this case the company is located on a site with several separate buildings or blocks. Each block contains several rooms, as illustrated in Fig. 5.22.

Block	Rooms
G	15–28
H	583–607
I	56–93
J	94–156

Figure 5.22 Block and room numbers

There are several disadvantages to storing both Block and RoomNo in **EMPLOYEE** with the rest of the data about the employee:

- At the moment the room numbering reflects the haphazard growth pattern of the company buildings. If the rooms are numbered to be more logical (e.g. block A has rooms 1–50, block B rooms 51–62, etc.), the Employee records will have to be searched to change both the room number and the block it is in.

- If the block reference is changed so that the blocks have names instead of letters (e.g. block H becomes the Brunel Block, block J the Stevenson Block, etc.), all the Employee records will have to be searched for references to the blocks and updated with the new name.
- If the room numbers are unique, then there is no need to store the block reference each time. So long as there is one look-up table to establish which room is in which block, we need only store the block reference in one place; all other references to it are redundant.

The third normal form will help with these problems.

Third normal form (3NF)

Definition. An entity is in 3NF if, and only if, it is in 2NF and no non-key attribute depends on any other non-key attribute.

Therefore, to get into 3NF we must remove attributes that depend on other non-key attributes:

- Decide on the direction of the dependency between the attributes
- If A depends on B, create a new entity, keyed by B, with A as an attribute (A may be a set of attributes, B may be a compound key).
- Leave B in the original entity and mark it as a foreign key, but remove A from the original entity.

To work out whether A is dependent on B or vice versa we must discover whether, given a value for A, there is only one possible value for B. If so, B is dependent on A. Relating this to our example, we can work out from the situation outlined in Fig. 5.22 that given any value of **Block** there is more than one corresponding value for **RoomNo**. Since each block contains many rooms. Therefore, **RoomNo** is not dependent on **Block**. However, for any given block of **RoomNo**, there is only ever one possible corresponding value for **Block**. Therefore, **Block** is dependent on **RoomNo**. We therefore create a new entity keyed by **RoomNo** with **Block** as an attribute, and remove **Block** from the original **EMPLOYEE** entity. **EMPLOYEE** (2NF) gives two 3NF entities:

EmployeeNo +	→	1. EmployeeNo +	2. RoomNo +
Name +		Name +	Block
Block +		RoomNo*	
RoomNo			

A foreign key, marked by an asterisk, in this case **RoomNo***, means that a non-key attribute in one entity is the key of another entity.

The total list of 3NF entities is:

COURSE = CourseCode +
CourseDescription

EMP_ON_COURSE = CourseCode +
EmployeeNo +
DateJoinedCourse +
AllocatedHours

EMPLOYEE = EmployeeNo +
Name +
RoomNo*

LOCATION = RoomNo +
Block

The update problem caused by storing **RoomNo** and **Block** in **EMPLOYEE** has now been resolved. If the blocks are ever renamed we need only update the appropriate occurrence of **LOCATION** (in the implementation terms the appropriate record in the Location file). Similarly, if the rooms are renumbered, the relationship between room and block is only updated in one place.

It is useful to represent these normalized entities and their relationships diagrammatically, using the same conventions as in E–R modelling. Relationships can be worked out automatically using the following rules:

1. Given two entities A and B, if the key of A is a sub-set of the key of B then the relationship of A to B is one to many

2. Given two entities P and Q, if P contains a foreign key F and F is the single key of Q, then the relationship of P to Q is many to one

To apply to these rules we need to be clear about the keys to the entities. In our example we have the situation illustrated in Fig. 5.23

- The key of **COURSE** (CourseNo) is part of the compound key of **EMP_ON_COURSE** (CourseNo + EmployeeNo). Rule 1 applies; therefore the relationship between **COURSE** and **EMP_ON_COURSE** is one to many.

- Similarly, the key of **EMPLOYEE** (<u>EmployeeNo</u>) is part of the compound key on **EMP_ON_COURSE** (<u>CourseNo + EmployeeNo</u>). Rule 1 applies; therefore the relationship between **EMPLOYEE** and **EMP_ON_COURSE** is one to many.
- **EMPLOYEE** has a foreign key. **RoomNo**, which is the single key of the entity **LOCATION**. Rule 2 applies; therefore the relationship between **EMPLOYEE** and **LOCATION** is many to one.

The completed diagram in Fig. 5.24 shows the relationships between the entities.

What we have achieved once normalization is complete

Normalization provides a useful and rigorous check on the less formal activity of E–R modelling. The recommended approach to data modelling is to adopt the intuitive E–R modelling approach first, then use normalization to check that the entities produced are logical data groups, with no redundant data. We suggest that you check that the Just a Line entities listed above are normalized.

Once this is done, we will have achieved a minimal data model on which to base the implementation of the system. Once we get to the stage of designing computer files, whatever implementation technology we choose there will be other factors to take into consideration. We may decide deliberately to introduce some redundancy into the file designs, in order to make the system more convenient in some way—easier for the client to use or to cut down on file access time. For example, in the Just a Line system we decided to retain **LastOrderDate** in the **CUSTOMER** entity because this date is so often used in conjunction with the customer details (see Chapter 8). Every time the mail shot is processed we go right through the customer file printing out customer details of customers who have ordered within the last year. It involves less processing to update that file every time the customer puts in a new order than to search for and retrieve the date from the relevant order record every time we need it. Although this redundancy goes against the spirit of data modelling, at least it is introduced knowingly, and the required updating is therefore built into the system.

SUMMARY

Data modelling uses two techniques—a top-down approach. E–R modelling, and a bottom-up approach, normalization. E–R modelling starts by intuitively identifying objects (entities) about which the system is required to store data. Appropriate attributes are then allocated to each entity. Normalization starts

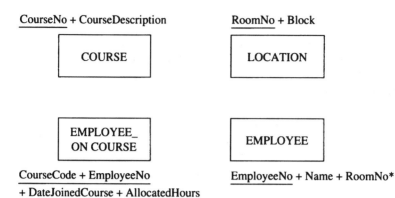

CourseCode + EmployeeNo
+ DateJoinedCourse + AllocatedHours

Figure 5.23 Staff short course entities and attributes

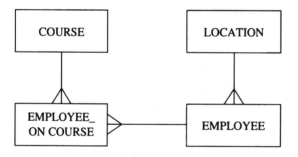

Figure 5.24 E–R diagram of staff short course example

with the smallest meaningful data items in the system and organizes them into well-formed entities. Normalization is a useful check that the entities identified during E–R modelling are logical data groups and that there is no redundant data.

EXERCISES AND TOPICS FOR DISCUSSION

5.1 (a) From the information presented in Fig. 5.2, list the candidate keys.
     (b) State which of the candidate keys would make the best primary key. Give reasons for your choice of primary key and justify your rejection of the other candidate keys.

Data model

5.2   Draw E–R diagrams of the following situations:

- A tree has many leaves;
  a leaf is on only one tree.
- A manager manages, at most, one laundrette;
  a laundrette is managed by only one manager.
- A car has one car-owner;
  a car-owner may own several cars.
- A hockey team has many players;
  a player may only play for one team.
- An author writes many books:
  a book may be written by several authors.
- A father may have several children:
  a child has only one father.

5.3   Examine the E–R diagram in Fig. 5.25 and state which of the following
       statements is true:

(a) A course can only be on one scheme.
(b) A scheme has only one course.
(c) A student does not have to be on any scheme.
(d) A student must be on one scheme only.

5.4   In your group medical practice each GP has many patients but each
       patient may be registered with only one GP. Assume that a GP can be
       identified by Name and a patient by PatientNo.

(a) Draw an E–R diagram to model this situation.
(b) How does the model change if patients are allowed to be registered
     with more than one GP?

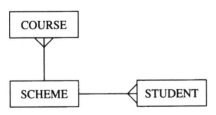

Figure 5.25 E–R diagram of student course example

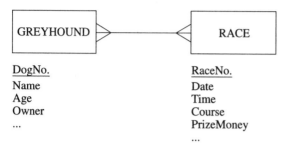

DogNo.   RaceNo.
Name   Date
Age   Time
Owner   Course
...   PrizeMoney
                          ...

Figure 5.26 Many to many relationship

5.5   Simplify the many to many relationship shown in Fig. 5.26 by introducing an intersection entity. Find a name for the new entity and list its attributes.

5.6   Fenland College of Knowledge wish to record information about students and their assignments. A fragment of the current, manual, recording sheet is shown in Fig. 5.27. Student numbers uniquely identify students, subjects are identified by subject code and assignments are identified by subject code and assignment number.

    (a)   Write entity descriptions for the entities STUDENT, SUBJECT and ASSIGNMENT, underlining keys.

Student No.	Name	Subject	Lecturer	Assignment No.	Description	Grade
32	J. Crerar	IS	G.L.	1	E–R model	B
		SML	C.R.P.	2	clock prog	C
45	I. Seath	C++	S.B.	3	lift program	C

Figure 5.27 Fragment of recording sheet concerning students and their assignments

    (b)   Draw an E–R diagram showing relationships between these entities.

This is a much more difficult exercise than the previous ones—do not be discouraged if you find it hard.

5.7   An animal shelter keeps a record of the treatment prescribed to each animal in its care. Details are recorded on a treatment card: a typical example is shown in Fig. 5.28. Animals are uniquely identified by their number. The shelter is divided into blocks of animal cages: one block for dogs, one for cats and one for animals with infectious diseases. Each block has a unique number. Describe the data on the card in unnormalized form, in first normal form, in second normal form and in third normal form.

NAME: Fred		BREED: Collie cross		NUMBER: 87	
BLOCK NO: 6		TYPE: Isolation		Block Y NAME: Tara	

Start Date	Condition	Drug code	Drug name	Dosage	Days
31/8/xx	bite on right hind leg	123	Trib	1 × 80 mg twice a day	10
31/8/xx	infection	234	Metron	3 × 200 mg once a day	8
6/9/xx	fleas	567	Nuvan Top	once every 10 days	

Figure 5.28 Animal treatment card

5.8 A company sells its kitchen-ware products by means of a team of salespersons who organize kitchen-ware parties in their customers' houses. Products are supplied to the customers from the nearest warehouse. A salesperson may have several warehouses in his or her sales area. The company keeps records of the total value of sales per customer for each salesperson:

Salesperson No.: 369
Name: Webster
Sales Area: South East

Customer Number	Customer Name	Warehouse Number	Warehouse Site	Total Sales(£)
46732	Bailey	34	Landbeach	453.56
26777	Sadler	23	Cottenham	205.03
23331	Bloxham	12	Waterbeach	34.99

Describe this data in unnormalized form, in first normal form, in second normal form and in third normal form.

5.9 A hospital doctor's list contains the data described below. Assume that a doctor will only be in one department on any one day. A doctor is uniquely identified by his or her doctor number, a patient by his or her patient number and a GP by his or her GP number.
Dr'sList = {DrNo + DrName + DrAddr + DrPhoneNo +
{Day + Dept +

{Time + PatientNo + PatientName + PatientAddr +
GPNo + GPName + GPAddr + GPPhone}}}

Describe this data in first, second and third normal forms.

5.10 The People's Prose Book Club operates a mail-order book club. Members select books from titles on offer for any particular month. The club keeps track of member details and the books they have ordered on a membership record card. An example of a membership record card is outlined below. Membership numbers, title numbers and publisher codes are allocated by the book club.

Member Number	Name	Address
452	Ms E. Gorse	8, The Beeches, Waterbeach

Date Ordered	Title Number	Title	Publisher Code	Publisher Name
2/4/96	34	Plato and Pleasure	86	Finn
2/4/96	45	Loaves and Fishes	23	Browne
14/5/96	23	Armour	23	Browne

Describe this data in unnormalized, first, second and third normal forms.

REFERENCES AND FURTHER READING

Beynon-Davies, P. (1991) *Relational Database Systems*, Blackwell Scientific Publications, Oxford.

Date, C. J. (1991) *An Introduction to Database Systems*, Vol. 1, 5th edn, Addison-Wesley, Reading, Mass.

Goodland, M. (1995) *SSADM Version 4: A Practical Approach*, McGraw-Hill, London.

Howe, D. R. (1989) *Date Analysis for Data Base Design*, Hodder & Stoughton, London.

Robinson, B. and Prior, M. (1995) *Systems Analysis Techniques*, International Thomson Computer Press, London.

ENTITY LIFE HISTORIES

6.1 INTRODUCTION

Each of the techniques that we have met in Chapters 4 and 5 provides a different view of the problem area and the evolving system. Data flow diagrams give us a picture of the movement of data through the system at various levels of detail. It is tempting to read a data flow diagram from left to right and from top to bottom, but this would not be accurate. Data flow diagrams do not include considerations about the sequencing, iteration or timing of events in the system. It is not part of a data flow diagram to describe the order in which processes operate on data, nor how many times a particular process may need to be carried out.

Figure 6.1 shows part of the current level 1 data flow diagram for the Just a Line system. The diagram does not tell us whether the customer places an order before receiving details of the cards, or whether Harry and Sue send details to potential customers in the hope that they will then place an order. The data flow diagram is equally vague about when a payment is made. We have no way of knowing whether all orders must be paid for in advance, whether Harry and Sue operate a cash on delivery system or whether credit is available.

The important point is that this lack of detail about the order of events in the system is not a fault in the data flow diagram. As we said at the beginning of Chapter 4, all models represent an abstraction, or view of the system. The role of a data flow diagram does not include modelling sequence, timing or iteration in the system.

The view of the system provided by the data model is of the relationships between data objects. The data model ignores the system processes, and so considerations of sequencing and iteration are not included.

It is possible to introduce the concepts of sequence and iteration into process definitions by means of *if ... then* statements and *while ... do* loops,

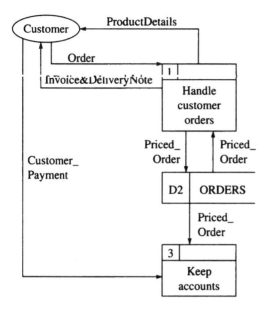

Figure 6.1 Part of the level 1 data flow diagram for the Just a Line system

but these definitions are only used to describe the lowest-level processes on a data flow diagram. They do not give a picture of the system as a whole.

To obtain a view of the ordering of events in a system, we need to use entity life histories. This is a diagrammatic technique which provides a picture of all possible biographies for any occurrence of a particular entity in the system. For example, in the current (manual) Just a Line system, the life of a customer entity is as follows:

- Creation—each time a customer places an order
- Amendment—if the customer's details (such as the address) change during the life of the order
- Deletion—when the order is delivered or when it is cancelled

The entity life history for a customer in the current Just a Line system can be seen in Fig. 6.2. The notation for the diagram is explained in detail later in the chapter. The diagram gives us a picture of the events listed above. It is interesting in that it shows that Harry and Sue have no way of keeping a record of customers, except for those who have an order currently being handled by the system. Because they give a different perspective on the system, that of ordering and timing of events, entity life histories often highlight interesting details that may be missed in other structured models.

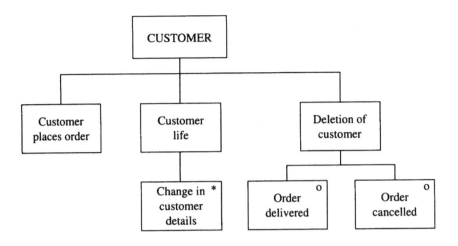

Figure 6.2 Entity life history of a customer in the current Just a Line system

6.2   DEFINITIONS AND NOTATION

Some definitions relating to entity life histories

- An *entity* is a data object of interest which has been identified in the entity relationship model. In the Just a Line system, customers, orders and cards are all objects of interest, giving us the entities CUSTOMER, ORDER and PRODUCT.
- An *event* is something that happens in the *real world*, that causes an entity (or more than one entity) to be updated. For example, a customer may move house or the price of a product may change. These are both events which will respectively affect the entities CUSTOMER and PRODUCT.
- An event may have an effect on one or more entities. We need to distinguish between events and their effects because a single event may appear as an effect in the life history of several entities. An event such as a price change will certainly affect the PRODUCT entity and may also affect the entity ORDER.

Notation for entity life histories

Entity life history (ELH) notation provides constructs to express sequence, selection and iteration of events in the system. Figure 6.3 illustrates sequencing. The diagram is read from left to right, so that event 1 in the diagram must take place before event 2, and event 2 before event 3.

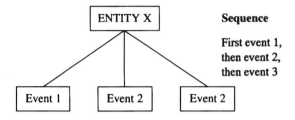

Figure 6.3 Representing sequence in entity life histories

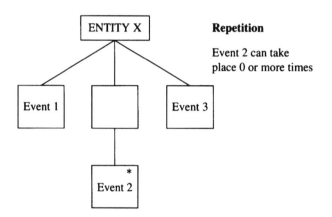

Figure 6.4 Representing iteration (repetition) in entity life histories

Figure 6.4 shows how iteration (or repetition) is represented in entity life histories. The asterisk, *, in the event 2 box shows that this event may occur any number of times, or it may not occur at all. The blank box in this diagram is part of the entity life history structure. Such boxes are usually give an appropriate label (see the two example ELHs in the next section).

Alternative events are shown in Fig. 6.5. In this diagram either event 2 or event 3 will take place, but not both. Figure 6.6 is very similar, but in this diagram event 2 may occur or it may not. There is no alternative event.

Although entity life histories are read from left to right, there are a few cases where this imposes an unnecessary constraint on the ordering of events in a system. An example of this from Just a Line would occur if it were possible for customers to pay for their cards either when they order (before they receive the invoice) or when the goods are delivered with the invoice. In this case we want to show that different orderings of the 'Send invoice' and 'Customer payment' events are possible. Figure 6.7 illustrates the double-line notation which indicates that certain events can take place in any order.

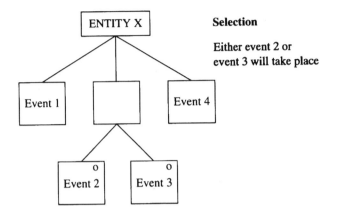

Selection

**Either event 2 or
event 3 will take place**

Figure 6.5 Representing selection in entity life histories

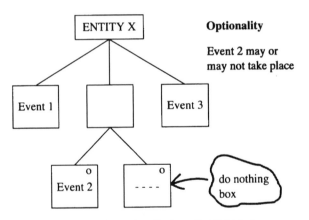

Optionality

**Event 2 may or
may not take place**

Figure 6.6 Representing optionality in entity life histories

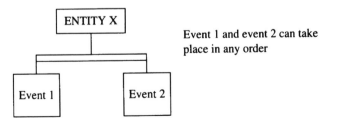

Event 1 and event 2 can take
place in any order

Figure 6.7 The double line indicates that there is no restriction on the ordering of events 1 and 2

It is important to remember that different types of symbol (*, o, etc.) cannot occur at the same level from the same box. To preserve the structure of the entity life history we use blank boxes as in Fig. 6.4.

6.3   HOW TO CREATE AN ENTITY LIFE HISTORY

The first step is to identify all the events that affect the system data, and note whether their effect on each entity is to action one of the following:

- Create a new occurrence (e.g. when a customer places an order this will create an occurrence of the entity ORDER).
- Update an occurrence (e.g. if details of the order are altered).
- Delete an occurrence (e.g. when the details of an order are removed from the company's records).

It is important not to confuse events with the processing that they initiate. Different events may trigger the same process; for example, a customer's details will be amended if the customer gets married and therefore changes her name, or if she moves house and so changes her address.

It may take more than one event to trigger a process; for example, a particular product line may be sold out and it is decided not to stock the line any more. These two events together trigger the process of deleting details of this particular product. On the other hand, the company may decide to discontinue the product and simply write off the unsold items. In this case the decision to discontinue the product is the only event needed to trigger the deletion process.

In entity life histories we do not normally record events which have no effect on the state of an entity. For example, if a customer wants to know which cards he or she has ordered, this enquiry will not affect the ORDER or the CUSTOMER entities.

Since each occurrence of an entity must be created, and eventually be deleted, we must check that events exist to trigger creation and deletion. If no deletion triggering event exists, we must create a system *housekeeping* event to prevent the file growing in an uncontrolled manner.

Example ELH from Just a Line—entity PRODUCT

We will assume a data dictionary definition of the entity PRODUCT as:

PRODUCT = ProductCode + ProductDescription + PacketSize +
CostPerPacket

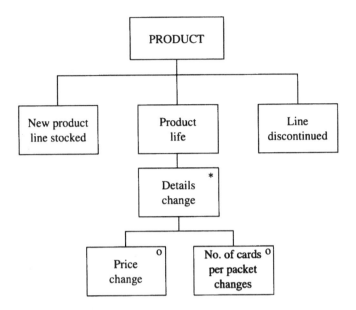

Figure 6.8 The PRODUCT entity life history

We now need to identify all the events that may affect PRODUCT and decide whether each event creates, amends or deletes an occurrence of the entity. This can be done by means of an entity event matrix.

Event	*Effect on PRODUCT*
new product line stocked	create
price increase on product	amend
different number of cards per packet	amend
product becomes best selling line	no effect
decision to discontinue product line	delete

Figure 6.8 shows the live history of the PRODUCT entity. An occurrence of the entity is created when a new line is stocked. This is followed by the PRODUCT life which may consist of any number of amendments, including zero. Each amendment may be either a change in price or a different number of cards in a packet. Finally, the occurrence of the PRODUCT entity is deleted when the line is discontinued.

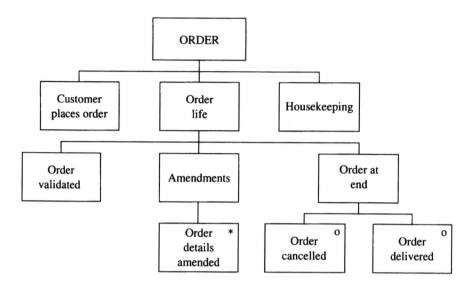

Figure 6.9 The ORDER entity life history

A second example ELH from Just a Line—the ORDER entity life history

We will assume a simplified data dictionary definition of the ORDER entity:

ORDER = CustomerNo + DateRequired + {OrderLine}

Event	Effect on ORDER
customer places an order	create
order is validated	amend
order details are changed	amend
the order is cancelled	amend
the order is delivered	amend
one year after completion of order (housekeeping)	delete

It may seem strange that the events of cancelling and delivering an order amend the entity instead of deleting it. This is because Harry and Sue wish to keep records of past orders for one year. You can see the ORDER entity life history in Fig. 6.9. Exercise 6.1 at the end of the chapter tests your understanding of the diagram.

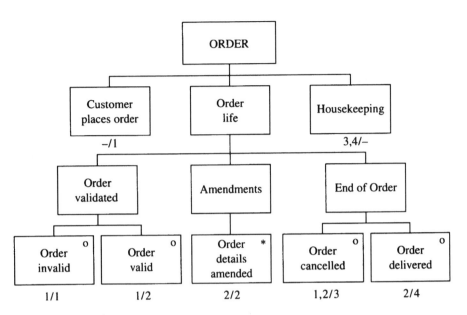

Figure 6.10 The ORDER entity life history with status indicators added

Status indicators

Numbers can be added to the event boxes on an ELH to show which state the entity is in at any particular time and place restrictions on the sequence in which events can happen. These numbers are known as status indicators. Figure 6.10 shows a more detailed version of the ORDER entity life history with status indicators added. The status indicators give us the following extra information about the ORDER entity:

- When a customer places an order the occurrence of the entity ORDER moves into state 1 (it has been created, but nothing more).
- When validation of the order takes place one of two things may happen. Either the occurrence of the ORDER entity is invalid, in which case it stays in state 1, or the order is valid and so moves into state 2. Validation can only occur when the order has been created and is in state 1. This is expressed by the status indicator lines 1/1, which appears under the Order invalid event box and 1/2 which appears under the Order valid event box.
- The status indicator line 2/2, which appears under the Order details amended event box, means that an amendment to an order is not an event which changes the state of the entity. It also tells us that order details can only be amended once the order has been validated.

- The status indicator, 1,2/3 defines the conditions under which an order may be cancelled. The order may have been placed but is invalid (state 1), it may have been placed and validated (state 2), or it may have been placed, validated and subsequently amended (state 2); in each of these cases it can be cancelled and so moves into state 3.
- An order may be delivered when it has been validated or when it has been validated and amended. It may not be delivered when it has simply been placed or if it is found to be invalid. This is shown by the status indicator line 2/4 under the Order delivered box which moves the order into state 4.
- Finally, the line under the housekeeping box 3, 4/- shows that an occurrence of the ORDER entity can only be deleted after it has been cancelled, or when it has been delivered. Once an order has been placed, it must go through the validation process and cannot be deleted until it has been either cancelled or delivered.

Status indicators are also useful as reference points for other modelling techniques. Process definitions often refer to the state of an entity, for example 'If CUSTOMER is in state 2 . . .'

SUMMARY

Each entity life history records *all* the events that can affect an occurrence of *one* entity during its lifetime. An ELH records the *relative timing* of events. This information about timing constraints (for example an order must be placed before it can be amended or delivered) is vital for our understanding of the system, and is not recorded in any of the other models.

The diagrammatic presentation of the information in the ELH makes it easier for the system developer to understand and to explain to the client.

The notation for entity life histories is simple and straightforward, but the different symbols can be combined to produce complex and expressive models of the developing system.

ELHs are used in many structured methodologies, such as SSADM and JSD (Jackson Systems Development). It is also thought that models produced by this technique may be suitable for object-oriented analysis and design (see Chapter 8).

EXERCISES AND TOPICS FOR DISCUSSION

6.1 Study the diagram of the ORDER entity life history (Fig. 6.10) and answer the following questions which relate to it:

(a) Which event creates an occurrence of the ORDER entity?

(b) Can an order be cancelled just after it has been placed?

(c) How many times can an order be amended?

(d) Is it possible for an order to be delivered and then cancelled?

(e) If an order is to be deleted, it must be in one of two different states. What are these states?

6.2 The information to be recorded about an entity X is as follows: either event 1 will occur, or event 2 followed by event 3. Which of the diagrams in Fig. 6.11, (a) or (b), represents this information correctly?

6.3 There is a deliberate mistake in the entity life history in Fig. 6.12. What is it?

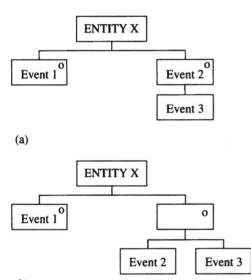

(a)

(b)

Figure 6.11 ELH diagram. Exercise 6.2

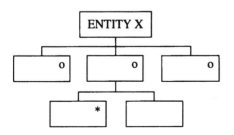

Figure 6.12 ELH diagram. Exercise 6.3

6.4 In the required system for Just a Line details are recorded about regular customers. An occurrence of the CUSTOMER entity is created when a customer places his or her first order. The entity is amended when the customer is added to the mailing list. Customer's details may change during the life of the entity, and finally the entity occurrence is deleted when the customer moves out of the area or when he or she has not placed any order with Just a Line for over a year. Draw an entity life history for the CUSTOMER entity in the required Just a Line system.

6.5 In Fig. 6.13 you will find an entity life history of an entity INVOICE. Describe this life history in English.

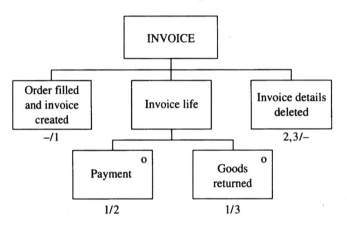

Figure 6.13 INVOICE entity life history

REFERENCES AND FURTHER READING

Crinnion, J. (1991) *Evolutionary Systems Development*, Pitman, London.

Goodland, M. (1995) *SSADM Version 4: A Practical Approach*, McGraw-Hill, London.

Robinson, B. and Prior, M. (1995) *Systems Analysis Techniques*, International Thomson Computer Press, London.

COMPLEMENTARY TOOLS, TECHNIQUES AND APPROACHES

In this chapter we introduce recent techniques and approaches to system development that complement the structured techniques described in Chapters 4, 5 and 6. The growing availability of automated tools to support all stages of the system development process has made it possible for developers to adopt new approaches to their work and to involve the client much more directly in the development process. We discuss the technique of prototyping, the use of CASE tools and the implications of both of these for the system developer and the client.

The increasing use of computers in safety-critical applications has highlighted the necessity for a more rigorous approach to system development in an attempt to guarantee the correctness and reliability of software. We explain what is meant by formal notations and how they contribute to this objective.

Finally, in this chapter we discuss briefly some of the problems that arise from the traditional way of developing and designing software systems based on their functionality and describe an approach that seems to offer some of the answers: object orientation.

7.1 PROTOTYPING

Designing anything involves building at least one model of it. A model offers us an abstraction, a particular view, of the object that is to be constructed. Children experiment with models using materials such as sand, paint and Lego bricks. If a house is to be built or extended, several different models are made: these can include the architect's plans, the structural engineer's drawings and even the customer's rough sketches of what the house should look like.

Designing systems, like designing houses, involves modelling. In Chapters 4, 5 and 6 we have already seen several examples of widely used modelling techniques offering a diversity of views of the system that is to be built. These techniques include such varied models as data flow diagrams, which show the movement of data in the system, entity–relationship models, which illustrate relationships between data objects, and the entity life histories, which show how data changes through time. Each of the techniques discussed shows a different aspect of the developing system, yet they all have one thing in common: a model created in one of these ways will always be just that—a model. However much care, time and effort the developer puts into the model, the model will never itself become a working system. CASE tools, which are discussed in the next section, allow the developer to create versions of these models which can be manipulated and altered as the client requires, but even these dynamic models have to be implemented in code before the system is actually working.

Prototyping, on the other hand, is based on the concept of a working model. There are different ways of prototyping and different uses of prototypes, but what is common to all these is that the system developer and even the client will be able to see and experiment with part of the system on the computer from a relatively early stage in the development process.

What is prototyping?

In common with many words in computer science, prototyping can mean very different things to different people. It is essential that a system developer, using prototyping with a team of other developers or when communicating with a client, makes sure that everyone concerned shares the same understanding of what the term 'prototyping' means. The following sections describe some of the most widely used prototypes.

Screen layouts The most basic prototype consists of non-functioning mock-ups of sample screen and report layouts. The system developer will be able to demonstrate to the client exactly what will appear on the screen when entering data, for example, or what a typical management report will look like. The client can request changes to the designs and the models can be refined until the client is satisfied. With this sort of prototype the system developer will not, however, be able to demonstrate or experiment with the way the screens work or interact with each other. It is not possible actually to enter data or produce a report. The screens are simply design layouts and there is no working system behind them.

The disposable prototype The power of modern fourth-generation languages makes it possible to build a system very much more quickly than with third-generation languages, such as COBOL or FORTRAN. With a disposable prototype, a model of the system (or part of it) is developed very quickly and refined in frequent discussions with the client. The model simulates the functionality of the proposed system, so that the client can see what it will do, but it is not backed up by detailed structured design. It is similar to a dress designer who makes up the pattern for an exclusive outfit in cheap material to see how it will look. Once the designer and client have tried out various ideas on this model, and are happy about the design of the final garment, the actual outfit is made up exactly like the model, but in a fabric of a much higher quality. Prototypes like this, in dress design or systems development, are very helpful in capturing requirements at an early stage in the development process, particularly if the client is not sure exactly where the problems lie. In the area of computer systems these prototypes are also useful models for designing and refining the user interface—what the system will look like to the people who are actually going to use it.

One of the most important things about this sort of prototype is that it is sooner or later discarded, for all but documentation purposes. It is very tempting for designer and client alike to allow the model to be developed as the basis for the final system, but this is a path to disaster. The essence of prototyping like this, to capture client requirements, is speed. There is no place here for the detailed analysis and design which are essential for robust, reliable and maintainable systems. Keeping a prototype which has been built in this way, and developing it to become the final system, is as inappropriate as a dress designer selling the model made up in cheap material as an exclusive outfit. If the system developer decides to build this sort of prototype, it is also essential to decide exactly when and how it will be set aside, and then ensure that this is done when the time comes.

The evolutionary prototype Evolutionary prototyping is often referred to as rapid application development. This prototype differs from the others in that, from the outset, the aim of the process is for the model to develop into the final system. This means that the system will be developed more quickly than by other, more traditional, methods and that the cost should be lower. It is important that extensive and detailed analysis of the problem is carried out before prototyping begins, otherwise the final system will be like a house built on sand. In this sort of prototyping, modern automated tools really come into their own; most developers will not attempt to build an evolutionary prototype without a CASE tool and a fourth-generation language.

Prototyping and the client

With prototyping, the relationship between the developer and the client is much more that of a partnership than one of expert and customer. In the following sections we discuss the advantages and disadvantages of prototyping from the client's point of view, and explain what the client will be expected to contribute to the development process.

The advantages of prototyping for the client The most obvious difference between prototyping and other techniques is that the prototype is a working model. When the client evaluates what is demonstrated, it is a live system, not a paper-based image of it. The client can have hands-on experience of the system during the development process and will be able to react to the design of the system before it becomes fixed. The client will find that seeing and experimenting with a dynamic model of the system makes it much easier to sort out exactly what the system should do and how it should look.

Effective prototyping will involve the client, not merely in discussions with the system developers but also in realistic simulations of work situations. It will be possible to see how the system will perform in relation to tasks in the organization. If, for example, a particular report is produced at the end of each month, the client would be able to see from the prototype how the data for the report would be collected, entered, selected, ordered, formatted and finally printed. If the layout of the final report is not exactly what is wanted, it can be changed with relatively little effort. Examining and playing with a prototype is thus a very good way for the client to get to know the system and to judge its strengths and weaknesses in different situations.

The client's involvement in the system development process has many positive effects. It enables much easier communication with the developer about ideas, opinions and any changes that are to be made to the system. The client will also find that it is much easier to understand what the developer says about the system, while sitting in front of a screen, than poring over documents and diagrams. The client's continuous involvement in the system throughout its development means that little, if any, training is needed on how to use it when it is finally delivered. This, of course, applies equally to any members of staff who have been involved in the development process. In this way considerable savings can be made on staff training costs.

Even if the developer decides that a particular system is not suitable for prototyping, and that it will be developed in a more traditional way, it is still likely that prototyping will be used in the design of the user interface. This is the area which, more than any, benefits from a prototyping approach, since it is this which determines how the system will appear to the users. Details such as how the system will respond to a password (perhaps by a row of Xs, a row of dashes or simply a message welcoming the user to the system) or the most effective design of a screen used in data entry, are the sorts of problems and decisions that are almost impossible to make effectively unless the client can actually see what will appear on the screen. At the start of the development the client may, for example, be quite set on a blue background with yellow text for all data-entry screens. It is only by seeing such a screen on the computer that the client can decide whether the screen is really what is wanted.

The design and refinement of the user interface is one of the most important aspects of almost all information systems. No matter how good the system is in other respects, if it is not user-friendly no one will want to use it (see Chapter 8). In large organizations, it is obviously not possible for everyone who is going to use the system to express their opinion on how it will look, but it is important that as many people as is practical, and certainly the principal users, have the opportunity to see what they will be working with.

The demands of prototyping on the client For a client who is keen and able to play a part in the development of the system, the advantages of the prototyping approach far outweigh the disadvantages. The client's involvement in the development process brings an awareness of what is going on and means less frustration with apparent delays or lack of progress. When the developing system seems to be deviating from what the client asked for, the problem can be pointed out to the developer and together they can discuss the solution or necessary compromises. The client's attitude to the system tends to be more positive when prototyping is used as the development method, since involvement from the earliest stages brings a strong feeling of identification with the growing system.

While this is an excellent way of developing a system, it does demand considerable input from the client in terms of time and effort. It is this degree of involvement that can be a real disadvantage of prototyping, from the client's point of view.

For successful prototyping it is essential that the client understands from the start just how much time and effort will be required. In large organizations this means that staff at all levels may be needed to contribute to the development process. The client must be available to help define and, if necessary, endlessly redefine models of the emerging system, screen and report layouts, and the various functions that the system is to perform. This can be very time-consuming and disruptive to the client's business, especially when staff are also involved.

However, there is no doubt that with a client who is able to contribute fully to the development process, the technique of prototyping offers the possibility of systems that are developed faster, more cheaply and that are much more likely to do what the client wants. A project such as Just a Line, for example, would benefit greatly from prototyping, either in the early stages for capturing requirements or to create an evolutionary model which will eventually develop into the final system.

Prototyping and the system developer

Since there are several different views of prototyping and since every problem is unique, it is difficult to generalize about what happens when prototyping is used to develop a system. The following section describes one way in which part of the Just a Line system might by prototyped. We then discuss the advantages and disadvantages of prototyping from the system developer's point of view.

Prototyping Just a Line The use of prototyping does not mean that the developer can dispense with the traditional tasks of early systems development. The first step in a case such as Just a Line would be to carry out a feasibility study and decide whether it is really worth developing a software system for the company.

It is also important to establish early on that the Just a Line problem is suitable for prototyping. From the interview notes we know that Just a Line is a fairly small company with fairly standard problems of disorganized order processing, stock control, accounting and almost no marketing strategy. We can see how the overall system could be broken down into these four areas, which could each be prototyped separately, and then integrated to form the complete Just a Line system. We can also tell from the interview that Harry and Sue are very keen to modernize the running of their business and seem willing to help in any way they can. What is not clear is the amount of time either or both of them can spare to help with the prototyping process. This is something the developer would have to find out. It would also have to be established whether Harry and Sue are agreeable to this method of proceeding and whether they understand and accept the amount of involvement required on their part.

In dealing with a larger and more complex system, the developer would now probably investigate the range of software tools available and decide which is appropriate for the job in hand. These tools are described later in Sec. 7.2 on CASE. We will not discuss them further here since the development of a prototype for Just a Line does not merit the use of expensive, sophisticated tools.

Having decided how to proceed and drawn up an initial project plan (as described in Chapter 10), the system developer must now investigate the problem more fully and identify the various parts of the system that are to be developed. There are many ways in which this can be done; the method chosen will probably depend on the developer's own past experience and preferences. One possible way would be to develop a high-level model of the problem area with Harry and Sue, using some of the structured techniques described in Chapters 4, 5 and 6. Whatever method is chosen, the developer should have a sound idea of both the data and the principal functions of the system.

In the case of Just a Line, we can identify the separate areas of marketing, order processing, stock control and accounting. The developer now takes one of these areas, marketing for example, and examines it in greater depth. In order to get a clearer idea of what exactly the clients want in terms of (say) a mail shot to regular customers, the developer may start to experiment with various ideas on the computer and invite Harry and Sue to comment and

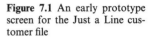

```
Just a Line Customer File

Name _____

Address_____

Phone No_____

Customer Code_____
```

Figure 7.1 An early prototype screen for the Just a Line customer file

suggest improvements. Some fourth-generation languages, such as dBASE III, allow the systems developer to design screens using a screen painter which automatically generates code from the screens.

Figure 7.1 shows an early prototype screen for the Just a Line file of regular customers. The screen would be used by Harry and Sue when adding new customers to their file for checking customer details. At present the screen simply shows the name, address and phone number for each customer, together with a Just a Line customer code. The developer will now show the screen to Harry and Sue who can then express their opinions and make suggestions.

The developer will try to incorporate all Harry and Sue's suggestions into the screen design and will then demonstrate what has been done, to invite more comments. Figure 7.2 shows a more sophisticated version of the screen, with additional fields to allow more customer details to be kept on file. In this version of the screen, the customer code has been altered to customer number and has been moved to a more prominent position, since this is how the Just a Line computer system will uniquely identify each customer. The address is more clearly displayed and an extra field has been added to show the date of

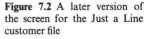

```
              Just a Line
            Customer File

Customer Number      _____

Name                 _____

Address              _____
                     _____
                     _____

Phone No             _____

Date of last order_____
```

Figure 7.2 A later version of the screen for the Just a Line customer file

the customer's last order. This new screen will now be shown to Harry and Sue. The cycle of demonstration and refinement will continue until both developer and client are satisfied with what has been produced.

Once it is clear exactly what the clients want from the part of the system under discussion, the developer may decide to back-track and build it using traditional methods of system design. In the case of Just a Line, however, it is likely that the customer screen prototype will be optimized so that it runs as efficiently as possible, fully tested and eventually integrated into the rest of the system.

Throughout this whole process Harry and Sue will be regularly consulted and asked to experiment with the developing system. The developer may set up special exercises for them to carry out, which make it possible to see how effective the system is. The developer will want to measure their performance in terms of speed, accuracy, and the number and types of mistakes made, as well as establishing how user-friendly they find the system to work with. Harry and Sue will be an integral part of the development process. They must be prepared to make decisions about their system and to take responsibility for them. Prototyping is hard work for everyone concerned, but it is also rewarding and generally results in a system that both developer and clients can be proud of.

The advantages of prototyping for the system developer Many of the advantages of prototyping for the system developer result from direct involvement of the client, such as better communication and more meaningful feedback on the way the system is developing.

The tasks of capturing the nature of the current problem and the client's future requirements are much less prone to error and misunderstanding when using a live prototype (rather than static paper models). This applies also to prototypes of the user interface, which allow the developer to show the client from an early stage exactly what the system will look like to its users.

Quite apart from the improved client communication, working with a live dynamic model offers the system developer other advantages. Static models, fixed in the stages of the traditional system life cycle, are at best cumbersome and at worst impossible to change. Yet, in developing systems, change is the norm—whether because of errors discovered, outside factors such as changes in the VAT rate or simply the client changing his or her mind. The prototype model is built to accommodate change; the developer expects to have to go round the loop of demonstrating to the client and refining the model several times before agreement is reached.   •

The inherent flexibility of the prototype model allows the designer to evaluate design decisions before they become fixed. Progress of the system in relation to the client's wishes can be monitored and alterations can be made accordingly. By setting up realistic simulations, such as a typical mail shot, the developer can judge how the system will perform and identify where improvements can be made.

Whatever precise interpretation a system developer gives to the term prototype, the basis of the approach is the live dynamic model. It is a model, together with the increased client involvement that it encourages, which gives prototyping its advantages as a method of developing software systems.

The disadvantages of prototyping

So far, we have emphasized all the advantages of prototyping. We have mentioned the extra time and effort that has to be put in by the user, but it may appear that the process is all plain sailing for the system developer. Unfortunately, this is not the case; any reader who has got the impression that prototyping is simply a license for hacking is going to be disappointed.

Prototyping is essentially an iterative process. The developer has to realize that it will not be right first, or even fifth, time round. This constant revising and refining is often difficult to accept for a more traditional software system developer who has been used to using a methodology. Many developers understandably feel protective about code that may have taken a lot of time and effort to write and may now have to be scrapped.

Not only is the methodological way of viewing system development inappropriate for prototyping but the traditional job definitions no longer apply either. The systems life cycle demanded the participation of systems analysts, systems designers and programmers—all of whom were specialists in their own particular area, but who needed to know a little about what the others were doing. A developer who is prototyping all or part of a system needs to be adept at capturing requirements and designing programs and must be able to program in at least one high-level language. The traditional analyst–programmer split no longer applies, and a developer who cannot follow a system through from the initial idea to the final implementation will be of little use in prototyping a system.

Effective prototyping demands not only people who have been trained in a new way but also more powerful software tools than the traditional methodologies. Prototyping needs speedy implementation and flexibility of software produced. For this, fourth-generation languages are essential, and for systems of any size CASE tools will also be needed. These are discussed more fully in Sec. 7.2.

Whereas communication with the client is much easier using prototyping, the amount of communication needed between different software developers working on a project can be much more difficult. If a system is split up into different areas for separate development of prototypes, it is essential that these separate parts can all eventually be integrated into one single, cohesive system. This involves a large overhead of communication between developers proto-typing the separate parts. There can come a point, with a large and complex system, where it needs to be split into so many separate parts that the communication overhead makes prototyping impractical as a development method. The nature of prototyping means that it is really a one- or two-man job. It will always be useful in developing certain parts of systems, such as the user interface, but it has not yet been proven as a suitable method for developing large and complex systems as a whole.

This problem of communication between developers is aggravated by the fact that prototyping is not a methodology and therefore has no underlying structure to aid management of the system development project. Traditional methodologies divide the development process into distinct stages and pre-scribe reviews and wall-throughs at specific points. The technique of proto-typing has none of these in-built milestones. New working guidelines have to be devised round the activities and deliverables of prototyping and, unless it is effectively managed, the development of a system using prototyping can easily get out of control.

Conclusion

Although prototyping does have drawbacks, both for the developer and the client, there is no doubt that with the right people, in the right circumstances, it is a fast and effective way of developing high-quality systems, and can encourage a friendly, productive relationship between the software developer and the client. In cases where it is not appropriate to use prototyping as the main development approach, it is still useful for the developer to prototype those areas of the system, such as the user interface, where client involvement is essential.

7.2   CASE

One of the anomalies of the computer industry has been the apparent reluctance of systems developers to use computers to help them in their work. For years now, computers have helped to run offices, build bridges and guide space probes, but it is only relatively recently that they have begun to be used as an aid to developing systems. If a client employs a single developer or a small software house to build a system, their principal tools until coding starts will probably still be pencil and paper. If, on the other hand, the system is developed by a large, modern software company, it is very likely that a CASE tool will be used in the development process.

What is CASE?

CASE stands for 'computer aided software engineering' and, like so many words in computer science, it incorporates a wide range of meanings. At the most general level a CASE tool can be any piece of software that assists in the development of a system. This can include compilers, debuggers and any automated design aid, such as a program that draws lines and boxes on the screen. At the top end of the range, however, the most sophisticated CASE tools include complete sets of integrated programs which guide the developer through the whole process of building and managing a system. Many CASE tools are specifically tied to a particular methodology. Some of the best known include IEW and IEF, which are CASE tools for James Martin's Information Engineering, and Automate, which supports the SSADM methodology. Other tools, such as Teamwork and Software Through Pictures claim to be more general and to fit in with different approaches to system development.

CASE tools and structured techniques

CASE tools automate the system development process, including modelling techniques such as those which we looked at in Chapters 4, 5 and 6. Using a CASE tool a designer can, for example, quickly build up a data flow diagram from boxes and other symbols provided on the screen. Hard copies of diagrams drawn with the aid of a CASE tool do not appear very different from those drawn carefully by hand or with a simple drawing package. Unlike a human, however, the CASE tool remembers all the details of every diagram that it has drawn.

Let us imagine that the developer has drawn the Just a Line context diagram (see Fig. 4.4) with a CASE tool and now wishes to explode the diagram and move down to level 1. All the inputs and outputs from the context diagram are recalled and automatically produced on the screen so that they can be incorporated into the new level 1 diagram. This will be constructed by moving the symbols provided by the CASE tool into the required position on the screen, adding data stores and internal data flows between processes, and labelling all the symbols on the diagram. As the developer draws the level 1 diagram, the tool automatically checks that the work is consistent with any previous diagrams for the Just a Line system. When the developer wants to move on to build the level 2 data flow diagrams, the CASE tool will explode each process, showing the relevant inputs and outputs. If the developer wants to make a change to one of the data flow diagrams later on, the CASE tool will register the effects of the change and automatically update the relevant diagrams. It does not allow the developer to infringe the balancing rules described in Chapter 4.

As well as checking consistency between different levels of diagram, the CASE tool can also create links and provide cross-checks between different types of model, such as data flow and entity–relationship diagrams. The CASE tool's repository (a huge, automated data dictionary) forms the basis for a whole network of connections between all the different models of the system. This sort of cross-checking, to ensure consistency between all the models of the system, is a major feature of all CASE tools and can save the system developer many hours of tedious and tiring work.

Some of the more sophisticated CASE tools use models of the required logical system to generate code, database files and menus automatically. Entities in the data model become database files, attributes become fields, process names in top-level data flow diagrams become top-level menus and lower-level process names become lower-level menus. This means that a CASE tool can assist and support the developer throughout the entire development process.

CASE tools and the client

There is no doubt that CASE tools can be a great help to the system developer, but how does this affect the client and the quality of the final system? As we mentioned in the previous section, a hard copy of a diagram drawn with a CASE tool does not look very different from a similar diagram drawn by hand. It will, however, be very much easier for the developer to make any changes the client suggests to the CASE diagram, since it will not be necessary to redraw the whole diagram each time. The client may also be shown diagrams on the screen, in which case the developer can help to make the required changes. Diagrams such as these, which can be altered on the spot, are extremely useful for experimenting with ideas about the design of the system: 'What would happen if part-filled orders were stored in a separate file?', 'Suppose we combine the processes of ordering and control of stock?'.

With a *live* diagram on the screen it is relatively easy to try out ideas and to see the effect various changes would have on the system as a whole. Used in this way, with a close partnership between the developer and client, CASE tools are invaluable in prototyping, since they greatly facilitate fast production of prototypes. CASE is particularly useful in the rapid development of evolutionary prototypes where the working model is progressively refined to become the final system.

Many people enjoy having the chance to play with a computer and a sophisticated diagramming tool, but some clients will never feel entirely comfortable viewing a diagram on the screen. They need to see the hard copy in front of them and to be able to pore over it at their leisure. It is important that someone who feels like this is allowed to have a hard copy of the diagram and plenty of time to study it. Any changes required cannot be made instantly, but they will still be a lot less trouble for the developer than going back to the drawing board. What is most important is that the client is not bemused and bewitched by the impressive technology of the CASE tool. It is essential that clients fully understand everything they are shown at each stage of the development process and that they are entirely happy about the way the system is progressing.

CASE—who benefits?

One of the principal claims for CASE tools is that they increase the productivity of the system development process. This can imply two different things: first, that there are considerable savings made in time, money and effort by the system developer and, second, that the final system produced is of a higher quality than a system developed without automated aids.

There is little doubt that CASE tools can greatly facilitate the work of the system developer in many ways. Systems can be analysed, designed and implemented more quickly using automated tools, and much of the tiresome side of the job, such as detailed checking of diagrams and charts for consistency and completeness, can be carried out by the CASE tool. All this is a great boon for the system developer, but how does it affect the client? As long as the final system is of a high quality, within the agreed budget and delivered according to schedule, does the client really care how it has been built? CASE tools are not magic. Just as an architect can design a mediocre building in spite of using the latest tools and techniques of the trade, so can a system developer, using the latest CASE technology, still produce a sub-standard system, whereas another can produce a system of high quality without the help of any automated tools.

CASE is no guarantee of quality. What is beyond doubt is that these tools do save time and money in the system development process. The result of this should be that such savings will not be swallowed up by software development firms, in buying and maintaining the CASE tool, but will be passed on to clients in the form of higher-quality systems which are delivered on time and within budget.

Understanding CASE

The whole area of CASE is shrouded in a blanket of terminology: you can hardly read even two paragraphs on the subject without being faced with some cryptic vocabulary—repository .. lower CASE ... reverse engineering are only a few examples. The following selection of terms and their explanations does not claim to explain all there is to know about CASE, but we hope that it will help anyone who wants to discover more about the subject to find their way through the jungle of jargon which surrounds it.

CASE | Computer aided software engineering. This, in its widest sense, can include any piece of software that assists in the system development process. However, a CASE tool is usually a highly sophisticated collection of software which can help developers in their work, especially in the areas of diagrams, cross-checking and documentation. CASE tools aim to automate the whole development process, from the initial identification of customer requirements to automatic code generation. Several CASE tools may be necessary to cover all aspects of a particular development.

Workbench | This includes all the tools necessary for a particular task. An analysis workbench, for example, may offer tools such as automated data flow diagrams, entity–relationship models, process definitions labelling and definition facilities, and different types of report on the models produced. All tools in a particular workbench are integrated and designed to work together. There is also integration between different workbenches in the same CASE tool.

Repository | This is also referred to as the encyclopaedia or dictionary. It is the core of any CASE tool, holding all the information about the problem area and the computer system. The repository enables cross-referencing between diagrams, models and workbenches, to ensure overall consistency. It instantly reflects any changes in the developing system.

Upper CASE | Tools which support the analysis and design of software systems.

Lower CASE | Tools which support programming and testing.

Re-engineering | Restructuring of inefficient or badly constructed code using a CASE tool.

Reverse engineering | Sometimes the documentation of a program is so sparse or confused that it is impossible to work out what the program was supposed to do in the first place. The process of reverse engineering feeds an old, inefficient piece of software into a CASE tool to find out its original purpose.

IPSE | Integrated project support environment. These are CASE tools for the management of system development projects. They offer automated support facilities for project management, such as schedule planning, cost estimating, version control, time accounting and problem recording.

Advantages of CASE tools

There are many advantages for a software developer in using CASE tools. The tools are based on structured techniques, such as entity relationship modelling, which have been tried and tested by countless system developers. CASE does not involve a reversal of former approaches to the development process; the tools simply offer a faster, more efficient and less tedious way of doing the job. Many of the system developer's most time-consuming tasks can be carried out by the CASE tool repository, which can perform endless cross-checking which would be too time-consuming to do by hand. This leads to fast, accurate detection of errors, omissions and inconsistencies.

Communication with the client during the development process can be greatly facilitated by using a CASE tool. CASE tools make comprehensive use of graphics and allow diagrams to be produced and altered with ease. This means that, when errors are discovered or when the client is not happy with a diagram, it is a relatively simple task to make the required changes. CASE tools facilitate and encourage reworking of models to ensure that the final design is exactly what the client wants.

The production of full, consistent documentation using a CASE tool is very much easier and more accurate than documenting a system developed by hand, since every item of data about the system is held in the central repository of the CASE tool. This is especially important on systems that take several man-years to develop, since it is likely that many different people will be working on the system during its lifetime. The extensive documentation produced and the speed of reworking mean that systems developed with CASE are more easily maintainable than systems developed by hand.

For developers who use prototypes as the basis of their work, all the advantages of prototyping, such as rapid development and improved communication with clients, are enhanced by using a CASE tool to build the prototypes.

On the management side, the advent of IPSEs (see the definition in the previous section) means that the technical details of developing a system can be totally integrated with the management of the development project. Project management is discussed further in Chapter 10.

Perhaps the most important advantage of CASE tools for the system developer is that using a CASE tool can be fun. With automated aids, the developer is free to concentrate on the creative side of the work, sure in the knowledge that the boring, repetitive tasks will be performed speedily and accurately by the CASE tool.

Some criticisms of CASE

Any new tool or technique gives rise to criticisms and CASE is no exception. CASE tools are very expensive and represent a major investment for a software development company. Since many of the tools are tied to a particular methodology, this involves a strong commitment to that methodology on the part of the company. This commitment, together with the size of investment, means that a development company will probably become fixed in a particular way of developing systems, rather than moving ahead to new techniques and approaches. A CASE tool involves further expense for the company in terms of time, effort and money since it needs to be maintained in the same way as any other piece of software. Moreover, there is a learning curve associated with the tools and specialized training is often needed. A software company would have to take this into account when considering whether it is worth investing in CASE.

The use of mathematics and logic in developing more correct, reliable systems is largely ignored by the CASE industry, yet this is considered by many experts to be an essential part of the development of computer software, particularly with regard to safety-critical and security-critical systems. The role of formal languages, based on mathematics and logic, is discussed in the following section.

The CASE tool can support, but must not replace, the work of the system developer. Development of software systems requires skills and talents, such as creativity and good communication, that cannot be performed by an automated tool. There is a risk that a poor developer may be able to blind the client with the science of the CASE tool, but it is important to remember that there is no substitute for good software systems developers who know their job.

Conclusion

It is as yet too early to say whether CASE tools fulfil all their promises. In the next few years there will probably be tools on the market that subsequently fall by the wayside and others that will attract large amounts of interest and investment. We will only be able to decide whether system development using CASE really does lead to better, more robust and maintainable systems once these systems have aged and weathered some years of use. There is no doubt, though, that CASE tools are here to stay. Software developers of the future will probably be as horrified at the idea of designing systems by hand as today's train drivers are at the thought of manually stoking the engine.

7.3 FORMAL NOTATIONS

For well over a decade, researchers have suggested that the use of formal notations (formal languages based on mathematics and logic) could play a valuable role in the development of software.

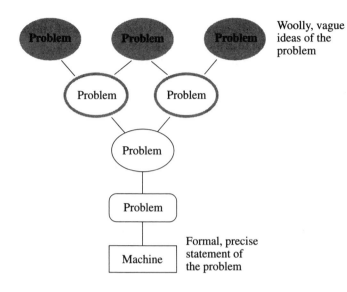

Woolly, vague ideas of the problem

Formal, precise statement of the problem

Figure 7.3 A view of the development process

In this chapter we first explain the different terms used in the area of formal notations and give two small examples relating to the Just a Line case study. We have used Just a Line here for the sake of continuity and because we did not want to introduce another case study at this stage. However, in reality, a developer would be most unlikely to use a formal notation for a simple data processing application like Just a Line. We examine some of the problems in software system development where the use of such formal notations may be helpful. We look at the ways in which formal notations can offer a solution to some of the problems in software development and finally we discuss some of the commonly voiced objections to using them.

What are formal notations?

Figure 7.3 repeats the diagram we discussed in Chapter 1. This shows the system development process as a series of descriptions, or specifications, of the problem which are gradually refined until a description is arrived at which can be understood by a computer.

The original accounts of the problem, which come from the clients, are most likely to be in a natural language, such as English, with perhaps a few diagrams and sample forms to help explain the situation. The final description will be in a programming language, since this is the only kind of language that a computer understands. What we are interested in is the question of which languages or notations to use for the intermediate stages of development.

So far in this book we have introduced several different notations which can be used to describe particular aspects of a problem. Data flow diagrams illustrate the objects in the system and the relationships between them, and entity life histories show how the data changes over time. Formal notations are simply another type of language which can be used to specify the problem area, although it can be seen from the explanations below that they are very different from the structured techniques that we have used up until now. Here are explanations of some of the terms in use.

Notations	These are symbols or groups of symbols which can be given meanings. Thus IV and 4 are both notations for the number four and ♠ ♥ ♦ ♣ are notations which represent the four suits in a pack of cards. Notations are simply ways of writing down parts of a language.
Formal notations	These are also referred to as formal languages or formal specification languages. The *formal* part of them means that these languages are governed by explicit, well-defined rules. We can contrast this with natural languages, such as English, where the rules are loosely defined and vary in different areas and in different situations. For example, the way you ask your friend for a loan is rather different from the way you ask your bank manager. Formal notations have very clear rules which are based on mathematics or logic. In the formal language of arithmetic, for example, we learn and use the rules of precedence when manipulating numbers. The formal language Z, which we will look at later in this chapter, is based on rules from predicate logic and from set theory.
Formal specification	This is a description of a problem which is written in a formal language.
Formal methods	The use of formal notations in developing a software system is often referred to as formal methods. This can be misleading since there is no inherent concept of a *method* in the sense of a particular way of developing a system. Formal notations are merely languages which the system developer can use instead of, or as well as, other techniques to describe the problem area. By formal methods we simply mean that formal notations are being used to specify all or part of the problem.

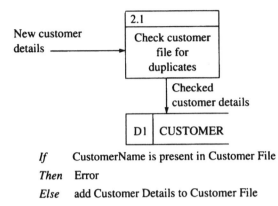

If   CustomerName is present in Customer File

Then   Error

Else   add Customer Details to Customer File

Figure 7.4 Part of the data flow diagram and process definition for the checking of new customer details

A small example of formal notations from Just a Line

As one of their requirements for the new system, Sue and Harry have asked for a price list/order form which can be sent out to regular customers. The new Just a Line computer system will therefore include a file with records of all the company's regular customers. Each time an order is received from a new customer the file is updated by adding the new customer's details. Obviously, Harry and Sue want to be sure that no customer appears in the file more than once. The system will therefore have to perform some kind of check each time a new customer is added, to make sure that the details are not already in the file.

The system developer may choose to describe this checking operation by using the techniques of data flow diagrams and process definitions which we have already looked at in Chapter 4. Figure 7.4 shows the relevant section of the data flow diagram and the extract from the process definition.

Alternatively, the system developer may decide to use a formal notation, such as the formal language Z, to describe how the file must be checked before a new customer's details are added. The Z language uses schemas (or boxes) which are divided into two parts. The top part contains variables, their types and any constraints on their use. The bottom part contains operations that can be performed on these variables and the results of these operations.

Figure 7.5 shows a Z schema to check for duplicate customer entries in the customer file and to add new customer details. The meanings of the symbols used and an explanation of the schema follow the diagram. Don't worry if you feel that the schema might as well have been written in ancient Greek—Z is a language that has to be learned like any other, even if parts of it look vaguely familiar. This example is included here simply to show what the language

```
┌─ Add Customer to File ──────────────────────────────┐
│                                                      │
│  CustomerFile, CustomerFile´ : Name  ⇸ Details       │
│                                                      │
│  CustomerDetails          : Name  ⇸ Details          │
│                                                      │
├──────────────────────────────────────────────────   │
│                                                      │
│  dom(CustomerDetails?) ∩ dom(CustomerFile) = { }     │
│                                                      │
│  CustomerFile´ = CustomerFile ∪ CustomerDetails?     │
│                                                      │
│                                                      │
└──────────────────────────────────────────────────────┘
```

Glossary:

⇸	Partial function
dom	Gives the left-hand side of the function, in this case the customer's name
∩	Set intersection
∪	Set union
{ }	The empty set
?	Input data
´	Data after an operation has been performed on it

Figure 7.5 A Z schema to add non-duplicate entries to the customer file

looks like. A Z specification will always include a natural language description of what the schema is trying to express, but as this has already been explained earlier, it is omitted here.

The top half of the schema contains declarations of CustomerFile (the old customer file before the customer's details are added) and CustomerFile´ (the file containing the new details). Both of these files are made up of series of records. Each record contains the customer's name which is linked to the particular customer's details. The data to be input is CustomerDetails? which also contains a customer name and details. In Z, all inputs are identified by the symbol ?. Figure 7.6 shows an example of the customer file and the data to be input.

The bottom half of the Z schema in Fig. 7.5 shows what happens when a new customer is added to the existing customer file. The top line expresses the pre-condition that the new name to be added must not already be in the customer file. This is shown by the symbol ∩, which intersects the customer names of the old file and the new customer to be added. The empty set symbol { } indicates that there is no overlap between the set of names in the old

Customer File	*Data to be input*
Briggs ⟶ Briggs' details	Browne ⟶ Browne's details
Clark ⟶ Clark's details	
Davis ⟶ Davis' details	
Evans ⟶ Evans' details	
Jones ⟶ Jones' details	
Milton ⟶ Milton's details	
Pryce ⟶ Pryce's details	
Wood ⟶ Wood's details	

Figure 7.6 An example customer file and data to be input

customer file and the new name. This means that the new customer is not yet on the file. This situation is shown in Fig. 7.7(a).

Once the pre-condition is satisfied, the last line of the schema states that the new customer file, CustomerFile′, is equal to the old file CustomerFile, with the new details added. If the customer's details are already on the file, the pre-condition will not be satisfied (see Fig. 7.7b). In this case the customer's details will not be added since this would cause duplicate entries on the file.

Specifying part of the Just a Line stock control system in Z

Judging by the interview in Chapter 3, the Just a Line stock control system is rather haphazard. In order to get a clearer picture of what happens, the developer has decided to use the formal language Z to specify some of the processes involved in stock control.

Each card line bought in by Harry and Sue is recorded as available stock, together with the quantity available for customer ordering. Quantities in the system are represented as natural numbers (whole numbers starting from 0). As customers usually place their orders for cards in advance, stock that has been ordered is marked as allocated, together with the associated quantity.

The basic types in the specification are cards and natural numbers, which are represented in Z as [Card, Natural]. This means that everything in the specification will be represented in terms of cards, numbers or some relationship between the two types.

There are three separate lists or files recorded by the system: the total stock, which is a file of card lines, the file of available card lines and the file

Existing customer file

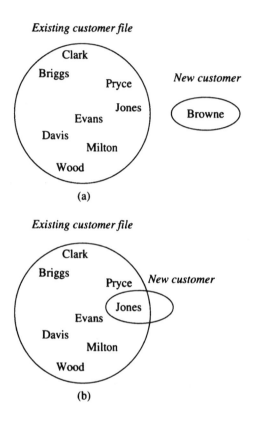

(a)

Existing customer file

(b)

Figure 7.7 (a) The pre-condition that ensures no duplicate is satisfied. (b) The pre-condition fails, since Jones is already on the file

of allocated card lines, both of which are represented by a relationship between cards and numbers. Every card line stocked by Just a Line appears in both the available and the allocated files. If none of the card lines is available or if none has been ordered, the relevant entry records a quantity of 0.

As an example, the three files in the system might read as follows:

Stock	*Available*		*Allocated*	
Summer Meadows	Summer Meadows	12	Summer Meadows	0
Local Scenes	Local Scenes	10	Local Scenes	4
Cute Kittens	Cute Kittens	0	Cute Kittens	6
Old Masters	Old Masters	3	Old Masters	0
etc.	etc.		etc.	

The StockState schema is shown below:

```
__StockState_____
 stock: ℙCard
 available: Card ⇸ Natural
 allocated: Card ⇸ Natural
_____
 dom available = stock
 dom allocated = stock
```

This represents the information that is stored in the system. The two lines in the bottom half of the schema are the system invariants. These are facts that must always remain true whatever operations are performed on the data in the system. In this case the invariants state that all card lines in stock should appear on the files of both the available and the allocated cards.

The following schema specifies the starting state of the Just a Line stock control system:

```
__InitialStockState_____
 StockState
_____
 stock = { }
 available = { }
 allocated = { }
```

The schema shows that initially all three files are empty.

The schema below specifies how the system changes when a new card line is added to the Just a Line stock, assuming that no orders have been placed for the new card:

```
__AddCardLine_____
 Δ StockState
 card? : Card
 qty? : Natural
_____
 card? ∉ stock
 stock' = stock∪{card?}
 available' = available∪{card?↦qty?}
 allocated' = allocated∪{card?↦0}
```

The first line of the schema, Δ StockState, indicates that the data stored in the system is going to be changed by the operation. The next two lines represent inputs by the user of the system of the name and quantity of the new card line. The bottom half of the schema checks that the card line which the user wishes to add is not already in stock and, assuming no duplication, the new card name is added to the stock file, the card name and the quantity available are added to the available file and the card name and the amount 0 are recorded in the allocated file.

The schema to add a card records accurately what happens, but is not very friendly to the user. Z allows the definition of free types which record responses that the system makes to the user. Part of the free type, Report, for the Just a Line specification is shown below:

$$Report \triangleq \{Card\ added,$$
$$Card\ deleted,$$
$$Card\ already\ in\ stock$$
$$Amount\ on\ order,$$
$$Card\ not\ stocked, \ldots\}$$

The response 'Card added' may now be added to the schema for the operation to add a new product line. In addition, a response may be used in a schema to represent the case where the user tries to add a card line that is already in stock, as shown below:

```
__DuplicateCardLine_____
Ξ StockState
card? : Card
qty? : Natural
result! : Report
_____
card? ∈ stock
result! = Card already in stock
```

In this case, the first line of the schema, ΞStockState, indicates that this operation will not alter the data in the system. The system output, result!, tells the user why the operation has failed.

In addition to upgrading the stored data in the system, Harry and Sue must be able to extract useful information from the stock control system. As an example, the following schema represents a successful operation to find out how much of a particular card line is already allocated:

```
__FindAmountAllocated_____
Ξ StockState
card? : Card
amount! : Natural
response! : Report
_____
card? ∈ stock
amount! = allocated (card?)
result! = Amount on order
```

Problem areas in software system development

One of the principal objectives of a software system developer should be a system which fulfils the client's requirements. Unfortunately, many developers fail to achieve this aim. Despite the use of structured methods, large numbers of software systems are delivered late, cost far more than the original estimates and need constant maintenance. The stage of the system life cycle euphemistically known as maintenance and modification generally takes up more time and resources than all the rest of the stages put together.

It is reasonable to expect that a client will want modifications made to a system in the course of time. More comprehensive reporting facilities may be needed, for example, or the client may wish to computerize part of the system which was previously handled manually. Progress involves change, and modification in this sense is a natural part of system development.

Maintenance, on the other hand, is when the developer has got it wrong. Maintenance is a blanket term which can cover everything from fixing small errors in program code to unravelling major misunderstandings about what the system is supposed to do. This is not the result of natural progression and change, but of an unacceptable level of mistakes made in the development of a system.

Errors can be made at any point in the development process, but the most difficult to find (and the most costly to fix) are those that occur in the early stages. If the developer does not fully understand the problems and requirements of the client, the specification of the new system is not worth the paper it is written on. Even if the developer has a very clear idea of what is needed, it must be possible to express this in such a way that anyone reading the specification, and in particular a programmer who has the job of coding from it, will have absolutely no doubt about what is required. If we look at Fig. 7.3 again, we see the development process viewed as a series of specifications. For the process to be successful, each specification must be describing the same thing. If the program code, which is the final specification in the series, does not correspond to the original problem, it means that there has been a serious mismatch somewhere along the way. This is what happens all too frequently in software system development.

Unless a major effort is made to deal with this problem it is only going to get worse. Each year, increasingly complex systems are being demanded by clients, and more software systems are being used in situations where their accuracy and reliability are a matter of life or death. Today, software controls nuclear power plants, manages flight control systems and monitors seriously ill patients in hospitals. Expectations of what computers can do are increasing all the time, but do we really have the technology and the expertise to keep abreast of them?

Software system development is still a relatively young industry. We can compare its situation today with that of civil engineering one hundred years ago. In the heyday of Victorian England, engineers such as Stevenson, Telford and Brunel attempted ever more ambitious projects. There were many spectacular successes, but also some equally spectacular disasters, such as the sinking of Brunel's mighty ship, *The Great Eastern*. Over the years, civil engineering has evolved from the status of a craft, where design was based mainly on experience and rule of thumb, to a discipline where design is based on sound engineering principles. In order to achieve the status of software engineering, this is the path that software development must follow, so that systems in the future will be more robust, more reliable and, most important of all, they will be what the client wants.

How can formal notations help to solve the problems of software development?

It is now widely accepted that to eliminate the problems of system development, much more effort must be expended in the early stages of the development process, i.e. more effort should be put into the early specification of the problem. As we said in the previous section, errors made near the beginning of the development process are the most expensive to find and the most difficult to correct. These early stages of development are too often rushed through—in order to leave time before installation of the system to correct errors, most of which, ironically, are made at this early stage, because it is rushed.

The traditional requirements specification document is notoriously ambiguous, incomplete and inconsistent. Some of this is due to lack of precision and rigour in the techniques available. Although the structured techniques introduced in Chapters 4, 5 and 6 are widely used in system development, none of them has a sound theoretical basis. There is often, for example, no single correct way of interpreting a problem in data flow diagrams, nor a way of proving such diagrams to be logically consistent or complete. Natural language, which is used extensively in specifications, is often imprecise and ambiguous. Both natural language and (graphical) structured techniques can be of immense benefit to the software system developer, but in cases where consistency and precision are essential these techniques are frequently inadequate.

The software system developer has to transform the client's informal description of a required system into a series of working programs. Traditionally, the recommended way of doing this is to step through the system life cycle, producing relevant deliverables from each stage. Our view of the system development process in Fig. 7.3 shows a series of specifications which are gradually refined until acceptable by a machine. Whatever way we look at the overall process, we can see that the developer has to describe the problem and the required system in some kind of language or notation at each stage of development. These descriptions not only specify the problem but are also used by the developer to record design decisions and reasoning behind these decisions. If the notation used for the descriptions is a formal language, this will benefit the developer and the system in several ways.

Primarily, what we are doing when writing a specification in a formal notation is describing the problem in an abstract way. We are using just the symbols allowed by the notation and manipulating them according to the rules of the notation, without having to worry about what they refer to in this particular instance. We use the language of mathematics all the time to abstract in this way. For example, if we needed to know how many chairs to put in a school hall for an assembly of all the children, we would not go about it by first putting in an arbitrary number of chairs, then assembling all the children and seeing how many children could be seated in a chaotic game of musical chairs. Physically manipulating chairs and children is hard work, and inefficient. The results might even be inconclusive. We might find that even after we had apparently got all the children seated, that one or two had been temporarily absent and were now chairless. We would be wiser to get a piece of paper and write down the number of children in each class: reception class 30, middle class 27, top class 19; total 76.

The numbers are abstract descriptions of the problem. We do not need to know what they refer to in order to manipulate them and arrive at the answer of 76. We have included a reference by writing down the names of the classes, but we do not need this to do our calculation. Furthermore, this answer is more convincing than the one arrived at by the musical chairs method.

What we are doing in this very simple example is using the formal language of mathematics to model our problem. What is true of the mathematical model is also true of the real-world problem. A formal specification of a system provides a model of some aspects of the system's behaviour. Engineering disciplines use mathematical models to understand the physical properties of the system being studied. The behaviour of dams, the atmosphere, oceans and continental plates can be described by differential equations representing the basic conservation laws of physics. In order to predict reliably how a construction will react to any given environmental situation, engineers construct a mathematical model which is capable of being analysed under the proven laws of mathematics. In the same way, system developers can construct models of the system under consideration. Manipulation of such a model reflects what will happen in the real system, and is easier to understand, reason about and evaluate than trying to manipulate the whole system with all its clutter. The ability to view the system in an abstract way allows the developer to concentrate on the parts of the problem that are currently important, and to leave other details until later on.

The power of abstraction is not the only advantage of using a formal notation to model a system. A further benefit comes from the fact that it is only possible to use formal notations if you are clear about what you are doing. Writing in a formal language is hard. The software developer is forced, by the language, to be consistent and to be precise. This is especially true where the language is executable, like the skeleton of a program, or where automated tools exist that can perform tasks such as type checking and detecting syntax errors. One such tool for the Z language is Formalizer, which has been developed by Logica in Cambridge.

A formal notation helps the developer to record decisions logically, to think clearly about them and to reason more easily. The right notation frees the developer from worrying about the intricacies of manipulating the language to concentrate on the problem in hand. As a comparison, think how much easier it is to perform multiplication and division with Arabic rather than with Roman numerals. In the early stages of the development of a system a formal notation, like structured techniques, helps developers to impose some order on the jumble of informal spoken specification. It forces them to ask questions and helps them to reason about the problem area and the early stages of the system.

Specifying the system in a formal language means that the developer can formalize the problem area at an early stage, rather than waiting for the formality of the coding. This means that internal inconsistencies, ambiguities and inaccuracies can be discovered and corrected sooner, and therefore less expensively.

Unambiguous communication is very hard to achieve. In developing a system of any size the software developer will need to communicate unambiguously both with the rest of the development team and with the client. Provided that the team members are all trained to understand a formal notation, a formal specification forms a more reliable basis for communication than an informal specification. The formal notation forces the team to build a specification that is as clear and precise as possible. If all members of the team 'speak' the same formal language and can fully understand the specification, then the risk of ambiguity in communication will be reduced to a minimum. Communicating with the client is a different problem; this is discussed in the next section on objections to the use of formal notations.

A formal specification can form the basis of good documentation. This is important in the struggle to improve the maintainability of systems. If a software developer comes back to work on a system after a gap, the precision of a formal specification will make it easier to remember the details of the problem. If the developer stops working on the system altogether, such a specification will help successors to understand what is going on. If the system is up and running, it is true that the developer can always look at the code, but program listings can be complicated by the inclusion of code to cope with many different system requirements such as response time, storage and the user interface. Because a formal specification is an abstraction, which concentrates simply on what the system does, it will give the developer a better overall understanding.

If we go back again to the diagram of the development process in Fig. 7.3, we can see that there has to be some way of ensuring that each description or specification of the problem is actually describing the same thing. This is one of the major problems of system development. There is no way of being 100 per cent certain that any specification corresponds exactly to the client's informally expressed requirements. However, if the developer is able to build a formal specification early on in the development process, and if all subsequent descriptions are expressed formally, then there can be a certain amount of confidence that the final program does at least do what the specification intended.

Objections to the use of formal notations

One of the most common objections to the use of formal notations is that clients will never be able to understand the resulting formal specification. As clients are the main source of information about the required system, it is essential that they understand the developer's specification of requirements. There are two answers to this objection.

First, it may be possible to educate clients so that they can understand the formal notation used. This is not impossible, but seems a rather unrealistic aim in most cases. The second answer to the objection is that the developer should be able to interpret the formal specification in a language that the client understands. Just because something is written down in a formal way, it does not mean that it cannot be described informally, using a language that the client feels happy with, whether it be natural English, diagrams or both of these.

It can be argued that using a formal notation to write a specification is too cumbersome and long-winded if the program is to be written in a fourth-generation language (4GL). This is because coding in the 4GL is so much faster than writing the specification itself. It is true that the value of using a formal language must, to some extent, be influenced by the choice of implementation technology and by the type of system to be developed. It would, for example, be a case of massive overkill to write a complete formal specification for the Just a Line system.

Allied to the above point is the issue of user expectations. There is always going to be pressure on system developers to produce software as fast, and therefore as cheaply, as possible. If a formal notation is used, the time before any code is written is inevitably going to be longer than if a technique such as prototyping is employed. Clients and managers have to be convinced that time spent at the specification stage will lead to time saved in debugging and at the testing and implementation stages.

Formal notations are often perceived by both managers and developers as something alien and which will require considerable retraining. They are unwilling to commit themselves to the investment that retraining would involve, although, ironically, many are quite happy to invest an equally large sum of money in a CASE tool.

In spite of the advantages that using formal notations can bring, many managers are wedded to the traditional structured methodologies. Popular methodologies, such as SSADM or Information Engineering, offer clear milestones for project management. This makes them very attractive to a manager charting the progress of a software system development. Progress can be recorded in terms of measurable events. The client can be told when a particular stage in the system development has been completed, and a date can be estimated for completion of the next stage. Formal notations are not a methodology, and do not at present form part of any of the widely used methodologies. They do not have any in-built milestones which can help in the management of a project. This means extra work for the project manager in monitoring progress and controlling the development of the system. Project management is a very important part of any system development, but it is a pity to discard a potentially useful tool, such as formal notations, simply because it does not look good on a chart.

Conclusion

There is today a pressing requirement to produce software systems that are reliable and error free. Research indicates that many of the problems with systems developed using traditional methods stem from an inadequate or ambiguous specification of requirements. A new approach is needed. Formal notations are not without problems and are not the answer for every type of system. However, they do seem to offer a promising approach. Many benefits will accrue from putting more effort into the early stages of software system development, but what will be achieved primarily is a consistent and unambiguous specification. Managers and developers must be convinced that investing more time and effort in the early stages of system development will result in savings much later on and that this makes sound economic sense.

7.4 OBJECT ORIENTATION

Why do we need a new approach to software design?

The structured approach to software development addressed many of the problems that caused the software crisis (see Chapter 2). Software systems developed over the last twenty-five years using structured methods have shown significant improvements. However, as the problems tackled by software developers have become larger and more complex, it has become apparent that structured methods are not a complete answer. Despite all the effort that has been put into improving the software development process, the software crisis is growing worse each year. It is still rare for a project to be delivered on time, within budget and without serious bugs; even more worryingly, software produced using structured techniques has proved to be very hard to maintain.

The significance of maintenance cannot be overemphasized. Software projects of any size take a long time, and therefore cost a great deal, to develop. Understandably companies who have invested huge amounts of money in a software application expect it to function for a significant amount of time. During its lifetime an application will be required to change in order to fix bugs, to accommodate system enhancements and to meet new requirements. The software will accumulate a great many makeshift patches and fixes. Unfortunately, each time a change is introduced or a bug is fixed the chances of introducing new bugs are increased.

Three things are commonly identified as making software hard to maintain:

- Functional decomposition
- Poor modularity
- Visibility of data

Functional decomposition Structured methods use a functional approach to software design, i.e. the structure of the software is based on top-down functional decomposition. The system is partitioned into functional sub-systems; the system is viewed as a number of separate processes, each of which represents a separate activity. Data passes freely between the sub-systems. For example, the Just a Line system (see Fig. 7.8) is divided into three functional sub-systems:

- Handle customer orders
- Order stock
- Keep accounts

Data, in the form of priced orders and supplier invoices, is passed between these sub-systems.

A program produced from a functional design echoes the design structure—the modules of the software are functional units. This functional structure has proved to be one of the things that makes such software hard to maintain. During the lifetime of a software application the types of change most often implemented are changes to the required functionality. If the structure of the software is based on its functionality, any change in functionality can affect the underlying program structure. The essential shape of the

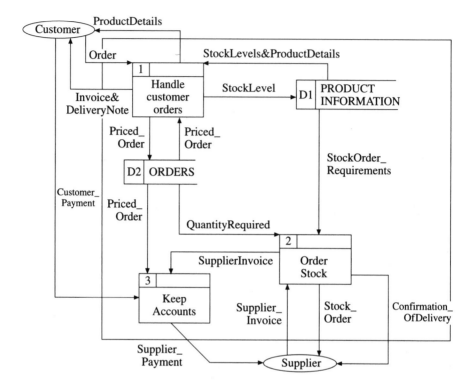

Figure 7.8 Just a Line: Level 1 diagram of the current system

software becomes masked and soon disappears entirely. It does not take long for a program to degenerate into a fragile incomprehensible monster that no one dares touch.

Poor modularity It is unusual for programmers to maintain their own code. The norm is for maintenance to be done by someone who has never seen the code before. Often maintenance is the lot of new, inexperienced programmers. The task of these programmers is made more difficult the more of the code they have to read and understand. If modules are properly decentralized, then each module is autonomous—it is self-contained and independent. If this is the case, a maintaining programmer need only read and understand the module he or she has to change, or perhaps that and one or two closely related modules. If a program module is not autonomous the programmer may find that he or she has to read and understand large sections of the rest of the program in order to understand it well enough carry out the required update.

Poor modularity is one of the causes of the well-known knock-on effect of introducing changes. The more autonomous the module, the less chance there is of a small change to one module causing a chain reaction throughout the program. Functional decomposition unfortunately does not promote properly decentralized modules.

Visibility of data Another cause of the knock-on effect of introducing changes is high visibility of data—data being too visible and therefore too accessible to parts of a program that do not need to access it. Changes made to the data in one part of the program cause mysterious errors and unpredictable behaviour in other parts of the program. The most notorious culprit in this respect was the COMMON block of data in early FORTRAN programs. This was a block of data to which all parts of the program had unlimited access. Block structured programming languages introduced the concept of scoping which limited data visibility. However, it did not entirely succeed in limiting data visibility to those parts of the program that needed it and the knock-on effect of changes continued to be a problem.

For software to be easier to maintain four things are required:

- Software structure needs to be based on something less liable to change than its functionality. Programs need to have a robust structure.
- Data needs to be less visible.
- Code needs to be easy to understand so that maintenance programmers who come across it for the first time are not given an impossible task.
- Program modules need to be as independent as possible. If this can be done, the effect of any change will be isolated to the module being changed. This should also limit the amount of programmer has to understand when he or she makes a change to a module.

Background to object orientation

Since the late eighties object orientation has been the latest bandwagon for software development. The ideas on which object orientation are based have been around for much longer. The first object-oriented programming language was Simula, developed in the late sixties, to support computer simulations of real-world processes. Decomposition in a Simula program was not based on functionality but the real-world objects to be simulated in the software. Ideas generated by the Simula team were taken up and developed at the Xerox Palo Alto Research Center, where the Smalltalk-80 programming language was developed, originally to program the Dynabook, an early type of laptop computer. There are now several object-oriented programming languages, the best known of which are Smalltalk, C++ and Eiffel.

The initial interest in the ideas of object orientation focused on programming language issues. However, methodologists such as Booch, Rumbaugh and Jacobson have applied the ideas of object orientation to the whole software development process—analysis, design and implementation. New modelling techniques, the object-oriented equivalent of the structured modelling techniques, have been developed to model the application domain in object-oriented terms.

One of the most widely adopted object-oriented methodologies is Rumbaugh's Object Modelling Technique (OMT). OMT builds a model of the real-world problem and adds implementation details at a later stage without fundamentally altering the model. There are four stages to OMT: analysis, system design, object design and implementation. The aim of the analysis stage is to obtain a clear understanding of the problem and build a model that will serve as a basis for the design and implementation stages. The analysis model is divided into three:

- The object model which shows the static structure of classes in the problem and their interrelationships. This is derived from E–R diagrams.
- The dynamic model which describes interactions among objects and with the effect of changes to objects over time.
- The functional model which describes data transformations. This is similar to data flow diagrams.

Each of these three models is drawn at all four stages of system development. Detail is gradually added to transform the basic model seamlessly into an implementation model.

Object-oriented terminology

Object orientation has its own specialized vocabulary which has to be mastered if the technology is to be understood. Many of the terms were introduced by Smalltalk and were new to the programming community because they referred to novel concepts. The principal terms are introduced in Fig. 7.9. The underlying concepts are explained below.

Object-oriented concepts

Objects The basic building block of object-oriented software is the object. Software objects are derived from and model the real-world objects in the application domain. Each object in the real world has an associated pattern of behaviour and each has to store and maintain data about its status. A car, for example, can start, move forward, turn, move backwards and stop. It maintains information about how much petrol it has in its tank, the temperature of its engine, its speed. In the same way a software object packages together data and behaviour. A software object retains certain information and knows how to perform certain functions. To represent the car as a

Object terminology

Object	Software packet containing data and methods (procedures) for operating on that data
Class	Template or factory for creating objects
Instance	Reference to an object that belongs to a particular class
Method	Procedure that is part of an object
Message	Request from one object to another that it execute one of its methods
Encapsulation	The packaging together of data and methods into an object
Information hiding	Making the internal details of a module inaccessible to other modules
Inheritance	Mechanism which allows a class to reuse methods and variables already defined in another class
Polymorphism	The ability to hide different implementations behind a common interface

Figure 7.9 Object terminology

software object, its behaviour—start, move, stop, etc.—will be translated into methods and its data—temperature, speed, amount of petrol—into variables. An object-oriented system is made up of such objects which collaborate and communicate with each other by message passing.

A system which is structured into objects has its structure centred round the data in the system, rather than the functionality. The structure is therefore less vulnerable to changing requirements because such changes are more often to the system functionality than to the data; over the lifetime of a system, its data remains relatively unchanged. In the case of Just a Line, for example, we can assume that the company's business will continue to be concerned with cards, customers, orders and payments, but the functionality required of these objects will probably change over time.

Software objects model objects in the real world. This offers a conceptual simplicity which promotes ease of understanding. For this reason object-oriented programs are easier to maintain.

Class An object is defined in terms of its class. When we specify that a class will have certain variables and methods, we determine that all objects of that class, i.e. all instances of that class, will have the same structure—just those variables and just those methods. We can think of a class as being an object factory, a template for all objects of that class. In data modelling terms, the relationship between a class and an object is conceptually similar to the relationship between an entity and an occurrence of an entity.

Message passing In an object-oriented system objects interact with each other by sending each other *messages* requesting particular services. A message normally takes the form of the name of an object followed by the method to be executed. The initiating object is referred to as the *client or sender*, the receiving object as the *server or receiver*. When a server object receives a message it executes the appropriate method. This approach is radically different from the functional approach. In a functionally designed program, *data* is passed between processing units; in an object-oriented program *messages* are passed between objects. For example, suppose we wanted to calculate the factorial of 20 (an integer). What we would probably do, in a functionally designed program, would be to write a procedure that calculated factorials. We would then call that procedure, sending it the number 20 as a parameter and expect it to return the result of the calculation. In an object-oriented program, the class of integers would be defined with factorial as one of its methods. The number 20 would be an object of the class. The object 20 could therefore be passed the message factorial; it would understand the message because factorial was one of its methods and would then execute the factorial method and return the result.

Encapsulation and information hiding Packaging related data and methods together is called encapsulation. The encapsulation mechanism provides three desirable software properties:

- Proper modularity
- Data abstraction
- Information hiding

Modularity Encapsulation promotes modularity—the package, i.e. the object, that results from the encapsulation of data and methods becomes the building block of the system. The modules produced are autonomous, self-contained and independent.

Data abstraction The data inside an object can only be accessed by using the object's methods—methods designed to ensure that the data is handled properly. We can think of the data as being surrounded by a protective outer ring of methods (see Fig. 7.10).[*]

The rest of the world cannot directly access that data; it can only pass a message to the object requesting it to execute one of its methods. This method in turn will access the data in the recommended manner. The methods represent the object's public interface; all the world knows of an object is the names of its methods. This provides the abstraction—all the module's clients need to know about it is the information provided in the external interface.

---

[*] This view of an object (see Taylor, 1990) is clearly illustrated in the type of diagram shown in Fig. 7.10. However, it is more usual to represent objects and classes as rectangles (see Fig. 7.12).

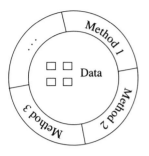

Figure 7.10 Data inside an object is surrounded by a protective ring of methods

The internal representation of the module's data and methods is irrelevant to the client.

Information hiding Encapsulation ensures that the internal representation of the data and of the methods is hidden. The external interface of an object does not tell the world details of how data is stored or how a method calculates a result. For example, suppose we want to define a counter to keep track of the score in a game. Let us suppose that we want to define it, in accordance with the rules of the game, so that the score can be incremented by one when a goal is scored and decremented by one when a foul is made. To implement this counter in a programming language that does not support encapsulation, we might declare a variable 'Score' to be an integer and write procedures to increment and decrement it as desired. However, the variable 'Score' will be visible to other parts of the program and as it is implemented as an integer there is nothing to stop other parts of the program using normal integer arithmetic to inadvertently add 5 to it, or subtract 10 from it, or even multiply it by 100. The data is not protected. However, if Counter is implemented as an object, its representation is hidden—the rest of the world does not know whether the variable, Score, is implemented as an integer, a cardinal or a pointer to an integer (see Fig. 7.11).

We can define two methods, increment and decrement, and implement them so that the rules of the game are adhered to. We can then rest assured that our Score variable will only be updated by invoking those methods. Information hiding is enforced.

Information hiding has another great benefit. If we want to change any of the internal representation of the object we can do so without affecting any other part of the program—any client object. We can, for example, change the algorithm we use to perform a calculation without changing the public interface of the object. If we wanted to change the way our counter is implemented so that every goal increments the score by 2 and every foul decrements the score by 2, we can implement this without any change to the

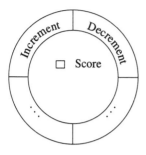

Figure 7.11 Counter implemented as an object—the representation of the variable Score is hidden

interface. A goal still increments the score and a foul decrements it, just as it always did. The two methods are still increment and decrement; they are just implemented differently. We might also decide to change the representation of the data from an integer to a pointer to an integer. This can also be done without having any effect on the external interface.

Encapsulation and information hiding, therefore, provide double protection. Data encapsulation protects the data from unintentional corruption by other parts of the program. Separation of the external interface from the internal representation means that there can be no reference to the internal representation of an object in any other part of a program. This protects the rest of the program from the 'knock-on' effects of performing upgrades. Many modern programming languages, e.g. Modula-2 and Ada, support encapsulation and information hiding—these ideas are not confined to object-oriented programming languages.

Inheritance Inheritance is a mechanism whereby classes can be defined in terms of each other; one class can be defined as a specialization of another. The specialized class automatically includes the method and variable definitions of the more general class. In object-oriented terms the sub-class *inherits* the characteristics of the super-class. The sub-class can then add features to reflect its specialization, change or delete inherited features. For example a possible Just a Line class, Customer, may be specialized into two sub-classes, LocalCustomer and RetailCustomer. These will share attributes such as name and address, but RetailCustomer may have extra attributes such as contact name and delivery address.

Polymorphism and dynamic binding The term polymorphism means the ability to define program entities (e.g. methods) that take more than one form. Polymorphism linked with an inheritance hierarchy allows a single message to be interpreted differently different objects. Dynamic binding means that it is

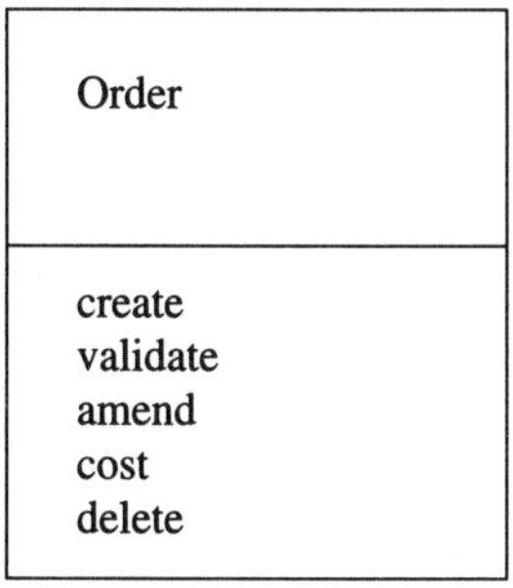

Order
create validate amend cost delete

Figure 7.12 Order class from the Just a Line system

not until run-time that it is decided which particular version of a method will be invoked by any given message. For example, if we redesigned the Just a Line case study using an object-oriented approach, we might define Order, Customer and Product as classes. Figure 7.12 shows the Order class with methods such as create, validate and amend.

In Just a Line, an order for a local customer will not be exactly the same as an order for a large retailer. The local order may have a delivery charge which is added to the total. The retailer's order will be unlikely to have a delivery charge and will probably be large enough to qualify for a wholesale discount. Figure 7.13 shows the super-class, Order, with two sub-classes: Local Order and Retail Order.

Local Order and Retail Order are specializations of the general or super-class, Order. The sub-classes inherit the variables and methods unchanged from the super-class, except for the cost method. This will be defined for Local Order, to include a possible delivery charge, and for Retail Order, to include a possible discount, making it an example of polymorphism.

Conclusion

The decomposition of an object-oriented system is based on the concept of an object. Objects in the real world become components of the software design and code. Structuring programs into objects offers conceptual simplicity, promoting ease of understanding which improves requirements capture, documentation and maintenance. Such a structure is more robust and less vulnerable to changes in requirements, because it is data, not function, based and data is less likely to change than function. Encapsulation of data and methods produces a modularity which localizes the effects of changes. Objects form cohesive reusable components. The inheritance mechanism combined with polymorphism and dynamic binding allows reused objects to be tailored to fit a new application.

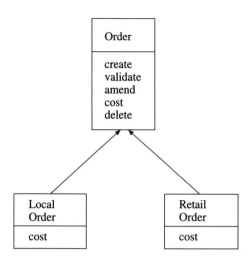

Figure 7.13 Inheritance in the Just a Line system. Local Order and Retail Order are sub-classes of the super-class Order

SUMMARY

Many software developers feel that traditional structured methods are no longer adequate to cope with the increasing variety and complexity of systems that are required today. In this chapter we have examined four different approaches which are gaining in popularity and which all have something new to offer to software system development.

Prototyping enables the construction of dynamic models of the evolving system and encourages participation of the client throughout the development process. CASE tools bring a new lease of life to the structured methods with automated drawing aids, consistency checks and links between all stages of the system development. The use of formal notations to describe a system results in a specification which is more precise, concise and less prone to ambiguity than traditional specification documents. Object orientation provides a view of software development that is based on objects and addresses many of the problems associated with the traditional, functional approach.

These new approaches and techniques should not be viewed simply as alternatives to each other, nor to traditional development methods. In Chapter 2 we mentioned the tool-box approach to system development where the developer selects the appropriate techniques and methods according to the problem in hand. These recent techniques and approaches can be seen as new additions to the tool-box which bring a greater element of choice to the system development process.

EXERCISES AND TOPICS FOR DISCUSSION

7.1   Design a prototype screen which will be used to enter details of an order for a Just a Line customer and calculate the amount owing. Using someone else in the group as the client, demonstrate and refine your customer order screen.

7.2   Design a report for Harry and Sue which will allow them to see how well various lines have sold during the past year. The report should be detailed enough to show seasonal variations in demand. Discuss and refine the report layout with another member of the group.

7.3   If you have access to a CASE tool, copy one of the diagrams from the Just a Line system in Chapter 4.

7.4   'CASE tools will never really solve the problems of the software developer, since they address the symptoms rather than the causes.' Discuss in your group what is meant by this statement and to what extent you agree with it.

7.5   'There is no point in using a formal notation since the average user could never understand it.' Discuss this statement in your group. What tools and techniques would you find helpful when communicating with clients?

7.6   'The most important thing about formal notations is the questions they make the designer ask about the system.' Discuss the above statement. What, in your opinion, are the advantages and disadvantages of using formal notations in the development of a system?

7.7   Study the Z schema in Fig. 7.5 which adds new customer details to the Just a Line customer file. How does this schema differ from the one in Fig. 7.14 on page 174 which also adds new customer details to the file? How will the schema in Fig. 7.14 react if a user tries to enter details of a customer who is already on the file?

FURTHER READING

Booch, G. (1994) *Object-Oriented Analysis and Design with Applications*, 2nd edn, Benjamin/Cummings, California.

Crinnion, J. (1991) *Evolutionary Systems Development*, Pitman, London.

Diller, A. (1994) *Z. An Introduction to Formal Methods*, 2nd edn, John Wiley and Sons, Chichester.

Edwards, P. (1993) *Systems Analysis and Design*, Chapter 6, McGraw-Hill, Watsonville, California.

Jacobson, I. (1992) *Object-Oriented Software Engineering: A Use Case Driven Approach*, Addison-Wesley, Wokingham.

Lantz, K. E. (1986) *The Prototyping Methodology*, Prentice-Hall, Englewood Cliffs, N.J.

┌─ Add Customer to File ──────────────────────

CustomerFile, CustomerFile′ : Name ↠ Details

CustomerDetails : Name ↠ Details

───

CustomerFile′ = CustomerFile ∪ CustomerDetails?

└───

Glossary:

- ↠ Partial function
- ∪ Set union
- ? Input data
- ′ Data after an operation has been performed on it

Figure 7.14 A Z schema to add non-duplicate entries to the customer file

Maude, T. and Willis, G. (1991) *Rapid Prototyping, The Management of Software Risk*, Pitman, London.

Meyer, B. (1988) *Object-Oriented Software Construction*, Prentice-Hall, Hemel Hempstead.

Potter, B., Sinclair, J. and Till, D. (1991) *An Introduction to Formal Specification and Z*, Prentice-Hall, Hemel Hempstead.

Rumbaugh, J., Blaha, M., Premerlani, W., Eddy, F., Lorensen, W. (1991) Object-Oriented Modeling and Design, Prentice-Hall, Hemel Hempstead.

Sommerville, I. (1995) *Software Engineering*, 5th edn, Addison-Wesley, Wokingham.

Taylor, D. A. (1990) *Object-Oriented Technology: A Manager's Guide*, Addison-Wesley, Wokingham.

Vonk, R. (1990) *Prototyping. The Effective Use of CASE Technology*, Prentice-Hall, London.

IMPLEMENTATION ISSUES AND NEW TECHNOLOGIES

During the software development process there are many issues that must be considered by the developer and many decisions to be taken. Some of the factors that influence these decisions are known from the start of development, others only become apparent as work on the system progresses. Every system is different, with its own individual set of circumstances. In this chapter we introduce some of the issues that a system developer would have to bear in mind while developing a system such as Just a Line.

- Compatibility with existing systems
- Selecting software
- A typical integrated package
- Implementing the Just a Line mail shot
- Multimedia
- The user interface
- Buying hardware
- Networks
- The Internet
- Security
- Time and cost

8.1 COMPATIBILITY WITH EXISTING SYSTEMS

No system exists in a vacuum. A system for running a department in a college, for example, is part of the overall system for that college and this, in turn, is part of the educational system of the country. The department system has to fit in with the larger college system and also with all the other departments that make up the college as a whole.

Within the Just a Line company the separate systems, such as marketing, taking orders, stock control and accounting, all have to work together. The

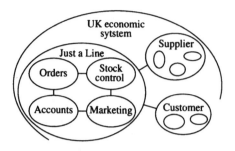

Figure 8.1 Just a Line and related systems

Just a Line system as a whole has to work with the systems of their suppliers and also the systems of their larger customers. All these systems, together with many others, form part of the economic system of the country and are affected economically by changes in this system, such as an increase in VAT, changes in interest rates and periods of recession.

Figure 8.1 shows the interrelationships between the different parts of the Just a Line company, their suppliers, their customers and the overall economic system. Because of the network of relationships surrounding Just a Line, the system developer will have to look further than the immediate area which is to be automated. It is very important that the new computerized Just a Line slots into place as neatly as the old manual system and that there is minimal disruption of the present balance between the various systems.

The situation is simplified for the Just a Line developer since Harry and Sue do not as yet have either a computer or software. This means that the system developer is free to choose the most appropriate machine and software for the Just a Line system, without being constrained by what the client has already purchased.

Two of the most important issues to consider in the development of the Just a Line system are the links with the systems of large customers, such as major retail stores, and the links with the Just a Line supplier. We already know from the initial interview with Harry and Sue that their present supplier issues a standard invoice. The supplier's invoice system is very closely related to the Just a Line system, but is not part of it. It is very unlikely that the supplier's invoicing procedures can be changed in any way by the system developer, but it is the developer's responsibility to ensure that the new automated Just a Line procedures for dealing with supplier invoices dovetail neatly with the supplier's existing system.

8.2 SELECTING SOFTWARE

In the early days of systems development the only choice of implementation was in a third-generation language such as COBOL or FORTRAN. All software had to be written from scratch, which meant that coding took up a large proportion of the overall development time. The advent of high-level fourth-generation languages (4GLs) improved the situation in several ways. There is no generally accepted definition, but a 4GL will have the following characteristics:

- 4GLs are very much more powerful than languages of previous generations. On average, one line of fourth-generation code corresponds to ten lines of code in a third-generation language.
- Third-generation languages are procedural. The programmer has to describe in detail *how* every task is to be carried out by computer. With fourth-generation languages, however, there is no need to do this; the programmer merely has to define *what* must be done. In other words, 4GLs are much more *problem oriented* than their predecessors.
- Fourth-generation languages are essential for prototyping (see Chapter 7).

In the Just a Line system the developer has a choice of four options for implementation:

1. Programming in a third-generation language (3GL).
2. Programming in a fourth-generation language.
3. Using a general-purpose integrated package. This is a set of programs which incorporates such facilities as word processing, spreadsheet, database and report generators. These are ideal for small business systems such as Just a Line.
4. Automating separate business functions, such as accounting or stock control, with specific application packages.

In making this choice the developer must consider all the relevant circumstances. Each system is individual, but it is still useful to weigh up the overall advantages and disadvantages of the different implementation methods.

Advantages of programming in a 3GL:

- The client gets a tailor-made system that will cater specifically for his or her particular needs.
- Requirements peculiar to the client organization can be built into the system.
- The software can be simpler and more compact than software developed with a package, because it is purpose built for a specific system.
- With good documentation, it should be relatively easy to make modifications to the system.

The advantages of programming in a 4GL are as for 3GLs, plus the following:

- Program development is faster, requires fewer programmers and is therefore cheaper.
- It is possible to produce prototypes using a 4GL.

Advantages of using a general-purpose package:

- Packages are relatively inexpensive method of implementation.
- Using a package saves hours of time and effort that would have to be spent on coding.
- Packages are designed to be portable. This means that it is possible for the client to purchase new hardware, yet still run the same software on it.

The advantages of using a specific application package are as above plus the following:

- Application packages have been tried and tested and can usually be guaranteed to work.
- Application packages can be installed and run with a minimum of effort.
- Time is saved on development and documentation.
- It is possible to get an unbiased opinion of the package from existing users.

Disadvantages of programming in a 3GL:

- *Effort.* If a system is to be programmed, a team of programmers will be given a specification from which they design, code and test the system. This is a very labour-intensive process compared with other methods of development.
- *Cost.* Because of the amount of work involved, a programmed system will nearly always be considerably more expensive than one implemented using a package
- *Time.* Writing programs and documentation is very time-consuming and can easily cause a development project to over-run predicted deadlines.

The disadvantages of programming in a 4GL are similar to those for a 3GL, but the time and effort required are less:

Disadvantages of using a general-purpose package:

- Although a general-purpose package, such as a spreadsheet, supports certain classes of application, some development is still required.

- General-purpose packages are limited in the type of application that they will support.

Disadvantages of using a specific application package:

- Application packages are not written for a particular client. It is therefore unlikely that any package will exactly fit a company's needs.
- It is sometimes impossible to modify a package because the suppliers do not release the source code. Where change is necessary the client may have to alter the system requirements.
- With a package, errors in the system can be difficult to trace and correct.
- The client is dependent on the supplier for general maintenance of the package.

Just a Line is a typical small business system. Harry and Sue's current office equipment probably consists of a typewriter, a filing cabinet and possibly a calculator. These could easily be replaced by a word processor, a database and a spreadsheet in an integrated package such as Microsoft Office, Symphony or Lotus 1-2-3. Obviously, the disadvantages listed above for implementing with a general-purpose package still apply, but an integrated package would fit Harry and Sue's present requirements pretty well and is certainly a cost-effective proposition.

8.3 A TYPICAL INTEGRATED PACKAGE

An integrated package which would be suitable for the Just a Line system could include the following modules:

- Word processor.
- Spreadsheet (with powerful graphics facilities).
- Database.
- Communications (to link up in a network with other machines running the package.
- Several packages also have their own programming or project processing language.

Each of the modules has all the usual facilities for the type of application, plus the ability to link up and exchange data with any of the other modules.

Harry and Sue need a system that is simple to learn and to use, yet is sufficiently powerful and flexible to be genuinely useful to them. In integrated packages, simplicity is achieved by standardization. Activities such as executing commands, accessing menus and entering data are carried out in the same way in each of the modules. This means that the package can be learnt quickly and is easy to use, even for people like Harry and Sue who are new to computers. The power of integrated packages comes from their ability to import and export data between the different modules. This allows many tasks to be performed which would otherwise prove to be cumbersome, time-consuming, expensive or simply impossible. The following are typical examples of what an integrated package can do:

- Incorporate a spreadsheet or graph into a word-processed document.
- Move data from the database into the spreadsheet so that it can be studied and analysed.
- Use the merge facility to send personalized, word-processed letters to everyone on a database file.

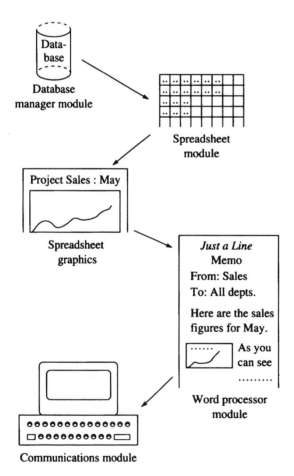

Figure 8.2 Combining modules

Figure 8.2 illustrates a series of tasks using a combination of modules. The stages are as follows:

- Transfer sales figures from the database to the spreadsheet.
- Perform calculations to compare with last year's figures and with predicted figures.
- Generate a line graph, bar chart or pie chart from the spreadsheet calculations.
- Incorporate the graph or spreadsheet into a word processor memo.
- Use the communications module to transfer the memo to other computers.
- With the package's programming language the whole operation can be performed without the user's intervention.

8.4 IMPLEMENTING THE JUST A LINE MAIL SHOT

Mail shots are an important part of Harry and Sue's new marketing strategy for Just a Line. Leaflets advertising the company's cards can be left in such places as libraries, baby clinics and church halls. The same leaflet, with a personalized order form, can be sent to regular customers of Just a Line. We will use a typical mail shot as a small example to show how part of the Just a Line system could be implemented in an integrated package.

- A file of customers is set up in the database manager module. The exact information held will depend on the developer's earlier analysis of what is needed for the system. This analysis will already be recorded in the data dictionary entry for Customer. To keep the example here as simple as possible, we will assume that the database file records each customer's details with the following fields: Customer Code, Name, Address, Town, Post Code, Phone Number, Date of Last Order.
- The mail shot is designed and set up in the word processor module. At this stage, the spaces where each customer's name and address will appear are filled with field names from the database file. These field names are enclosed in angled brackets (see Fig. 8.3).
- Harry and Sue decide that it is not worth mailing customers who have not ordered from Just a Line for more than twelve months. The query command is used with the database customer file to select only those customers who have placed an order with Just a Line within the twelve months. This is set up as a separate file of regular customers.
- The word processor file containing the mail shot can now be merged with the new database file of regular customers. Each customer's details will automatically be inserted into the relevant place on the mail shot. The result will be a printed mail shot with a personalized order form for each customer.

There's always time for –

Just a Line

Here at last is our exciting new range of cards–old prints of local scenes which will be a pleasure for you to send and for your friends to receive.

For this month only we have an extra special offer. Buy a pack of 10 cards (just £4.50) and we'll give you two more cards completely FREE!

Hurry–the offer closes at the end of the month, so fill in the form below or call in at Just a Line. We are always pleased to see you.

Best Wishes,

Harry and Sue.

Just a Line
Local Card Offer

Please send me _____packs of 10 local cards @ £4.50 each including postage and packing, PLUS 2 cards free with each pack.

I enclose cheque for _____

Name: <<Name>>_____

Address: <<Address>>_____

               <<Town>>_____

               <<Post Code>>_____

Figure 8.3 Design for the Just a Line mail shot

8.5 MULTIMEDIA

Multimedia—the combination of different forms of media in a computer-based system—has been one of the most exciting implementation developments in recent years. A multimedia system uses text, graphics, sound, photographs and video, both separately and in varying combinations, so that different kinds of information can be presented in the most appropriate ways. Multimedia systems to date are found mainly in the areas of education and training, in entertainment software, such as children's games, and in systems that provide information for the general public. A typical example of multimedia would be a system to be used in primary schools to teach children about the dangers of smoking. Such a system might use photographs to show how smoking damages the lungs, video interviews with children on why they choose not to smoke and animated cartoon characters to reinforce the message.

Although the underlying structure and functionality of multimedia systems are computer based, it does not follow that development of such systems can automatically be carried out in the same way as in a traditional software system. Some of the important differences between multimedia and traditional software systems include the following:

- Most multimedia systems are used more for information presentation than for data processing. The data in a multimedia system tends not to be in a continual state of change and the key factor is how the data is displayed to the user. This means that non-functional requirements of the system, such as ease of use and response time (see Chapter 3), must be a priority during development.
- Integration of the different media in the system is of prime importance. In this, the development of a multimedia system has more in common with the production of a film than with traditional software development.
- Developers of a multimedia system will probably come from a variety of backgrounds and possess very different kinds of expertise. A development team might include video professionals, graphical artists and sound technicians as well as computer scientists. This variety can make both communication between team members and the overall management of the system development much more complex than for a traditional software system.

Multimedia technology is changing rapidly. Although more and more systems are being produced, there are currently no established guidelines for development and it would be a mistake to think that the principles and procedures that are used in traditional systems are automatically applicable to multimedia.

8.6 THE USER INTERFACE

The user interface is the link between the human user and the computer system. It includes screens, reports, documentation and on-line help facilities— in fact any part of the system with which the user comes into contact.

There are many different types of problem that are found in the interfaces to software systems. Some of the most common are listed below:

- The displays are cluttered. This may be caused by trying to include too much information, or by inappropriate use of line, boxes and colour on the screen.
- The ways in which the user is expected to carry out various tasks may not be consistent.
- The terminology used for on-screen instructions is confusing.
- The error messages given by the system are patronizing and unhelpful.
- The manual is so convoluted that it might as well be in ancient Greek, as far as the average user is concerned.

The importance of a good user interface cannot be overemphasized. It does not matter how efficiently a system runs, how reliable it is or how easy it is to maintain—if nobody wants to use it, it is worthless. Today, almost everyone comes into contact with a computer in some way—even if it is only as the recipient of a computerized bill. The days when only trained technicians handled machines are long over, and increasing numbers of people are using computers as an essential part of their working life. Now, more than ever, it is vital that computer systems have the sort of interface that will make people keen to use them, and in order to achieve this, user interface issues must be considered at all stages of system development.

The user interface and the automation boundary

The scope of the interface for a particular software system corresponds to its automation boundary. The automation boundary encloses the area of the original (manual) system which is to be computerized. All the inputs and outputs of the new computerized system will cross the automation boundary. The automation boundary may enclose the whole of the original system, or only a part of it.

When deciding where the automation boundary lies, it is important to consider the allocation of functions between the computer and the user. For example, in the case of Just a Line, Harry and Sue decide that they wish only to computerize the customer orders and marketing sections of the business. Figure 8.4 shows the automation boundary for this reduced system.

A decision to computerize only the customer orders and marketing parts of the Just a Line system means that the task of checking whether cards ordered are in stock will have to be performed manually and that this information will have to be entered manually into the computer. The user interface of the Just a Line system will have to cater for this—perhaps with a

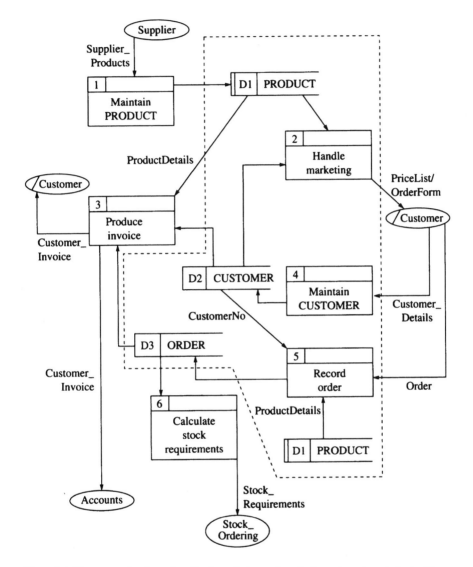

Figure 8.4 The automation boundary for the ordering and marketing sub-systems in Just a Line

screen such as the one shown in Fig. 8.5. On the other hand, Harry and Sue may decide that the best option is to computerize the whole of the original Just a Line system. In this case checking whether cards ordered are available or not will be done automatically, without involving the user. The interface will simply have to issue a warning message if any cards ordered are not in stock.

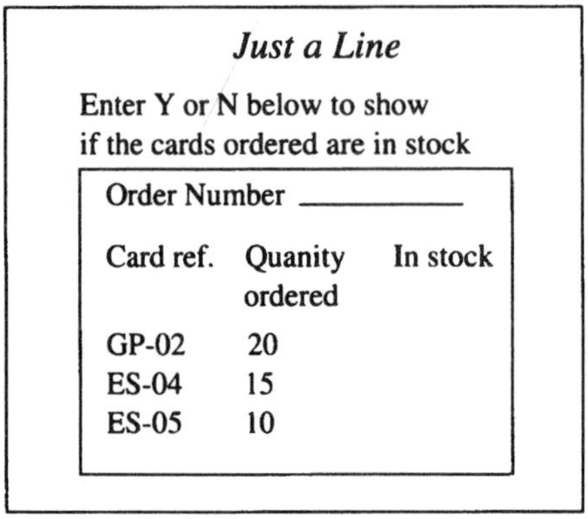

```
                    Just a Line

        Enter Y or N below to show
        if the cards ordered are in stock
        ┌─────────────────────────────────┐
        │ Order Number _____           │
        │                                 │
        │ Card ref.   Quanity    In stock │
        │             ordered             │
        │                                 │
        │ GP-02       20                  │
        │ ES-04       15                  │
        │ ES-05       10                  │
        └─────────────────────────────────┘
```

Figure 8.5 A screen to interface with the manual task of checking that cards ordered are in stock

The user of the system

As its name implies, the user interface of a system must be built to suit the user. This means that all parts of the system that are visible to the user should reflect the user's view of what is going on and how tasks are carried out. Task analysis is used to help the system developer to gain a sound understanding of the tasks currently performed by users, and then to translate these into equivalent tasks in a computerized system. In designing the user interface, the system developer must take into consideration such factors as the amount of previous experience the user has had with computer systems, the user's attitude to the new system and the amount of time he or she will make use of it.

Building the user interface is often a complicated juggling act, since there is nearly always more than one user. The client, who has commissioned the system, may have a managerial role in the organization and may therefore be an infrequent user of the new system. In some cases the developer may find that it is necessary to design a user interface that will support and encourage complete novices, while at the same time satisfying experienced computer professionals. The Just a Line system does not have this problem, since neither Harry nor Sue has had any previous computer experience. However, it would be a mistake to treat them simply as one user. First, they perform different roles in the Just a Line organization. Second, they may be completely different in their ability to learn and use the new system, and in their preferences regarding areas such as screen layout or on-line help facilities.

Whether there is one user or many, there is little doubt that the most effective way to design the user interface of a system is by prototyping. Diagrams on paper can give some idea of what individual parts of the system will look like, but they are static and so cannot give any idea of how the system will *feel* to an individual user. The technique of prototyping, which is discussed in Sec. 7.1, creates a dynamic model which allows the user to have hands-on experience of the system, before it is built.

Designing screens

One of the areas where prototyping with the user is most effective is the screen designs for the new system. The user can see exactly what the system will look like and can express preferences at a stage of development where it is still a simple matter to incorporate changes and new ideas. Working with the user, the developer can make suggestions and ensure that the final screen design not only reflects what the user wants but also that it conforms to the basic guidelines for good screen design. Some of these guidelines are listed below:

- The screen should be restful to look at, without dramatic colour combinations or a large number of flashing signals. Effects of this kind may be fun in a new system, but very soon become tiresome and distracting.
- Highlighting should only be used to pick out important information, not to add decoration to the screen.
- The screen should contain all the relevant information and no more. An overcrowded screen is tiring to look at and irritating to work with.
- The screen should be self-sufficient and self-explanatory. It should not be necessary to refer constantly to the user manual to find out what to do next or how to escape out of the screen.
- The overall design of the screens in a system should be consistent, so that, for example, error messages always appear on the screen in the same position and in the same format.
- If possible, the screen layout should reflect the layout of the associated source documents, for ease of input.
- Data on the screen should be presented in a logical sequence for the user. Related items, such as names and addresses, should be grouped together.
- It should always be obvious how to get out of trouble and how to find more help with particular tasks.

Interaction styles

The interaction style of the user interface determines the user dialogue with the system. In the early years of the systems development, all interaction between the user and the system was carried out by means of a command language. The user would have to type in commands, which were often lengthy and apparently meaningless, to tell the computer what was to be done. Since almost all computer users at that time were trained programmers, they were not troubled by having to type in commands such as 'cp Customer.mod Reg_Customer.mod' to copy a file. For a user who is fluent in the particular command language used, the facility of issuing commands to the system gives more control and freedom to the user than are found in other interaction styles.

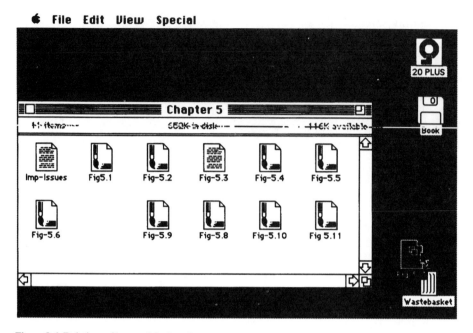

Figure 8.6 Deleting a file on a Macintosh computer

For those users who are not computer professionals, and particularly for the inexperienced user, a command language interaction style can be intimidating and off-putting. Fortunately, in tody's software systems, there are alternatives that give the novice user more support and encouragement in getting the most out of the system. One example of a user-friendly interaction style is direct manipulation, where the user actually moves objects on the screen corresponding to the tasks to be carried out. Users of Apple Macintosh computers, for example, can copy a file simply by dragging the file icon on the screen across from one disk to another and delete a file simply by dragging its icon to the on-screen wastebasket. This is shown in Fig. 8.6. The most widespread and commercially successful use of direct manipulation can be seen in the millions of computer games which are sold each year. Even children barely old enough to read can get hours of enjoyment from making the game hero jump over castle walls, slay monsters and finally find the key that will unlock the treasure chest.

For the Just a Line system a command language interaction style would not be suitable, since Harry and Sue have no experience of computer systems. They would probably have a lot of fun with a direct manipulation style, but would not be too happy about the time the development would take or would cost. We said in an earlier section that the Just a Line system is very suitable for implementation with an integrated package. Most packages dictate their own interaction style. This is one that the makers of the package have chosen as suitable for the type of system which the package will be used for. In many packages, the user's interactions with the computer are performed by means of menu selection. This means that the user is presented with a menu of possible options on the screen. When an option is chosen, a further menu of related sub-options may be displayed for the user to make another selection, or the particular task chosen may be carried out.

Menu selection offers the user a route map through the system. Figure 8.7 shows a sub-set of the menu hierarchy from the Just a Line system. At the top level, the menu options reflect the main areas of activity that were identified in the system—Maintain Customers, Handle Orders, Stock Control, Marketing. The user selects the required option by pressing the associated numbers, e.g. number 1 for the Maintain Customers option. A screen then appears showing the tasks associated with maintaining customers in the Just a Line system—the user can add a new customer to the customer file, delete a customer from the file, amend a customer's details, etc. Selection of the task to be performed is carried out in the same way as the main screen, by typing in the associated number, for example 1, to add a new customer to the file. This brings up the customer entry screen which enables the user to enter the code and details for the new customer.

Although an integrated package restricts the developer's choice in the design of the user interface for a particular system, there are still many issues to be determined and many decisions to be taken. Some of the factors to be considered in a menu-driven interface are listed below:

- How many items should appear on a menu?
- In what order should the options be listed?
- How should the options be named or described?
- What sort of prompt should be given to the user?
- How should the user respond—by typing in a number or by highlighting the required option?
- How should the system react if the user does not select a valid option? What sort of error handling is appropriate?
- Does the use of graphics and colour enhance the menu screen or act as a distraction?
- Should a quick route through the menus of the system be provided for experienced users?
- How should help be provided?

In a system such as Just a Line, many of these questions can be resolved by consulting Harry and Sue about their preferences. This helps to ensure that the system looks as they want it to and also gives them the feeling of being part of the system development process. User involvement is beneficial in all areas

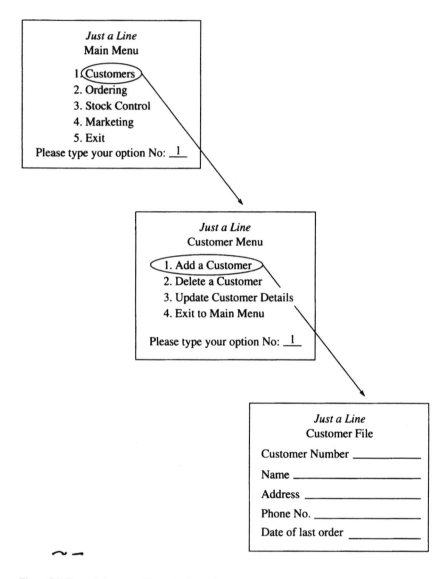

Figure 8.7 Part of the menu hierarchy from the Just a Line system

of the development, and in designing the user interface it is essential. An interface that is quick to learn, easy to use and matches the user's view of the tasks in hand means not only a happier user but also fewer errors and a more efficient and effective user performance.

8.7 BUYING HARDWARE

Computers come in all shapes and sizes and computer salesmen are adept at persuading customers that their particular machine is the best possible buy. It is often very difficult for buyers to obtain impartial advice on the relative merits of different computers. In the case of a company such as Just a Line, where the clients do not already have a computer, it is part of the developer's role to advise on the best machine for the system. The system developer will have to sit down with Sue and Harry and work out exactly what their requirements are. It should then be possible to identify the machine that best satisfies these requirements. The developer must not let the clients be bamboozled by sales talk into purchasing extra pieces of equipment that are not really needed. When deciding which computer would best suit a particular system there are many factors to consider:

- What amount of processing power is needed?
- What is the volume of data to be handled?
- Are response times critical? (How quickly does the user need to have results?)
- Does the machine have a 'friendly' operating system?
- Do the clients have any previous experience with computers?
- What software is available?
- What peripherals, such as printers, will be needed and what quality is required?
- How well will the machine fit into the target environment?
- How much support in terms of training and maintenance is provided?
- Is the machine capable of supporting future expansion and modifications to the system?
- How much does it cost?

In the case of Just a Line it seems likely that they would start small with probably a single personal computer (PC). The problems of the volume of data and the system response times are not relevant at present, but, since Harry and Sue are both new to computers, it is important that they will find learning to use the machine an easy and enjoyable task. The Apple Macintosh is widely considered to be one of the easiest computers for beginners, so it would certainly be worth their while having a look at that.

Although the Just a Line software needs are fairly standard at the moment (mainly database and word-processing facilities) future expansion may bring a need for more specialized software, so it is important to know which programs are available for particular machines. At present, IBM PCs have the widest range of software, and many other personal computers on the market are PC compatible, which means that they can run programs developed for the IBM PC. This is an example of a situation where the system developer and the clients would have to decide which factor has priority—ease of use (the Macintosh) or range of available software (a PC compatible machine). To complicate the issue further, the Windows 95 software, produced by Microsoft for the PC, claims to be the market leader in both functionality and ease of use. However, with so much available and so many factors to consider, there is no clear choice at present. When choosing computer equipment it is also worth finding out which computers are used by companies that the client does business with. In the case of Just a Line this would be their supplier and large customers such as John Lewis.

Finally, since Just a Line's business is in printed cards, it is essential that their own stationery is of a high quality. This means that, when choosing the hardware for the system, they must give special consideration to printers.

For a company in the position of Just a Line one of the most difficult issues to decide on is that of future expansion. If their new professional approach attracts larger customers, who will buy in bulk, the whole character of the business could change. On the other hand, Harry and Sue may decide that they are happier remaining a small local firm, selling direct to personal customers. In terms of their investment in computer hardware, the best that can be done is to keep as many options open as possible. The most suitable purchase at this stage is probably a stand-alone personal computer which could later be linked up with others in a network.

8.8   NETWORKS

If Just a Line's business takes off as Harry and Sue hope, a single personal computer will soon be inadequate and they will need to expand their hardware by means of a local area network (LAN). This will allow users to access the same data, use the same programs, send messages from one machine to another and to share expensive peripherals such as a laser printer. The topology (or layout) of the network will depend largely on the physical layout of the Just a Line premises. Figure 8.8 shows examples of three different types of topology.

(a) Star topology, based on a central computer
(b) Fully connected point-to-point topology, where each machine is connected to all the others in the network
(c) Multipoint ring, where the machines are linked by means of a shared bus

When evaluating different topologies and deciding which is the most suitable, there are certain questions that the system developer should bear in mind:

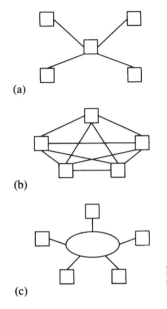

(a)

(b)

(c)

Figure 8.8 (a) Star topology; (b) fully connected point-to-point topology; (c) multipoint topology ring

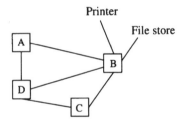

Figure 8.9 File and print server network

- Does the particular topology need a lot of cabling, thus putting up the cost of the network?
- If one machine breaks down, what will be the effect on the network as a whole?
- Are there any possible bottle-necks in the network?
- Will it need a complicated control system?
- How simple will it be to add more computers to the network?
- If a cheap network is chosen initially, is it compatible with more sophisticated models?
- Do the clients have any preferences?

As well as these questions, the developer should consider whether the network should include a file and print server. This is illustrated in Fig. 8.9. In this network machine B is dedicated to managing tasks such as scheduling file access and queueing print jobs. This is the most efficient way of managing these tasks, but it means that machine B cannot always be used for specific applications.

The alternative to including a file server is a peer-to-peer network where all the machines are stand-alone personal computers. This is less efficient overall than a file server network, but it is cheaper and can be upgraded to include a file server if necessary. In most cases there will not be an obvious solution to the problem of networking. The most efficient topology may involve so much cabling that it is prohibitively expensive. The network most suitable for future expansion may have a very complicated control system. It is up to the developer to consider all the relevant factors and to select the most appropriate network for each individual system.

8.9 THE INTERNET

At the other end of the scale from small, local area networks is the largest computer network in the world: the Internet. This is in fact a web of networks which connects millions of computers world-wide. The net is growing and changing so rapidly that it is impossible to give an accurate estimate of its size.

One of the main benefits for users of the Internet is the World Wide Web, which allows access to information on every conceivable topic, held on computers all over the world. Using client-server technology and graphical browser software, such as Netscape, the user can visit any number of different computer sites to view texts, photographs, graphics and videos. Other advantages for net users include the ability to communicate with other users via E-mail (electronic mail) and the opportunity of joining any number of specialized mailing lists.

The Internet has no central management and no overall owner, though individual networks are owned by government, business or other organizations. The lack of overall organization of the net has generated a lot of controversy in areas such as security, possible censorship of material and net 'traffic jams'.

If these problems can be resolved successfully, the Internet will have even more far-reaching consequences and will attract an even larger number of users. In future years Harry and Sue of Just a Line may well find that the most effective way of marketing and selling their cards is via on-line shopping over the net.

8.10 SECURITY

In almost every area today, computers play a crucial role in the management of information. This brings considerable benefits in that:

- Information can be retrieved faster.
- Inaccurate data can be speedily corrected.
- Information can be distributed easily and quickly to those who need it, even if they are remote from the information source.

There are, however, some areas where the information stored in a computer is of such a sensitive nature that any damage to it, or any access to it by unauthorized personnel, would be at best a nuisance and at worst a disaster. Such areas include defence, medicine, the nuclear industry, the stock exchange and many others.

To a certain extent, this problem has always been with us. Many manual systems in the past have been notoriously insecure; we only have to think of the communist spy ring of Burgess, McLean, Philby and Blunt to see that even top national security systems were not immune to leaks. However, the speed at which computers operate and their power to transmit information instantaneously over vast distances have both highlighted the problem and made it more acute. Legislation such as the Data Protection Act has made the general public aware of the importance of information and the power it gives to those who possess it, while advanced communications technology, such as the Internet, has opened up whole new issues such as ownership of data, rights of access and censorship.

The topic of computer security can be divided into two areas: damage to data and unauthorized access to data. Each of these can occur either accidentally or with intent. A breach of security in a system can take many forms, including the following:

- Data may be lost accidentally and no back-up copy has been made.
- Programs and data can be corrupted by viruses—deliberate errors that have been put into a system by someone wishing to destroy it.
- A junior employee may inadvertently enter part of the system to which access is forbidden.
- A dedicated hacker can penetrate most systems without too much trouble.
- A security breach which occurs initially by accident, such as an extra '0' added in error to a salary slip, may be knowingly repeated on other occasions.

Just as there are many types of security breach in computer systems, so there are many ways, both simple and complex, in which these systems can be made less vulnerable. In each individual system it is part of the system developer's job to decide the extent of security measures that are needed. Security procedures increase the complexity of a system. This increased complexity leads in turn to higher costs and a longer development timescale. Security procedures can also have an adverse effect on the user-friendliness of a system since, by definition, such procedures make access to the system less straight-forward.

In the case of Just a Line, the data that is to be stored is not of a confidential nature, so it will not be necessary to set up elaborate procedures to prevent an outsider reading the data. It could, however, be disastrous for Harry and Sue if someone were to gain access to the system and modify, or corrupt, the data in it. It would be equally serious for the company if data was lost and no back-ups had been made. Security considerations for Just a Line should concentrate on thorough, daily back-ups of all major files, and probably passwords to gain access to the system. On the other hand, a larger system, dealing with sensitive data, would require far more elaborate proce-dures. Some of these are listed below:

- The risk of unauthorized access can be reduced by a system of codes and passwords which may prohibit access to the whole system, or to certain parts of it.
- Important files can be protected as *read only*. Only certain users will have the means to remove the protection and write to the file.
- Users can be prevented from inputting invalid data by a series of validation checks during data entry. Data that is highly sensitive can be encrypted before being entered.
- Disinfectant programs are now available that combat many of the more common computer viruses.
- Better user training means less accidental damage.
- Terminals can be locked physically with a key.
- Rigorous housekeeping routines can be established to ensure regular back-up of files. Ideally, separate copies should be kept off-site, in case of fire or other physical damage.
- Data is a valuable resource. The system and its data should be fully insured.

8.11 TIME AND COST

There are two issues that inevitably dominate every system development project and two questions that the client asks more frequently than any other: 'How long will it take?' and 'How much will it cost?'. When proposing alternative ways of implementing a system, the developer will probably suggest a variety of solutions, reflecting the concerns of time and money. In the Just a Line system possible implementations could include the following:

- A minimal system, implementing only the ordering and marketing functions of the organization. This would run on a single, stand-alone personal computer and use an integrated package. The system would be relatively cheap and could probably be ready in a few months.

- A slightly more sophisticated system which includes the stock control part of Just a Line. This could also be implemented using a package, but could involve a small network of computers linking Harry and Sue's office to the shop/warehouse. This system would take longer to develop than the first option and would cost quite a lot more, since a number of computers are needed.

- A full implementation of all Just a Line's present functions (ordering, stock control, marketing and accounting) with potential to fulfil more sophisticated future requirements, such as a credit scheme for regular customers. This system could also use a package, but would probably be implemented with a fourth-generation programming language, to cater more precisely for the company's needs. A number of networked PCs would again be used in this system. This option would take much longer to develop and would cost considerably more than the first two systems, but might well prove more cost effective in the long run if Just a Line's business really takes off.

It is very tempting for clients, especially if they are first-time buyers, to opt for the cheapest, quickest system as being the least risk. Unfortunately, this often proves to be a very short-sighted choice. Computer systems play such an important part in business today that it can be dangerous not to computerize, or to automate only a small section of the organization, when business rivals have extensive, elaborate computer systems. It is part of the developer's job to analyse the situation of the client company and the role the new system will play in it, so that the client is led to make the most productive long-term choice of system. This may mean spending more money and waiting longer for the completed system. If financial considerations prevent initial implementation of the total system, a phased approach can be adopted: the system can be developed and delivered in separate modules over a period of time.

Once the decision on implementation has been made and the delivery date and cost agreed, it is important that these should be adhered to as closely as possible. Keeping a project within its timescale and budget is part of the job of the project manager. This is discussed further in Chapter 10.

SUMMARY

In this chapter we have examined many of the issues that a developer must bear in mind when deciding how a system is to be implemented. We have discussed topics as diverse as the user interface, integrated packages and system security. What is common to all these areas, however, is the difficulty of making general statements that would apply to all systems. Software is not like mass-produced products, such as cars or washing machines. Every software system is a one-off. The issues we have discussed in this chapter must be examined anew for each system and it is likely that the decisions taken will be different for each one. What is important is that the developer is aware of all the relevant issues and that informed decisions about the system are made both by the developer and the client.

EXERCISES AND TOPICS FOR DISCUSSION

8.1 At the beginning of this chapter we said that no system exists in a vacuum. Try to think of a system (not necessarily a computer system) that is completely independent.

8.2 Investigate two or three different makes of personal computer from the point of view of cost, ease of use and availability of software. Decide which you would recommend to Harry and Sue if you were developing the Just a Line system.

8.3 Examine the three different network topology diagrams in Fig. 8.8. Try to evaluate each one in terms of the criteria listed in this chapter.

8.4 Think about the interfaces of systems with which you are familiar in everyday life—the telephone system is one example. In a group, discuss whether the interfaces to these systems are satisfactory and how they might be improved.

8.5 Look at the screen that you designed in Exercise 7.1 and evaluate it in terms of the guidelines for good screen design listed in this chapter.

8.6 Discuss the relative security measures needed by the following systems:

- A system that runs a school library
- A system for a group of GPs
- A system for a vet
- A system that deals with bank accounts
- A system that guides a manned space probe

FURTHER READING

Crinnion, J. (1991) *Evolutionary Systems Development*, Pitman, London.

Shneiderman, B. (1992) *Designing the User Interface: Strategies for Effective Human–Computer Interaction*, 2nd edn, Addison-Wesley, Reading, Mass.

Sommerville, I. (1995) *Software Engineering*, 5th edn, Addison-Wesley, Wokingham.

TESTING AND HANDING OVER

We saw in Chapter 7 how, if prototyping is used as the method of developing a software system, the client takes an active part in each stage of development. With a more traditional development approach, however, the client's involvement is generally limited to the beginning and end of the development project. In the early stages of work on a system, client participation is essential to enable the developer to capture as exactly as possible the requirements for the system (see Chapter 3). Once the software product has been built, it is again the client who must make the final evaluation as to whether the finished system is actually what is wanted.

In this chapter we discuss the final stages of the software system development process—testing, user trialling and installation. We also look at the topics of system documentation and what happens to a system after it has been handed over to the client.

9.1 TESTING

Testing is often seen as a means of establishing that a program is error-free and that it does what is required. This is a very dangerous.point of view. It is virtually impossible to test a program so thoroughly that it can be claimed to be free of errors. In most cases, fixing one error gives rise to a host of others, which in turn have to be corrected and exhaustively tested. It is much more realistic to think of testing as a *process of finding errors*. When a stage is reached when the program appears to run perfectly, this does not mean that there are no more errors in the program, it simply means that those errors have not been discovered.

In Chapter 7 we discussed the topic of formal notations (specification languages which are based on mathematics and logic). In Section 7.3 we explained how the formal basis of specifications written in these language allows much more accurate testing of whether a program actually meets its specification. It is very much harder to test a program against a specification written using informal, structured techniques, such as data flow and entity–relationship diagrams. There is no way of proving conclusively that the program matches the specification, let alone that the specification reflects what the client originally wanted! Inadequate though it is, the testing process is still the principal tool available to developers to help them establish whether or not the system that has been built is what was required.

The testing process

Most software developers perform testing of a system from the bottom up. First, small program units are tested individually, to check that they have been coded correctly. This is usually carried out by the programmer who coded the program. These units are then combined into program modules which deal with specific parts of the system (examples from Just a Line are stock control, ordering and marketing). The modules are tested in the same way as the small program units, again usually by the programmer. When all known bugs have been eradicated, the system as a whole is thoroughly tested by the developer or team of developers.

In each of the above groups of tests a program or suite of programs is executed with predefined sets of data to see if the program behaves as expected and produces the desired results. The types of tests usually carried out fall into the following categories:

- Valid data which would be normal for the system. In the Just a Line system this would include entering details for a typical customer and an average customer order for some cards. Tests in this category also include boundary conditions, i.e. data which is not typical, but which is still within the correct range for the system. Examples of boundary conditions include the following:
  - A delivery charge of 0.00
  - An order for a very large number of cards
  - Items of data which completely fill the defined fields, such as an extremely long customer name or address
- Data which is invalid and should not be entered into the system. In Just a Line this could include:
  - A delivery date for 3/6/1892
  - An order for a card design that does not exist
- Data which is itself valid, but which is not acceptable to the system in its current state. Examples from Just a Line include:
  - Trying to enter details for a customer who is already on the customer file
  - Trying to amend an order which has already been supplied

Problems and Requirements List
for Just a Line

Problem or requirement	Source	Solution
1. No way of knowing who the regular customers are	Sue	Set up a file of all customers who place at least one order each year
2. Telephone orders are very time-consuming to deal with	Harry and Sue	Provide written order forms which can be sent out with mail shots
3. What is done with past orders?	Analysis—entity life history of Order	Create a separate file for past orders and delete any orders more than 1 year old
4. It would be nice to be able to see at a glance how various cards are selling	Sue	Set up a spreadsheet recording sales for all cards and produce a bar chart that shows comparative popularity of the different cards

Figure 9.1 Extract from the problems and requirements list for Just a Line

- Data which tests the performance of the system, such as the speed of response times and the handling of large volumes of data.

In a traditional system development project, the above tests are generally carried out by the development team without the participation of the client. Once the developer is reasonably confident that the system performs as required, the client is brought in and acceptance testing takes place. A useful basis for acceptance testing is the problems and requirements list, which was compiled during the system development. This is a record of all problems and requirements which are mentioned by clients in interviews or which are subsequently discovered during analysis of the system. The list initially records each problem or requirement together with its source. During the development of the system, as each problem is dealt with, this is also recorded on the problems and requirements list.

An extract from the problems and requirements list for the Just a Line system is shown in Fig. 9.1. For each problem or requirement that has been identified, the developer should create a test which will examine whether or not the system solves the problem or fulfils the requirement.

In acceptance testing, the system as a whole is under investigation in order that the client can assess whether it meets his or her requirements:

- Do the system functions cover all the tasks that fall within the automation boundary?
- How does the system cope with the problems and requirements that have been identified?
- How fast is the processing? Are results of queries and reports produced in a reasonably short time?
- Will the new system fit in well with what remains of the original manual system?
- Is the system easy to learn and simple to use?
- What is the quality of the supporting documentation?

All these and many other questions will be raised during the acceptance testing process. This is the point at which the client is agreeing to take delivery of the system and it is essential that what is handed over is fully satisfactory.

User trialling

In most development projects the system is handed over once the client is satisfied with the results of the acceptance tests, but sometimes a further period of more extensive testing may take place which is run entirely by the client. This is known as user trialling and differs from acceptance testing in the following ways:

- Trialling does not use tests that have been devised by the development team. The whole process is run by the client and the other users of the system.
- Test data is supplied by the client and should be *real* data wherever possible.
- Large volumes of data are needed to create a realistic situation.
- Users of the system must have some training before trialling can be carried out.
- Trialling involves a lot of planning, both for the developer and for the client organization.
- Trialling involves a lot of time and effort on the part of the client and users of the system.

In spite of the extra effort involved, particularly for the client organization, trialling repeatedly proves to be well worth this trouble in that it frequently uncovers fundamental errors in the system that have somehow slipped through previous testing procedures.

9.2   CHANGEOVER TO THE NEW SYSTEM

Once all the planned testing procedures have been completed satisfactorily, the system can be handed over to the client and the changeover from the old to the new system put into effect. There are several ways of carrying out the changeover; the method chosen will depend on such factors as the type of system that is being installed and the preferences of the client organization. The changeover will require careful planning on the part of both the developer and the client to ensure maximum efficiency and minimum disruption to the normal working of the client company. All changeovers involve extra work at night or at the weekend, both for the developer and for those members of the client organization who are most involved in the new system.

Methods of changeover

Four common methods of changeover to a new system are listed below, together with an indication of the advantages and disadvantages of each.

1. Direct changeover (also known as cutover)

   - The old system ceases to function and is completely replaced by the new system.
   - This type of changeover must be carried out at the weekend or during a holiday period.
   - Direct changeover is often used in on-line and real-time systems, where it is not feasible to run the old and the new systems in parallel.
   - Duplication of work for the client organization is minimized, since only one system is running at any time.
   - The changeover must be very thoroughly planned, so that the new system can take over with a minimum of trouble and run smoothly from the start. This is very important, since there is no old system to fall back on if things go wrong. If the new system had teething troubles, this can prove to be a disaster for the client company.
   - Once changeover has been completed, there are no results from the old system that can be compared to see how well the new system is operating.

2. Parallel running

   - In parallel running, the new system is installed alongside the old and the two are operated together until complete confidence in the new system has been established.
   - Parallel running is much less risky for the client than direct changeover, since the old system can simply continue running if problems arise.
   - Some of the results from the old system can be compared with those

from the new, so that the client can get an idea of how efficiently the new system is operating.
- Running two systems side by side creates a huge work load for the client organization. This means that in many companies parallel running would not be a practical method of changeover.

3. Pilot running

- In pilot running the system is run for a time in one area only. In Just a Line, for example, orders from customers who live in the immediate locality might be run on the new, automated system, while all other customers' orders would be handled manually as before. As Sue and Harry gain confidence with the new system, more and more customer orders will be handled by the computer.
- The advantages and disadvantages of pilot running are a combination of those for direct changeover and parallel running.

4. Phased implementation

- In phased implementation the system is installed gradually, so that the client and other users can become accustomed to one area of business at a time. In Just a Line the mail shot program should be installed at first, followed by the programs dealing with customer orders, stock control, supplier orders and finally the accounting procedures.
- In phased implementation part of the system can be (and often is) installed before the rest of the system has been completed. This gives the opportunity of valuable feedback from the client while the system is being developed. It also takes some of the pressure off the developer, since small parts of the system can be delivered when they are ready without waiting for completion of the whole system.
- Phased implementation would probably be the most appropriate method of changeover for the Just a Line system, since it allows Sue and Harry to concentrate on part of the new system and to become competent in using the system in stages. As their confidence increases, the new, automated system will gradually take over in all areas of their business.

9.3 STAFF REACTIONS TO THE NEW SYSTEM

When choosing a method of changeover, one of the most important factors for the system developer and the client to consider is that of staff reactions to the new system. All members of the client organization will be affected by the system to some degree, and will in turn be able to influence the system's success or failure.

On the positive side, many staff will welcome modernization of the organization. They will enjoy learning new skills and be keen to try out the new system. These members of staff may already have some knowledge of what a computer can do for them. They will be keen to use it to carry out repetitive and tedious tasks and appreciate its ability to work rapidly and accurately—without needing a coffee break!

On the other hand, many staff in the organization may feel hostile towards the new system. They may be reluctant to accept change in their patterns of work and be opposed to the idea of retraining. In some cases staff may see the new system as a threat to their jobs; they feel vulnerable to redundancy, enforced early retirement or transfer. Even if their job descriptions and salaries remain the same, these staff members are afraid that the most interesting parts of their work will be taken over by the new system, so that what they will actually be doing is much less skilled than before.

Since Harry and Sue are at present the only employees in the Just a Line company, these are not problems that they have to deal with. In all but the smallest organizations, however, the system developer is likely to find a variety of staff reactions to the new system. It is important that time and thought should be given to how these different reactions are to be handled. No matter how well designed and efficient the new system may be, if the staff will not work with it, it will be a failure.

9.4 DOCUMENTATION

One of the most important parts of the software system handed over to the client is the written documentation that accompanies the programs. This documentation serves several purposes:

- It enables developers to understand how the system has been built, so that it can be maintained and modified as necessary.
- It gives instructions for the day-to-day operation of the system and peripherals such as printers.
- It introduces new users to the system and allows them to find their way around it.
- It provides information that enables experienced users to exploit the system to its full potential.

Documentation of the development of the system

The documentation for developers, who will maintain and modify the system, should provide a complete record of the system development process from the initial client request to the final implementation and testing. Many of the documents that should be incorporated will already have been produced as deliverables during the development of the system:

- The original problem definition.
- Models of the current and required systems which were created during analysis such as the data dictionary, data flow and entity–relationship diagrams
- Descriptions of the system design, including module charts and pseudocode
- Details of hardware and software used
- Fully commented code for all programs that form part of the system
- The complete set of test plans, test data and results for the system

All these documents should contain extensive commentary which explains the reasoning behind the decisions taken during the system development. The documentation as a whole should show clearly not only *what* was done but *how* it was done and *why* it was done in that way.

Most of the documentation described here will be produced in parallel with the development of the system, but it is important that it is not forgotten once the system has been handed over to the client. Any changes made to the system during its lifetime must be recorded so that an accurate picture is maintained of the current state of the system.

Documentation for the operation of the system

The style and content of the documentation which covers the day-to-day running of the system will vary according to the size of the system, its complexity and the expertise of those people who are to perform the operating tasks. In a large organization, where the system may involve many different terminals and other pieces of hardware, operating duties will probably be carried out by trained technicians. Their responsibilities may include routine maintenance of equipment as well as the daily tasks which ensure the smooth running of the system. The documentation in this case can assume a certain amount of technical knowledge.

With a small organization, such as Just a Line, it is the clients who are in charge of the day-to-day running of the system. They will need instructions for relatively simple tasks, such as putting more paper in the printer and making regular back-up of files. Documentation in this case must be simple and clear; no technical knowledge can be assumed. Jobs that require specialist knowledge, such as fixing machines, should be covered by a maintenance agreement between the clients and the hardware suppliers. There should also be continuing contact with the developer of the system who can advise on problems concerning operation of the system software.

Documentation for novice users

It is very important that clients and users who are not familiar with computers receive full training in the use of the new system before they have to operate it on their own. Once the system has been delivered and the client is left in charge, it is the documentation, along with the on-line help facilities, that provide the main support for users. Although the system developer will maintain regular contact with the client organization for some time after delivery, it is simply not practical for users to consult the developer about every little query. For immediate solutions to the problems that arise, clients must be able to turn to the user documentation.

User documentation for any system must, above all, be easy to follow. The user manual is a reference document, not a novel which will be read through from beginning to end. Information that the user needs must be simple to find. This means that the manual must have a clear structure and a comprehensive index. For novice users the style of the manual is also important. Any technical terms used must be defined in layman's language and even very simple operations should be explained in full, preferably using diagrams. There should also be instructions on how to get out of trouble at all stages. Figure 9.2 shows an extract from a user manual which teaches inexperienced users how to create a spreadsheet.

Novice users are not interested in the advanced features of the system. Their priority is to perform basic tasks, such as entering data and producing reports. The section of the user manual that is aimed at new users must concentrate on enabling them to get started, to gain confidence with simple operations and to get out of trouble quickly and easily.

Documentation for experienced users

Experienced users of the system will not need to refer often to the user manual, and even then probably only to discover possible short cuts for frequently used operations or to read about the more complex features of the system. The documentation at this level can assume that the user understands technical terms and is already familiar with the basic workings of the system. Experienced users will not want them to get the most out of the system and to exploit its potential to the full.

9.5   THE POST-IMPLEMENTATION REVIEW

If all goes well, the first formal meeting of the client organization and the whole development team after delivery of the system is the post-implementation review. This typically takes place about three months after installation, by

6. Creating a spreadsheet.

1	2	3	4	5
1	TRICKY DICKY'S CARS OF CHARACTER			
2	FINANCIAL SUMMARY: JANUARY 1996			
3				
4	VEHICLE DESCRIPTION	COST	SOLD	PROFIT	%PROFIT
5	1962 Cortina	£15.00	£100.00	£85.00	567
6	1972 Volvo	£50.00	£110.00	£60.00	120
7	1956 Ford Popular	£10.00	£30.00	£20.00	200
8	1952 Rolls Royce	£500.00	£450.00	(£50.00)	−10
9				
10	TOTALS	TOTAL	TOTAL	TOTAL	OVERALL
11		OUTLAY	SALES	PROFIT	%PROFIT
12		£575.00	£690.00	£115.00	20
13				

6.1 Here is an example of a typical spreadsheet which you can create using the instructions in this section. While you are entering data don't worry about the look of the spreadsheet (justification of data entries, decimal precision, etc.). The spreadsheet will be tidied up after all the data has been entered. If you make a mistake while entering data into a cell, use the backspace key to correct it. If you want to change the contents of a cell after you have finished entering the data into it, you can simply overwrite with the new data.

6.2 Position the cursor on row 1 column 1. The spreadsheet refers to this as r1c1 and we will use that notation from now on. Make sure that you are in data entry mode (use the ESC key). Type the spreadsheet heading. Move the cursor to r2c1 and type the sub-heading.

6.3 You may find that a column isn't wide enough.
To fix this:
 − place the cursor on the column which you want to make wider;
 − enter menu mode (use ESC);
 − select the following commands to change the column to 20 characters wide from the default 10 characters:
LAYOUT .. CELL SIZE .. WIDTH .. 20 ..COLUMNS .. 1
return to data entry mode.

N.B. Remember that you can always use the ESC key to move back a level if you make a mistake while executing menu commands.

Figure 9.2 Extract from a user manual which teaches novice users how to create a spreadsheet

which time the clients will have got to know the system and can report on how it is functioning. The post-implementation review is a useful occasion for the developer to discover what lessons can be learnt from this particular system project. During discussion with the clients the following questions will probably be raised:

- How satisfied are the clients with the hardware and software supplied?
- Were the clients happy with their degree of involvement in the development of the system?
- How are staff of the client organization reacting to the system?
- To what extent does the system fulfil the original client requirements?
- How is the system performing in a live situation? Are response times fast enough and does the system cope efficiently with large volumes of data?
- How has the system affected the client organization in terms of turnover and future staffing levels?
- Does the client have any ideas for future enhancements to the system?

9.6 MAINTENANCE

It is tempting to view delivery of the completed system to the client as the end of the development process. The money is handed over, the client takes charge of the system and the developer moves on to new projects. However, this is very far from being the end of the story. In fact, the stage euphemistically known as *maintenance* frequently swallows up more time and money than all the other stages of the development process.

The blanket term maintenance can cover everything from fixing minor mistakes in coding to unravelling major misunderstandings about what the client wanted from the system. On top of this, maintenance is often used to describe modifications and extensions, which may only be requested after the client has been using the system for some time.

There are any number of reasons for a developer being called back by the client to change some part of the system. Some of these are listed below:

- The computer suppliers may have brought out a new version of their hardware and are gradually decreasing their support for older models.
- There may be new versions of the software that was used to build the system and support for previous versions is no longer available. Systems built using packages may be particularly vulnerable to this problem.
- Changes may occur which are external to the system and over which the client and developer have no control, yet which necessitate a change in the way the system operates. For example, a change in the ordering procedures of the Just a Line supplier may necessitate changes in the Just a Line system.

- There may be errors that have only become apparent after the system has been in continuous use for some time.
- The interface of the system may not be acceptable to those people using it. The staff of the client organization may not feel happy with the new system and may be reluctant to give up their former methods of work for it.
- In getting to know the system the clients may have identified extra features that would be useful to the organization and that they would now like the developer to provide.

Whether it is a matter of maintenance of modification and whether it is a major or minor change that is required, any work on the system after it has gone live is a complicated process. It is unlikely that the developers who worked on the original system are still available, since they will all have moved on to new development projects. This means that the people fixing the system will have to spend some time getting to know how it operates and how it was built. The quality of the system documentation (see Sec. 9.4) is of vital importance here.

If major changes to the system are needed, the whole development process may have to be repeated, but now the working system has to be preserved at the same time. It is not acceptable for an organization, which has become dependent on a computer system, to chose down while alterations to the system are carried out, so the developers have to work round the operational system, causing as little disruption to it as possible. Changes should be implemented by means of a fully documented change control procedure. This consists of forms detailing the required change (completed by the user) and the developer's estimate of the implications in cost and time.

All changes to the system, however small, have to be fully tested, installed and documented. Thus, even small changes involve a lot of work for the system developer. Moreover, it is often very difficult to predict accurately how much time, effort and money a particular change will entail, since an apparently minor change can cause a ripple effect in the system. Given all these problems, it is hardly surprising that the maintenance stage is the one that is least popular with system developers.

SUMMARY

Although it is at the coding stage that a computer system seems to come to life, there is still much work to be done before the development process is completed. This chapter describes briefly the final stages of a system development project, from testing through to installation of the system in the client organization. There are several different ways in which the changeover to a new software system can be achieved and it is important that the most suitable method is chosen in each case. Others factors, which influence how the system will be received by its users, should also be carefully considered. These include staff reactions to the new system and the quality of the supporting documentation. Finally, the chapter looks at what happens to a system after delivery, the purpose of the post-implementation review and the particular problems of maintenance and modification.

EXERCISES AND TOPICS FOR DISCUSSION

9.1 Write a set of simple user instructions for a program written in a computer language with which you are familiar. The program is to receive as input a series of whole numbers, terminated by a full-stop and output the largest number in the series.

9.2 Write a test plan for the above program.

9.3 Discuss which method of changeover would be suitable for the following systems:

- A system that runs a school library
- A system for a group of GPs
- A system for the delivery operations of a small dairy

FURTHER READING

Pressman, R. S. (1992) *Software Engineering: A Practitioner's Approach*, 3rd edn, adapted by Darrel Ince, European adaptation, McGraw-Hill, London.

Sommerville, I. (1995) *Software Engineering*, 5th edn, Chapters 22–24, Addison-Wesley, Wokingham.

Yourdon, E. (1989) *Modern Structured Analysis*, Chapters 23 and 24, Prentice-Hall, Englewood Cliffs, N.J.

10

MANAGING THE PROJECT

Up to this point we have been considered various activities which are part of the system development process. We have looked at frameworks for system development, at traditional and innovative modelling techniques, and at some of the many factors that the designer may have to take into account before implementation. What we have not yet considered is how the whole process is to be organized and evaluated.

Management of software system development has much in common with the management of projects in other areas, but at the same time the nature of computer systems also demands specific qualities and expertise from the project manager. In this chapter we look at how a small project, such as Just a Line system, might be managed. We introduce some of the techniques available to help the project manager and we consider briefly the concept of quality in the development of software systems.

10.1 WHAT IS PROJECT MANAGEMENT?

No project can run efficiently without some sort of management. Even something as apparently straightforward as preparing a meal of spaghetti requires organization, checking and control. The chef has to make sure that all the necessary ingredients are to hand, such as pasta, herbs and tomatoes. He or she must know the order in which the preparation and cooking should be carried out and must check to make sure that the whole process is proceeding as planned. If the pasta is cooked half an hour before the sauce is even started, the result will be an indigestible heap of soggy spaghetti!

If more than one person is involved, the problems of management become even more complex. On top of the tasks already mentioned, the head chef in our example has to assign various tasks to the team of under-chefs so that they do not end up with mountains of spaghetti and no sauce. The chef's role includes constantly encouraging and cajoling the team so that they produce

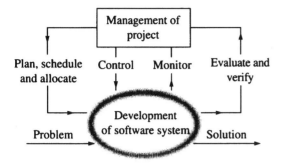

Figure 10.1 The development of the system and the management of the project

their best possible work, acting as mediator if there are any clashes of temperament among team members and liaising with the waiters so that the right dishes of food are ready at precisely the right moment. It is no wonder that head chefs in large restaurants hardly get time to do any cooking!

Developing software systems is no different from any other kind of project. The basic progression, from a vague notion of the problem to a solution which can be interpreted by a computer, is fraught with potential difficulties. Without a firm framework of planning, monitoring and control, and careful handling of the development team, such a project can very soon disintegrate into complete chaos. Figure 10.1 shows how the development of the system and the management of the development project can be viewed as separate, but closely related, entities.

10.2   WHY DO WE NEED PROJECT MANAGEMENT?

As can be seen from the example of a dish of spaghetti above, even an apparently simple sequence of actions needs a certain amount of management. In any project, somebody has to be able to plan what is to be done and to keep track of how things are going in relation to the plan. In all but the smallest projects this process of monitoring is important in controlling the overall costs and benefits of the project. If work is running late, or if costs are beginning to escalate, it is essential to discover this as soon as possible and to be able to see how the project as a whole is going to be affected. The sooner a problem is uncovered, the sooner corrective action can be taken and the possible effects of the problem curtailed.

Separating the management side of a project from the technical development side means that one person is responsible for organizing, planning, monitoring and controlling the project as a whole. These tasks are recognized as time-consuming and laborious, but essential for the smooth running of the project. Establishing a well-defined role for the project manager means that there is a clear point of contact for clients and an obvious person to whom team members can take their problems.

10.3   POSSIBLE DRAWBACKS

Project management is all about making the best use of resources, yet management itself takes up time, money and other resources. A skilled developer, who is acting as manager for a project, may have to spend a large amount of time on planning and administration instead of contributing to the actual development of the software system. This could be seen as a waste of technical expertise. The tasks of project management, such as producing a plan, monitoring progress and writing reports, are all expensive, in terms of both time and money.

Project management is not a magic wand. Many software systems are still delivered late, well over budget and often fail to fulfil the client's requirements. Nor is this a peculiarity of software systems; we only need to think of the projects to build the British Library or the Channel Tunnel to realize that other industries have the same problems. It is not surprising that there is a tendency to ask whether our present management methods are always worth the cost and effort put into them.

10.4   WHO IS INVOLVED IN PROJECT MANAGEMENT?

At the very simplest level, a system development project may involve only one person. Yet even here, that person is playing more than one role. If the system is for personal use, the same person represents the client, who has requested the system and who must be satisfied by the final product, the developer, whose task is to design and build the system, and the project manager, who plans, monitors and controls the progress of the system development.

In most situations these three roles are played by different people. Additionally, there may be many different clients or users and a large number of software engineers in the development team. An important part of the project manager's job is to liaise between these various parties and to ensure that development of the system progresses as smoothly as possible.

The development team

Right from the start of a project, it is essential for a project manager to have the best possible team for the job. The technical expertise required will vary according to the type of system to be developed, but there are other, more general, qualities that a project manager should look for when selecting the team. Some of these are listed below:

- Readiness to work hard
- Ability to listen
- Receptiveness to the ideas of others
- Ability to communicate
- Ability to co-operate with other team members
- Enthusiasm for the project
- Ability to cope with pressure

The team must act throughout the duration of the project as a cohesive unit. A team member who does not fit in, however brilliant they may be technically, can seriously damage the project's progress.

The project manager

As well as having all the qualities already mentioned for team members, a project manager must be good at dealing with people in general. This is important, both for the management of the development team and the relationship with clients. The project manager is the link between the client and the team. It is the manager's job to keep the client up to date on how the project is progressing and to keep the team informed about the client's reactions to the developing system. When things go wrong, it is the project manager who must identify where the problem lies, explain the situation to the client and somehow reach a compromise that satisfies everyone involved.

It is important for the project manager to have at least some technical expertise. This is necessary, firstly, so that the project manager is aware of and can appreciate the problems of the people developing the system and, secondly, so that the nature of the project is sufficiently well understood to identify the tasks and make accurate estimates of timings and costs. In a small project, the project manager will probably also be a member of the development team.

As well as technical skills, however, the project manager must have the ability to carry out other kinds of tasks which are specific to the management of the development project. A project manager must be able to:

- Plan.
- Estimate time and effort (and therefore costs) as accurately as possible.
- Identify and set sensible tasks for the team.
- Use prior experience effectively.
- Schedule work.

- Use resources efficiently.
- Monitor and control the progress of the project.
- Evaluate what is produced and insist on the importance of high-quality work.
- Identify quickly the cause of problems and be flexible enough to adjust previous plans if necessary.

If we add to this list of requirements that the project manager should be good at handling people and should have enough expertise to participate in the work of the project, we can see that a good project manager has to be all things to all men at all times!

10.5   PLANNING

If you look again at the list of project management skills above, you will see that several of these are concerned with making a plan for the development of the software system. Thus, a large part of the project manager's work has to be done before the actual development can get started.

Planning is basically a juggling act. A plan must reconcile what the system has to achieve with the resources available. Just as the objectives of the project will be different in every case, so the balance of resources will vary from one project to the next. Sometimes the client is prepared to spend plenty of money, but wants the system delivered within a very short time span; sometimes a developer with a particular type of expertise is not available; sometimes the client is unable or unwilling to spend much time in consultation about the development of the system. The project manager must have all this sort of information to hand in order to produce a workable plan.

It is important for the project manager to be able to identify areas of potential risk, such as inexperienced personnel, new technologies or problems of requirements capture, and to compensate for these by making contingency plans.

10.6   ESTIMATING

The ability to estimate accurately is crucial to the success of the project plan. It is essential for the project manager and the client to have as clear an idea as possible of the time a project will take and the costs it will incur. There are at present no formal methods or rules for assessing the time or cost of a project in advance. However, there are certain techniques that can help the project manager to produce more accurate estimates. When estimating the project manager should:

- Make sure that all relevant information is available.
- Divide the project into small, well-defined parts before assigning times and costs.
- Be realistic; an estimate is not a deadline, nor is it an optimistic guess.
- Make a realistic assessment of the risks involved in a particular project. This might include factors as diverse as the developers' lack of experience, potential conflict between clients and developers, using a new piece of software or a scarcity of adequate development facilities.
- Make extra allowance for contingencies, on the grounds that something is bound to go wrong.
- Make good use of historical data; this includes estimated and actual times and costs from previous projects, both from the project manager's own experience and from other people's.
- Reduce bias, by checking estimates with at least one other person.
- Distinguish between resource time and elapsed time. A job may require only one day's work on paper, but the time interval before it is completed is actually much longer because of factors outside the project manager's control. This is particularly important in the situation where team members are working on more than one project at a time.
- Practise estimating and keep a tally of the results, in order to identify personal strengths and weaknesses. Some people are naturally better at estimating than others, but everyone can improve with practice.

10.7 IDENTIFYING TASKS

In the same way as software system developers decompose a problem to help them to understand it better (see Chapters 4, 5 and 6), a project manager has to break down the project development into tasks and sub-tasks before the work to be carried out can be allocated. This is where it is essential for the project manager to have a knowledge of the nature of the work to be carried out. It is here also that a detailed methodology, such as those mentioned in Chapter 2, can be of great help to the project manager. A methodology prescribes the main decomposition of a system and the milestones in the development process. It also specifies the documents that are needed for each stage of development and the documents that should form the output.

Examples of some of the tasks that might be identified in the Just a Line development project are:

- Produce a set of levelled data flow diagrams for the required system.
- Create an entity–relationship model of the required system.
- Devise the test plan.
- Write user instructions.

Task Definition	
Project	*Just a Line*
Date	July 1996
Task Title	Design document to be used as price list and order form for mail shot
Task Reference	JL-T15
Sub-Tasks	Further interview with clients to finalize details Design first draft Agree design with clients
End Product	Agreed design for price list/order form
Constraints	Design should not exceed 2 sides of A4 paper Order form section should be separate so that it can be torn off for use by the customer
Resources	1 team member (output design specialist) Computer, printer Clients available for consultation
Estimated Effort	1 developer for 1 day
Actual Effort	

Figure 10.2 Task definition for Just a Line

A task should be as self-contained as possible with a well-defined boundary. The definition of the task should include a clear statement of the objectives, the end project of the task, any constraints involved in carrying out the task and the resources required. It should also give an estimate of the time required to complete the task and room for the developer to insert the actual time taken. These figures are useful for estimating similar tasks in future projects.

A definition for a task in the development of the Just a Line system is shown in Fig. 10.2.

10.8   DETERMINING AVAILABILITY OF PERSONNEL AND RESOURCES

The task definitions are an important part of the overall project plan, but on their own they do not provide sufficient information for the project manager to allocate and schedule the work to be carried out. It is also important to know exactly when team members and essential resources may be free for work on the project.

To record the availability of team personnel, charts should be drawn up which give details of each team member's weekly commitments and how much time is free to spend on tasks for this particular project. It is normal for developers to be working on more than one project at any one time. In this case, the project manager may have to negotiate with managers of other projects for the time particular developers may be available. This, of course, greatly increases the complexity of the overall project plan.

As well as weekly commitments and other project allocations, the availability chart for each team member should give details and dates of any planned absences during the project, such as holidays and training courses. A typical personnel availability form for a member of the Just a Line development team is shown in Fig. 10.3.

10.9   SCHEDULING

Once the project manager knows exactly what has to be done and the amount of time and resources available, it is possible to allocate tasks and schedule the work to be carried out. There are many automated project management tools on the market and they are of particular help in this area. They will produce a plan of work which aims to deliver the required system within specified time and budget limits, and which makes optimum use of the resources available. Automated tools are also invaluable when, inevitably, original plans have to be revised. No project ever goes entirely to plan; new tasks emerge, estimates turn out to be wrong, team members leave. Redrawing plans by hand can be a major headache, but automated tools considerably lessen the workload for the project manager.

The first step in the scheduling process is to identify milestones that will show that a particular phase of the project has been finished. In the development of the Just a Line system some of the milestones identified might be:

- Model of required system complete
- Interface designs agreed with clients
- Testing complete
- User documentation written

Personnel Availability	
Project	*Just a Line*
Date	July 1996
Name	Kate Simpson
Position	Analyst
Weekly Activities	**Average hours per week (max. 40)**
Work on other projects	7
Administration	1
Total non-project activities	8
Project Management	0
Availability for project tasks	32
Planned Absences	**Dates**
Training	4–7 August
Holiday	2–19 September

Figure 10.3 A personnel availability form for Just a Line

Milestones are essential for the project manager, not only in monitoring the project but in reporting back to the client on how development of the system is progressing.

In the same way as a software system developer uses graphical models to help to understand and organize the problem space, a project manager uses graphics in the form of charts as an aim to scheduling work and making optimum use of resources. Although there are many different types of charts, they mainly fall into one of two categories, bar and network charts.

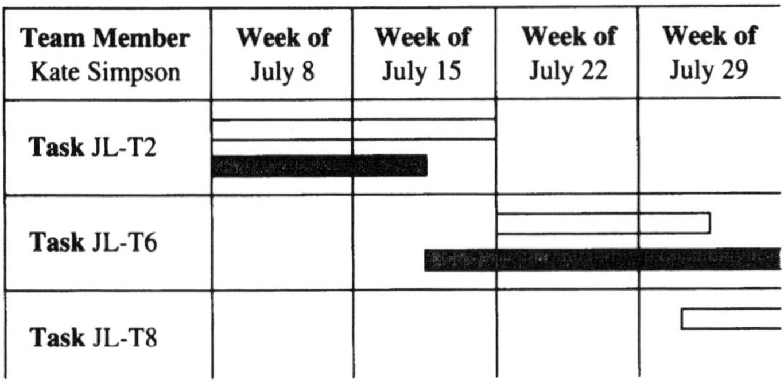

Team Member Kate Simpson	Week of July 8	Week of July 15	Week of July 22	Week of July 29
Task JL-T2				
Task JL-T6				
Task JL-T8				

Figure 10.4 A section of a simple bar chart from the Just a Line project

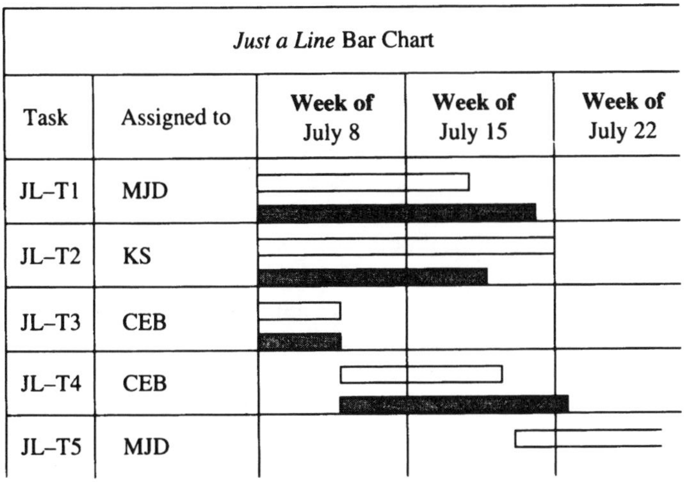

		Just a Line Bar Chart		
Task	Assigned to	Week of July 8	Week of July 15	Week of July 22
JL–T1	MJD			
JL–T2	KS			
JL–T3	CEB			
JL–T4	CEB			
JL–T5	MJD			

Figure 10.5 A more sophisticated bar chart for Just a Line

Bar charts

Bar charts (often referred to as Gantt charts) show the tasks to be carried out, together with the estimated and actual time for each task. They can also be used to show staff allocations to particular tasks and the dates they are expected to be working on them. This helps the project manager with the problem of scheduling staff who may be working on several projects over a period of time.

Figure 10.4 shows a section of a simple bar chart for the Just a Line project. The white bars show the estimated dates that a team member is expected to be working on a particular task and the shaded bars show the actual dates. We can see from the chart that Kate was allocated to task JL-T2 for the weeks beginning 8 July and 15 July, but in fact she completed the task before two weeks were up and so she was able to begin her next task (JL-T6) early. We can see that, at the time the chart was drawn up, this task was unfinished, but had already taken Kate longer than estimated.

Bar charts are a clear, convenient way of organizing and conveying information. They are the most popular *at-a-glance* way of monitoring projects, but they are limited in that they do not always give a good overall view of the project. On large projects it may be difficult to see from a bar chart how tasks relate to each other, or the effect on the project as a whole of a particular task taking much longer than estimated. Figure 10.5 shows a section of a more sophisticated bar chart which includes the tasks carried out by all the team members.

Network charts

Network (or activity) charts use a notation that overcomes these limitations. There are different variations on the basic idea of a network chart, of which the best known are PERT (program evaluation and review technique), CPM (critical path method) and CPA (critical path analysis).

On a network chart, tasks are represented by lines with the estimated duration of the task written below each line. Circular symbols represent events or project milestones and may be divided into four segments, as shown in Fig. 10.6. The first segment shows the milestone number, the second indicates the earliest estimated completion time for the task, e.g. week number, the third segment gives the latest time the task can finish without affecting the overall project and the bottom segment shows the contingency factor, i.e. the difference between the two times.

A network chart, such as the small example in Fig. 10.7, shows how the various tasks are dependent on each other, which tasks must be performed in sequence and which in parallel. Figure 10.7 shows a simplified chart for the design and implementation of a mail shot for Just a Line. Copies of the mail shot will be personalized and sent out to customers on the Just a Line file. We will assume that the file of customers already exists. The tasks represented in the diagram are:

T1—design personalized mail shot
T2—agree mail shot design with clients
T3—write test plan
T4—select and order pre-printed Just a Line stationery

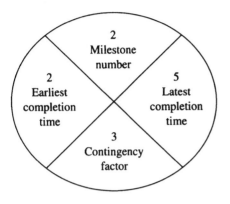

Figure 10.6 A project milestone as represented on a network chart

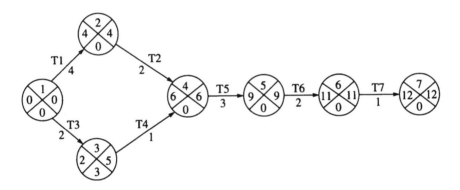

Figure 10.7 A simple network chart for the design and implementation of a mail shot for Just a Line

T5—write code to produce mail shot
T6—test
T7—demonstrate to clients

From the chart we can see, for example, that task T5 cannot be started until T1, T2, T3 and T4 are complete, but that tasks T2 and T4 can be carried out in parallel.

Once tasks and milestones have been established, the start and end dates for the project can be added to the chart. From the completed chart we can determine the *critical path*, the longest path on the network. The project manager must be able to identify the critical path, since it indicates which tasks must be performed on schedule so as not to cause delays in the project. Tasks that are not on the critical path can be delayed by the amount of time specified in the contingency segment without delaying the overall project. However,

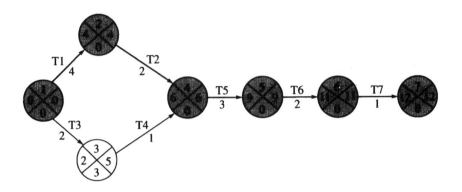

Figure 10.8 A simple network chart and the critical path

delays to tasks that are on the critical path will have an effect on the end date of the project. Figure 10.8 shows the critical path for the design and implementation of the Just a Line mail shot. The critical path is shown by the heavy lines and shaded circles.

Both network and bar charts are used extensively in project management. One method of scheduling that aims to combine the best features of each type of chart is the network–bar chart. This is simply a variant of a bar chart, but includes an indication of dependencies between tasks. In order to get a complete overall picture for the project plan, the project manager needs to make use of both network and bar charts, since each type of chart conveys different but essential information. In the same way as the various modelling techniques introduced in Chapters 4, 5 and 6 each give the developer a different perspective of the system, the various types of scheduling chart give the project manager different perspectives on how the project is progressing.

10.10   THE COMPLETED PLAN

The project plan, once completed, becomes the framework for the development of the software system. Individual project managers will have their own methods of documenting the plan, but this should incorporate all the following items.

- A summary of the objective of the project
- Network and bar charts showing scheduled start and completion dates and a high-level view of allocation of staff and resources
- A detailed list of resource requirements
- A detailed list of estimates costs

- A statement of an assumptions made in estimating, including risk assessment and contingency factor (extra time allowed for things to go wrong)

Appendices to the plan should include:

- Detailed task definitions
- Personnel availability forms
- Detailed schedules

Although it is important that the project plan is rigid enough to act as a framework for the development of the system, it is equally important that it is flexible enough to adapt to changing circumstances. Planning should be seen, not as a once-and-for-all activity, but as an iterative process. Change is a constant factor in the life of a project; it comes from the client, from the development team and from external circumstances. Wherever it comes from, the project manager must be prepared to react to it in the way that brings the most long-term benefits, or the least long-term damages, to the project as a whole. This often means making amendments to the plan—extending the task list, rescheduling staff and resources, or recalculating costs. It is a critical part of the project manager's job to strike the optimum balance between firmness and flexibility in the management of the project.

10.11   MONITORING AND CONTROLLING THE PROJECT

Once work on the development of the software system is under way, the main task of the project manager is to monitor and control the progress of the project. To achieve this, it is important to be able to measure how things are progressing in terms of time, cost and quality. At any given point the project manager should be fully aware of the following factors:

- The current status of the project with respect to the plan
- The cause of any deviations from the plan
- The corrective action that needs to be taken and the effect this will have on the project

Good communication is essential for firm project control. There has to be some mechanism through which the project manager can keep a constant eye on how the system development is progressing. This mechanism often consists of a mixture of:

- Reporting by members of the development team, either at the end of each completed task or at regular time intervals

- A series of pre-planned meetings and walkthroughs at which the current situation is assessed and future action determined

During walkthroughs, a specific deliverable, such as a required logical model of the system, may be examined by project team members as part of overall quality control.

10.12   WHAT HAPPENS WHEN THINGS GO WRONG?

Corrective action, if needed to put the project back on course, must be taken as soon as possible. The sooner deviations from the plan are spotted and action taken, the more likely it is that long-term damage to the project will be avoided. Corrective action can take various forms, the most appropriate of these depending on the particular problem under consideration.

In any specific case the options open to the project manager include the following:

- The completion date can be put back so that the project goes late.
- Team members can work overtime.
- More resources, such as extra system developers, can be introduced to work on the project. This is an attractive, but potentially problematic, alternative. Not only can it dramatically increase project costs, but the need to inform new team members about the nature of the development, the current status of the project and the team's methods of working can use up the extra resources that have been added and seriously disrupt continuity and team spirit.
- The overall aims of the project may be changed. This could mean that the original manual system is not fully automated or that the final implementation is less ambitious than originally intended. In an extreme case the project manager may have to consider scrapping the project altogether.

When things go wrong with a software project there is rarely an easy or an obvious way out. The option chosen will always represent a compromise between reduced benefits from the system and extra costs incurred in terms of money, time and effort.

10.13   SOFTWARE METRICS

We have already said that it is essential to keep firm control of a project and to be able to evaluate how it is progressing, but we have so far said little about how this control and evaluation can be achieved. How can the project manager tell if the project is falling behind schedule? How is it possible to ascertain if the work produced is of the required standard? What exactly is a *quality system*?

A body of knowledge which aims to help software developers and project managers with these problems is software metrics. Software metrics are measurements that quantify aspects of software, both for the development process and the final product. They can be used both to evaluate what has already been accomplished and to predict what can be achieved in the future.

The most successful software metrics to date are those that relate to the management of the software development process. Examples of these metrics are measurements of elapsed time, the effort expanded on a particular task and the cost of different activities. These measurements can be used as an aid to refining present plans and scheduling future projects.

Software metrics are also used increasingly to measure the *quality* of a software system, but this is a much more difficult area to quantify. It is very hard to find meaningful metrics for something as intangible as software and to interpret them in such a way that they will accurately predict how good a software system will be. Measurements that are often recorded include the complexity of the original problem, the number of lines of code in the final system and the number of faults in the system reported by the client. In practice, however, such measurements alone are a poor indication of the nature of the final system. It is hard enough to define what we mean by a *quality* system, let alone attempt to measure it.

10.14 STANDARDS AND QUALITY ASSURANCE

As software systems continue to play ever larger and more central roles in the world today, it is increasingly important for us to be able to produce systems of high quality. In order to do this we need first to be able to define accurately what we mean by a *quality system*. Unfortunately, this is much harder than it appears. To begin with, are we talking about quality from the point of view of the client or the system developer? For the client, quality means getting a system that does what is required of it, on time and at a reasonable price. The client will be interested in what the system can do, how user-friendly it is, whether it is reliable and how much it costs. The system developer will also be interested in these attributes, but on top of these he or she will be concerned with issues such as good program design, efficient use of resources and a well-structured database. Building a system is not like building a car or an aeroplane. Each system is individual and each will have its own set of quality criteria—in one case security of data may be of prime importance, whereas in another efficient use of resources may have top priority.

There are, of course, certain attributes that any good system should have. It should, for example, be reliable, easy to use, easy to maintain and, above all, it should satisfy clients and users. Standards do now exist, such as ISO 9001, which aim to capture these general attributes of software quality. It is now possible for organizations developing software to register conformance to ISO 9001 and indeed this is mandatory on many government projects.

Building quality into a system is only effective when carried out in conjunction with the people who are going to use the system. Users should be asked to specify what they consider as acceptable quality for the system interfaces. At the very least, users should be encouraged to scrutinize all input screen designs and output documents.

Quality systems do not come cheaply and it is essential that everyone concerned with the development of a system participates in the drive for excellence. In many large software organizations there is an independent quality assurance division which is responsible for assessing the software system. The quality assurance team on any project is sometimes viewed by the system developers with a degree of suspicion and even hostility. This is unfortunate, since they are there to help the developers, not to act as a police force. It is in the interests of everyone working on the project that a system of the highest quality possible is produced. There may also be a department that handles the configuration management of the system. Configuration management is responsible for documenting all modifications to the system and keeping track of all versions of it. This ensures that quality is maintained throughout any changes that the system may undergo in its lifetime.

In a small project, such as the Just a Line system, the project manager will have overall responsibility for quality assurance. This will involve careful monitoring and control of the development process and insisting on work of a high standard from all members of the development team. Each member of the team should feel responsible for the quality of their own work and team members should be encouraged to review each other's work in a critical, but positive, way.

The amount of time and effort put into quality assurance depends on the nature of the system. Safety-critical systems, where the consequences of failure are life-threatening, require the most rigorous quality assurance procedures. Examples of safety-critical systems that need this level of quality assurance are monitoring of hospital patients, flight control and nuclear plant control. This type of system may entail a justifiably high quality assurance cost which may equal or exceed the development cost of the system. In contrast, for a standard information processing system, such as Just a Line, the cost of an appropriate level of quality assurance may be as little as one-third of the development cost.

Structured walkthroughs are one of the most useful and effective ways of checking quality. These involve formal meetings as each milestone in the project is reached. During the walkthrough the developer who is responsible for the material being reviewed presents the completed work to a panel of peer reviewers, including the walkthrough organizer and a system developer who can judge the technical merit of the work. If appropriate, the user may also be present. Frequent walkthroughs during the project are an effective way of ensuring validation and verification of the developing system. Validation is concerned with matching the system to the customer's requirements. It asks questions such as 'Is the right product being developed? and 'Will the system be fit for the purpose for which it is intended?' Verification, on the other hand, is concerned with issues of internal correctness—'Does the system match its specification?' and 'Is the system being developed in the right way?'

Apart from walkthroughs, sound development methods, formal specifications, comprehensive documentation, rigorous testing and independent audits all help to ensure that the final system is indeed a quality product.

Software developers spend far too much time today on correcting mistakes which should never have been allowed to occur in the first place. Putting the emphasis on quality means trying to get it right first time round. Quality costs money, but the consequences of ignoring quality assurance issues can make all the difference between a system that is fit for the purpose and one that falls short of requirements.

SUMMARY

All system development projects need to be managed if the system is to be delivered on time, within budget, and if the best use is to be made of available resources. Together with technical excellence, good management is one of the keys to ensuring that the software produced at the end of the development process is of a high quality.

The job of the project manager involves a wide variety of tasks—from the technical, such as scheduling resources and monitoring progress, to the personal, such as dealing with the problems of individual team members. Today, automated tools and software metrics can alleviate many of the tasks of project management, but it is still the project manager who has overall responsibility for the efficiency of the development process and the quality of the finished system.

EXERCISES AND TOPICS FOR DISCUSSION

10.1 'I believe that large programming projects suffer management problems different in kind from small ones' (F. P. Brooks Jr). Discuss the particular problems that might arise in the management of a large project.

10.2 Does the development of a small system, such as Just a Line, need to be managed?

10.3 Imagine that you have been seconded to work on the Just a Line project. Draw up your own personal availability chart for the next three months.

10.4 Choose a small project which you will carry out on your own. For example, you could aim to write a program to add two numbers together in a programming language that is new to you.

(a) Make a list of the resources you will need for the project.

(b) Draw up a list of sensible tasks for this project and estimate how long each task will take you.

(c) Determine the order in which you will perform the tasks and see if it is possible for any to be carried out in parallel.

(d) Carry out the project, modifying your original plans where necessary.

(e) How accurate were your estimates? To what extent were you able to stick to your original plan?

FURTHER READING

Brooks, F. P. (1978) *The Mythical Man Month*, Addison-Wesley, Reading, Mass.

Crinnion, J. (1991) *Evolutionary Systems Development*, Chapter 15, Pitman, London.

Sommerville, I. (1995) *Software Engineering*, 5th edn, Chapter 3 and Part 7, Addison-Wesley, Wokingham.

Yourdon, E. (1989) *Modern Structured Analysis*. Chapter 16, Prentice-Hall, Englewood Cliffs, N.J.

CONCLUSION

In this book our aim has been to provide a gentle introduction to the process of software system development. For the interested reader, who wants to find out more about particular topics, we have included a full bibliography. The general theme of the book has been that there is no single best way of developing software systems, but we feel that the following guidelines may be useful.

- Rather than following a rigid methodology, a more flexible way of building a system is for the developer to gain a thorough understanding of the problem and then to select the most appropriate technique or tool at each stage of development.
- Every system is different. For successful development, careful investigation of the problem and its environment is essential.
- System developers should have a working knowledge of a wide range of development techniques. In this way they will have more chance of having the most appropriate tool at their disposal.
- The book describes separately several different types of technique that are used in the development of software systems: the structured techniques, formal notations and prototyping. These are not necessarily alternatives: in many systems a range of techniques may be used to complement each other.
- Software system development involves many skills. Reading about development techniques may make them appear easy, but using them to develop a real system takes time, effort and experience. There is no substitute for practice.
- Even the smallest software system development project needs proper organization and management. Techniques described in the book will help to ensure that the system is delivered on time, within budget and that it is of the required standard.
- As clients demand ever larger and more complex software systems, effective teamwork is an essential ingredient in the successful development of a

system. Software developers should not underestimate the importance of team and social skills.

- Many software projects today involve the modification or enhancement of an existing system. Most clients and users will already have some experience of computers and may have their own ideas about how the new system should be developed. Increased involvement of clients and users in a software project will influence the development process and the techniques and methods chosen.

- It is important that software developers should not become stuck in a particular way of developing systems, but maintain an open mind and a flexible approach to enable them to take full advantage of advances in technology and new approaches to development.

BIBLIOGRAPHY

Beynon-Davies, P. (1991) *Relational Database Systems*, Blackwell Scientific Publications, Oxford.
A thorough and easy to understand introduction to the topic.

Birtwhistle, G., Dahl, O., Myrhaug, B. and Nygaard, K. (1973) *Simula Begin*, Studentliteratur (Lund) and Auerbach Pub., New York.
The best known book on Simula and an excellent introduction.

Booch, G. (1994) *Object-Oriented Analysis and Design with Applications*, Benjamin/Cummings, California.
One of the founding-fathers of object-oriented analysis and design. Booch's notation and ideas have been inherited by most of the succeeding generations of methodologists.

Brooks, F. P. (1978) *The Mythical Man Month*, Addison-Wesley, Reading, Mass.
A collection of essays about project management. Easy to read, with lots of interesting ideas about managing software projects.

Brown, J., Loomes, M. and Stobo, J. (1991) *Discrete Mathematics for Computer Scientists*, Hatfield Polytechnic (now University of Hertfordshire), Division of Computer Science.
In-house notes which form an excellent introduction to the mathematics underlying formal specification languages. Suitable for complete beginners or as a refresher course. Lots of exercises and answers make this a good student-centred learning package.

Carter, R., Martin, J., Mayblin, B., and Munday, M. (1988) *Systems Management and Change—A Graphic Guide*, Paul Chapman in association with The Open University.
An unusual and stimulating introduction to the subject of systems in general.

Crinnion, J. (1991) *Evolutionary Systems Development*, Pitman, London.
Shows how prototyping can be combined with a structured methodology. Very good coverage of the structured techniques.

Date, C. J. (1991) *An Introduction to Database Systems*, Vol. 1, 5th edn, Addison-Wesley, Reading, Mass.
The classic text on the subject. Complete and thorough, but not for novices.

Davis, A. M. (1993) *Software Requirements: Objects, Functions and States*, Prentice-Hall, Englewood Cliffs, N.J.
A classic and comprehensive text on all aspects of requirements capture.

Diller, A. (1994) *Z. Introduction to Formal Methods*, 2nd edn, John Wiley, Chichester.
A comprehensive tutorial introduction to the Z specification language.

Edwards, P. (1993) *Systems Analysis and Design*, McGraw-Hill, Watsonville, California.
Covers the whole software development process. Good on CASE and prototyping.

Gane, C. and Sarson, T. (1979) *Structured Systems Analysis*, Prentice-Hall, Sydney.
One of the classic works on structured analysis and design.

Goodland, M. (1995) *SSADM Version 4: A Practical Approach*, McGraw-Hill, London.
A comprehensive guide to SSADM (the methodology recommended for many government contracts). This is a good example of a complete methodology.

Hawryszkiewycz, I. T. (1994) *Introduction to Systems Analysis and Design*, 3rd edn, Prentice-Hall, Sydney.
A detailed look at the modelling techniques used in systems development, well supported by an on-going case study.

Howe, D. R. (1989) *Data Analysis for Database Design*, Hodder & Stoughton, London.
An accessible introduction.

Jackson, M. (1983) *System Development*, Prentice-Hall. London.
The original book on JSD.

Jacobson, I. (1992) *Object-Oriented Software Engineering: A Use Case Driven Approach*, Addison-Wesley, Wokingham.
Describes Objectory, the first comprehensive, commercially available object-oriented method.

Kendall, E. K. and Kendall, J. E. (1988) *Systems Analysis and Design*, Prentice-Hall, Englewood Cliffs, N.J.
An encyclopaedic work on the subject.

Lantz, K. E. (1986) *The Prototyping Methodology*, Prentice-Hall, Englewood Cliffs, N.J.
Some interesting ideas on prototyping. The author treats prototyping as a methodology in its own right and does not relate it to the structured modelling techniques.

Layzell, P. J. and Loucopoulos, P. (1989) *Systems Analysis and Development*, 3rd edn, Chartwell-Bratt, Kent.
A readable introduction to structured systems analysis and design. The book covers all the structured techniques, functional design, file and database design, system implementation, etc.

Loucopoulos, P. and Karakostas, V. (1995) *System Requirements Engineering*, McGraw-Hill, London.
A very good introduction to the subject.

Maude, T. and Willis, G. (1991) *Rapid Prototyping, The Management of Software Risk*, Pitman, London.
Explains the technique of prototyping as part of the software engineering process with particular emphasis on the management of risk. The book includes a strategy for rapid prototyping, a discussion of the management of prototyping projects and an examination of different tools and techniques that are available.

Meyer, B. (1988) *Object-Oriented Software Construction*, Prentice-Hall, London.
An in-depth presentation of the methods and techniques of object-oriented design. Most of the book is about Meyer's own object-oriented language, Eiffel, but the first three chapters are essential reading for anyone interested in developing quality software.

Potter, B., Sinclair, J. and Till, D. (1996) *An Introduction to Formal Specification and Z*, 2nd edn, Prentice-Hall, Hemel Hempstead.
A very readable introduction to the Z specification language.

Pressman, R. S. (1992) *Software Engineering: A Practitioner's Approach*, 3rd edn, adapted by Darrel Ince, European adaptation. McGraw-Hill, London.
A comprehensive and widely used book on software engineering.

Ratcliff, B. (1987) *Software Engineering: Principles and Methods*, Blackwell, Oxford.
A good introduction to the area of systems development, including sections on JSD, formal methods and project management.

Robinson, B. and Prior, M. (1995) *Systems Analysis Techniques*, International Thomson Computer Press, London.
Detailed and clearly explained account of the modelling techniques used in structured systems analysis. Includes many exercises and answers.

Rumbaugh, J., *et al.* (1991) *Object-Oriented Modelling and Design*, Prentice-Hall, Englewood Cliffs, N. J.
Describes OMT, which has become one of the most widely adopted object-oriented methodologies.

Shlaer, S. and Mellor, S. J. (1988) *Object-Oriented Systems Analysis*, Yourdon. New York.
In spite of its title, this is not really a new approach to analysis. However, it does give a good introduction to data modelling and also covers data flow diagrams.

Shneiderman, B. (1992) *Designing the User Interface: Strategies for Effective Human–Computer Interaction*, 2nd edn, Addison-Wesley, Reading, Mass.
A classic introductory text.

Skidmore, S. (1994) *Introducing Systems Analysis*, Blackwell NCC, Manchester.
A very readable text, including a comprehensive discussion of fact-gathering techniques which may be used during analysis.

Sommerville, I. (1995) *Software Engineering*, 5th edn, Addison-Wesley, Wokingham.
A comprehensive introduction to the whole topic of software development. It includes sections on formal specification, different types of program design, CASE tools and project management. A useful reference book.

Sutcliffe, A. (1988) *Jackson System Development*, Prentice-Hall, New York.
An interesting, readable description of JSD, putting it in a context with other methodologies.

Taylor, D. A. (1990) *Object-Oriented Technology: A Manager's Guide*, Addison-Wesley, Reading, Mass.
A clear, simple overview of the concepts and significance of object technology.

Veryard, R. (1984) *Pragmatic Data Analysis*, Blackwell Scientific Publications, Oxford.
This is one of the few data modelling books that are not really about databases. Useful if you want to learn more about entity–relationship modelling.

Vonk, R. (1990) *Prototyping. The Effective Use of CASE Technology*, Prentice-Hall, London.
A good introduction to the technique of prototyping and how it can be used with CASE tools in the development of systems.

Yeates, D., Shields, M. and Helmy, D. (1994) *Systems Analysis and Design*, Pitman, London.
Covers the whole development process in an informative and accessible way. Includes an on-going SSADM-based case study.

Yourdon, E. (1989) *Modern Structured Analysis*, Prentice-Hall, Englewood Cliffs, N.J.
Good coverage of different types of system, structured modelling techniques, system analysis and design.

GLOSSARY

Words marked * have their own definition in the glossary

Abstraction: the process of ignoring currently irrelevant details of a problem in order to concentrate on the most important parts.

Acceptance testing: the final testing of the software system in the presence of the client. The system is then accepted by the client or further alterations are made.

Analysis: one of the stages of the traditional system life cycle*. Analysis involves investigation into and modelling* of both the problem area and the developing system.

Application package: software designed to be used for a specific business or application area such as accounting, stock control, payroll. Packages are usually designed for general use, not for a particular client.

Automation boundary: delineates the part of the system that will be computerized.

Bar chart: type of graph. A technique used in project management where such diagrams (Gantt charts) are used to help plan and schedule resources during the development of a system.

Bureau: organizations that offer general types of computer services. Some offer specialized services such as COM* or data preparation.

Business model: a model of the existing manual or computer system in the context of the organization, which is the system's immediate environment. The model is used to identify the implicit requirements of the business that must be incorporated into the new system.

CASE: Computer Aided Software Engineering. The use of software tools to automate the system development process. CASE tools can include any program that aids the system developer, such as a drawing program or a code debugger. However, the tools are usually much more sophisticated, covering a complete stage of the system life cycle*.

Class: template or factory for creating objects*.

CLDFD: Current Logical Data Flow Diagram. This is a data flow diagram* which is drawn to illustrate *what* happens in the current system without considering *how* it happens.

Client: the person who requests the new system and is the main contact point with the system developer. The client will generally also be a user* of the new system, but this is not always the case.

Client server: a system where one computer (the client) accesses data which is held on another computer (the server) via a network*. A common example of a client server system is the hole-in-the-wall cash machine.

COM: Computer Output to Microforms. Extremely compact method of recording of computer output on to microfilm or microfiche; widely used for storing library catalogues and back issues of newspapers.

Configuration management: systematic logging of changes to the system; version control.

Consistency: a specification is consistent if there are no internal contradictions between different views of the system.

Context diagram: the top-level data flow diagram* which is used to give an overall view of the current or required system.

CPDFD: Current Physical Data Flow Diagram. This is a data flow diagram* which illustrates *how* procedures are carried out in the current system.

Critical path: in project management, identification of the critical path highlights those areas of the system development where any delay will cause a delay in the project delivery date.

Data abstraction: the technique of hiding the implementation* details of a module behind a public interface*.

Database: all the data required to support the operations of an organization—collected, organized and maintained centrally and in such a way that it can be used by many different programs.

Data dictionary: a structured modelling technique which uses English and a small set of symbols to define the data in the system.

Data flow diagram: a widely used structured modelling technique which models the movement of data round the system. Data flow diagrams are made up of processes*, data flows*, data stores* and external entities*.

Data/information flow: one of the constituent symbols of a data flow diagram* The data flow is drawn as a directed line and is labelled with the name of the data.

Data modelling: the technique of building representations of a system based on the data objects or entities* that are found in it. The principal technique used in data modelling is the entity–relationship diagram*.

Data Protection Act: an Act of Parliament passed in the United Kingdom in 1984 to protect personal data held in a form that can be automatically processed and which concerns identifiable individuals. The Act stipulates that such data must be registered, protected against unauthorized access and that individuals have the right to examine and correct the data concerning them.

Data store: a symbol found on data flow diagrams*. Data stores represent data which is stored permanently by the system, such as product prices or customer details.

Decision table: a technique used in process definitions* in which different conditions and actions are laid out in tabulated form.

Decision tree: a technique used in process definitions* in which different cases are represented in a tree structure.

Decomposition: the process of breaking a problem down into successively smaller parts in order to understand it better.

Deliverable: the output from a stage in the system life cycle*. Deliverables in the early stages of the life cycle are generally in the form of documents and diagrams. In the later stages they also include program code and test results.

Direct manipulation: a widely used interaction style, where the user moves objects on the screen corresponding to the tasks to be performed.

Documentation: the documentation of a system includes many different aspects—instructions for the users and operators about the running of the system; information necessary to those concerned with system maintenance* including the documents generated as deliverables* during the system development.

Dynamic binding: the binding at run-time of a message to a particular version of a method*.

Entity: a unit or object of data which is part of the system under consideration and which is important in the development of the new system.

Entity life history: a structured modelling technique which illustrates how a data entity* is affected by events over the course of time.

Entity–relationship diagram: a structured modelling technique which identifies data objects in the system and illustrates the links between these objects.

Environment: the system environment refers to anything outside the system which affects it in some way—e.g. people or organizations generating or responding to system data.

External entity: one of the symbols found on a data flow diagram*. An external entity represents a person or organization which has links with the system, but which is not part of it.

Feasibility study: part of the system life cycle* which attempts to determine whether there is a practical solution to the problem under consideration.

File: organized collection of related data items.

Formal methods: the process of using formal notations* in the development of systems is sometimes referred to as formal methods. However, formal notations do not include any concept of method in the sense of a methodology*.

Formal notations: languages based on mathematics and logic which are used in the specification of computer systems.

Fourth-generation language (4GL): a high-level programming language where one line of code can be as powerful as up to 10 lines of code in an earlier-generation language. 4GLs are problem oriented, which means that the programmer only has to define *what* needs to be done, not *how* the tasks should be carried out. 4GLs are used widely in prototyping*.

Functional decomposition: breaking down a system into smaller parts in terms of its processes.

Functionality: what a system does in terms of the processes which it supports.

Functional requirements: the tasks that a system is to perform, what its inputs and outputs are, and how these are linked.

Gannt chart: see bar chart.

Hardware: equipment used by a system including printers, keyboards and VDUs, disk and tape drives.

Implementation: the stage of the system life cycle* where the design is translated into a programming language.

Implementation independent: an implementation-independent design can be implemented* in different ways, using different programming techniques or languages.

Information hiding: making the internal details of a module inaccessible to other modules.

Inheritance: mechanism which allows a class* to reuse methods and variables already defined in another class.

Inputs: data which is entered into the system by the user.

Installation: the stage in the system life cycle* where the system is delivered and set up at the client's premises.

Instance: reference to an object* that belongs to a particular class*.

Integer: a positive or negative whole number, such as minus 46, minus 7, 0, 17, 351.

Integrated package: suite of programs or modules supporting certain types of application, usually a database, a spreadsheet, a word processor and communications software, which facilitate the passing of data between the different modules and have a common way of doing things—similar keystrokes, etc. Examples are Microsoft Office and Lotus 1-2-3.

Interface: the system interface is its connection with the outside world. Data passed to or from other computer systems must be in a compatible form. The user interface* refers the user's view of the system, usually via a series of screens.

Internet: a vast network of networks that connect millions of computers throughout the world. The Internet supports the World Wide Web*, electronic mail links and a huge number of specialized mailing lists.

Intersect: an operation on sets which takes two sets and returns the elements which occur in both sets—e.g. intersecting the sets {dog, cat, mouse, hamster, gerbil} and {mouse, rat, cat} gives the set {cat, mouse}.

ISO 9001: international standard for quality assurance.

Life cycle: stages in the development of a system, each with a specified set of deliverables*.

Logical model: the collected models (both text and diagrams) which illustrate *what* the system does, omitting consideration of *how* this is achieved.

Maintenance: the final stage of the life cycle*, where errors are corrected and system modifications* carried out.

Message: request from one object* to another that it execute one of its methods*.

Method: procedure which is part of an object.

Methodology: recipe for developing a system. The detailed description of the steps and stages in system development, together with a specified list of inputs and outputs for each step.

Microcomputer/Personal Computer (PC): desk-top, stand-alone, single-user computer, for small business, education or domestic applications; usually relatively cheap (under £1000); can be connected to a variety of peripherals* and used in a network*.

Modelling: the process of building a representation of all or part of a system. This is carried out using techniques such as natural language, structured techniques, prototyping, formal notations or any combination of these.

Modification: changes of any size which are made to the system after it has been delivered to the client.

Module: section of a program often consisting of several procedures* and designed to execute a logically identifiable unit of data and associated routines.

Multimedia: the combination of different forms of media—text, graphics, sound, photographs and video—in a computer-based system.

Network: the linking of two or more computers, thus allowing them to communicate, share data and applications* and use the same peripherals*.

Network chart: diagram showing task dependencies and identifying the critical path*, used in project management

Non-functional requirements: the attributes of a system as it performs its job. Non-functional requirements include usability, reliability and performance.

Normal form: the process of normalizing* data—involves following a series of steps going from the unnormalized form through first, second and third normal forms. Higher normal forms have been defined for use if the system is to be implemented on a relational database*.

Normalization: the process of organizing data items into groups in such a way that no redundant* data items are stored. In this way unnecessary duplication of data is avoided.

Object: software packet containing data and methods (procedures) for operating on that data.

Operating procedures: instructions for computer operating and control staff, relating to the correct running of the system including use of peripherals*, use of stored files, acceptance of source data and distribution of output.

Operating system: suite of programs which control the operation of the computer and the application* programs; examples are MS-DOS, UNIX and Windows. The functions of an operating system vary according to the type of computer, but can include scheduling of jobs according to a priority system, control of multiprogramming, control of peripherals* including terminals, communication with the operator, allocation of storage and control of system software such as compilers and assemblers.

Outputs: the information which is produced by the system for the user.

Peripherals: machines other than computers which are an essential part of the system. Typical peripherals include disk drives and printers.

Physical model: concentrates of describing *how* a system works; physical models can be used to describe current and required systems.

Polymorphism: the ability to hide different implementations* behind a common interface*.

Portable: a portable program can be run on more than one type of computer.

Pre-condition: something which must be true before something else can occur, e.g. a customer must be on the Just a Line file before they can receive any mail shots.

Primary key: attribute which uniquely identifies an occurrence of an entity.

Procedure (in program): in programming terms a procedure is a section of a program normally designed to execute a logically district routine or function.

Process: in structured systems development a process is something that happens to data. A process is modelled in data flow diagrams* by a box with data flows entering and leaving. What happens in a process is described in detail in the related process definition*.

Process definition: a structured modelling technique which specifies* the lowest-level processes on a data flow diagram*.

Processing/order processing/data processing: data processing consists of manipulating (e.g. selecting, performing arithmetic operations, sorting) raw input data into a form that provides useful information from which decisions can be made. Order processing involves dealing with an order according to company policy.

Programmer: someone who transforms program or system specifications* into a computer programming language.

Prototyping: an iterative method of developing a certain kind of system instead of using traditional structured methods. Rapid prototyping involves constructing a working model of the system at a very early stage in development and using the model to identify user requirements. Once these have been established, the prototype is thrown away. Evolutionary prototyping is where the working model is used as the basis of the final system.

Pseudocode: a description, normally of a program or a process, which uses many of the features of a modern block structured programming language such as Modula-2 but has no rigid syntax. Features include the use of control structures (IF THEN ELSE, CASE, REPEAT) and a structured layout. Can be implemented in several different programming languages.

Redundant: a stored data item is redundant if it is never used, if it is stored in more than one place in a system or if it can be derived from other data stored in the system.

Report generator: a language for constructing programs to tabulate and summarize data in report form.

Requirements capture: the overall process of establishing exactly what the client wants from a new system. Requirements capture covers the three phases of requirements elicitation (identification), requirements specification (description) and requirements validation (checking).

Response time: a measurement of the time from when a computer is asked to process some data to when the results are produced.

RLDFD: Required Logical Data Flow Diagram. This is a data flow diagram* which is drawn to illustrate *what* should happen in the new system without considering *how* it will be implemented.

RPDFD: Required Physical Data Flow Diagram. This is a data flow diagram* which illustrates *how* procedures are to be carried out in the new system.

Schema: part of the Z* formal specification language. A schema is like a box which encloses related portions of mathematics and so partitions the specification*

Software: broad term covering the methods of using and controlling computers; includes programs and systems.

Software engineering: the application of sound engineering principles to the development of software systems.

Software metrics: measurements that quantify the system development and the final software product.

Source code: code in the language it is originally written in by the programmer, e.g. Modula-2, before it is translated into machine code.

Specification: a definition or description. For example, a specification of the functionality* of a system describes what the system does; a specification of the user interface* describes how the system will look to the people who are going to use it.

Spreadsheet: software that supports certain types of applications like financial forecasting, planning and modelling. Examples are Excel and Multiplan.

Stand-alone: a microcomputer/PC* which can operate independently without being linked to any other machine.

Stepwise refinement: a textual method of program design in which high-level processes are progressively decomposed into smaller and simpler steps.

Structure chart: a graphical method of program design in which high-level processes are decomposed into a hierarchy of sub-processes.

Structured English: a sub-set of English which is used in process definitions*.

Structured methodology: this is a good example of tautology, since no methodology would ever claim to be unstructured. For a definition, see the entry under Methodology*.

Systems analyst: usually a member of a data processing department. A systems analyst's work has traditionally been concerned with capturing user requirements, specifying and designing the new system. He or she will also be concerned with testing the system and maintaining it.

System boundary: defines what is to be considered inside the system and what will form its environment*. On a data flow diagram* the system boundary is defined on the highest level, context diagram*.

System developer/designer: sometimes used as alternative expressions to systems analyst* but more often used in a broader way to mean someone who does the work of an analyst and a programmer.

Third-generation language: programming languages such as Pascal, FORTRAN, COBOL which are oriented more towards the user and his or her problem than towards the machine, and are therefore considered to be more *high-level* than the languages that preceded them.

Time-sharing: a computer is apparently shared by several users* or jobs at one time. In fact, each user or job has sole use of the computer for a tiny fraction of time.

Tool-box approach: an approach to system development in which the developer is equipped with a 'tool-box' of tools and techniques such as prototyping*, data modelling*, data flow diagrams*, formal notations*, and chooses the ones most suitable for the problem in hand.

Topology: the layout of a computer network*.

Trialling: system tests done by the user once the system has been installed on site; usually, real past data is used.

User: any organization or person who uses the computer system to input or process data, or who receives the results of such processing.

User interface: the parts of the system with which the users come into contact, such as screens and reports.

Validation (1): the process of ensuring that what is being developed is actually what the client wants.

Validation (2): checks built into the system to eliminate data which does not conform to specified norms, such as format and range checks.

Verification (1): the process of ensuring that what is being developed is as free from error as possible.

Verification (2): re-entry of data for checking purposes; data is retyped and checked against the original entry.

Word processor: software to facilitate certain functions such as typing, editing and printing documents, checking spelling, formatting text, adding footnotes, etc. Examples are MacWrite II and Word.

World Wide Web: software on the Internet* that allows users to access information held on computers world-wide.

Z: a language which is based on mathematics and logic and which is used for the specification* of computer systems.

ANSWERS TO SELECTED EXERCISES AND NOTES FOR DISCUSSION TOPICS

CHAPTER 1

Exercise 1.3

Students should refer to the bibliography for suitable books. Pressman's *Software Engineering: A Practitioner's Approach* covers different approaches to the software life cycle in Chapter 1. Some of the most widely used life cycle models are the waterfall, the spiral and prototyping.

Exercise 1.4

Discussion on this question should include factors such as the amount of money available, the time allowed for development, the wishes of the client, the preferences of potential users, the nature of the local area. Decisions about the system boundary should consider both the physical area to be covered by the system and the topics to be included, such as maps, transport, local walks and cycle paths, medical centres, shopping and entertainment.

CHAPTER 2

Exercise 2.1

Points to be discussed could include:

- The *software crisis* proved that new methods were needed.
- Large systems will typically involve discussions with several users and will be developed by a team.
- Need for a systematic approach to capturing user requirements.
- Need to coordinate team work, common approach, common vocabulary.

- Importance of milestones for project management—estimating and controlling a project.

Exercise 2.2

Documents in the Just a Line system:

- List of card designs
- Price list
- Customer order form and delivery note
- Supplier order form
- List of stock in hand
- Supplier invoice
- Cash book

Exercise 2.3

Points to include:

- A methodology provides a mechanism to help the developer divide the problem area into manageable portions.
- A methodology provides compatible techniques to build useful models and the ability to verify and cross-check each step of the development.
- Distinct phases, sub-phases and tasks.
- Good project management guidelines, control and evaluation.

but:

- Many different types of system exist; no methodology will be suitable for all.
- Rigid adherence to a methodology may result in unnecessary work being done, and in useful techniques being ignored because they are not part of the methodology used.

Exercise 2.4

Stage	*Deliverable*
1. Problem definition	Problem definition—statement of problems, scope and objectives of new system.
2. Feasibility study	Feasibility study report—analysis of viability of project, rough cost–benefit analysis.

Stage	*Deliverable*
3. Analysis	Specification of requirements—logical model of required system may include required logical data flow diagrams, data dictionary, process definitions, data model and entity life histories.
4. System design	Several alternative solutions (physical).
5. Detailed design	Technical design specification, includes program specifications, hardware specifications, cost estimates and an implementation schedule.
6. Implementation	Working system, includes program listings and documentation, test plan, hardware, operating procedures, clerical procedures.
7. Installation	Operational system, trained users.
8. Maintenance	Operational system, modified and documented as required.

CHAPTER 3

Exercise 3.1

- Information which is already structured in lists or forms; e.g. the supplier's catalogue
- Information about company procedures and how certain tasks are carried out at present; e.g. how orders are handled and how the various bits of paper are filed.
- Measurements such as the number of customers or the average size of an order; e.g. free supplier delivery if Just a Line order more than £300 worth.
- Problems that the client has identified in the current system; e.g. hit-and-miss stock control.
- Definite requirements for the new system; e.g. the mailing list.
- Information that is not stated directly, but where there are definite 'vibes'. Examples of this might be where the clients complain that they are always rushed when the supplier's order comes in, whereas what is actually happening is that the supplier always delivers late; 'Customers

are so chatty' meaning 'It takes ages to find out what exactly they want'; 'It's just an overall feeling of being disorganized' meaning 'We're in a right mess'.

Exercise 3.2

There are many more questions that could have been asked. Some of these are:

- How long do you keep past orders?
- Approximately how many customers do you have at the moment?
- What is your target number of customers?
- How much money do you have to spend on the system?
- How many orders do you handle on average each week?
- To what extent do you want orders from large stores to become the main part of your business?
- What happens when you have a holiday?

CHAPTER 4

Exercise 4.2

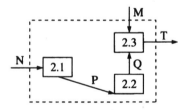

Figure E4.2 Correct version of child diagram (from Fig. 4.8)

Exercise 4.3(a)

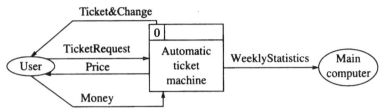

Figure E4.3(a) Automatic ticket machine: context diagram

Exercise 4.3(b)

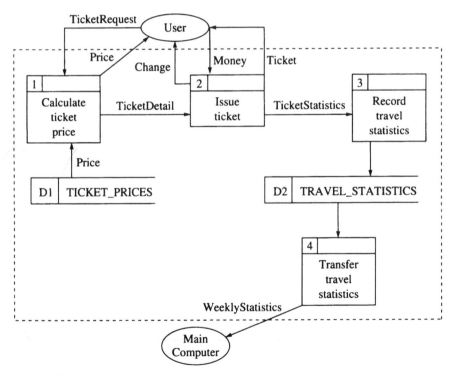

Figure E4.3(b) Automatic ticket machine: level 1 data flow diagram

Exercise 4.4

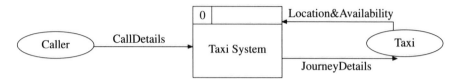

Figure E4.4(a) Taxi system: context diagram

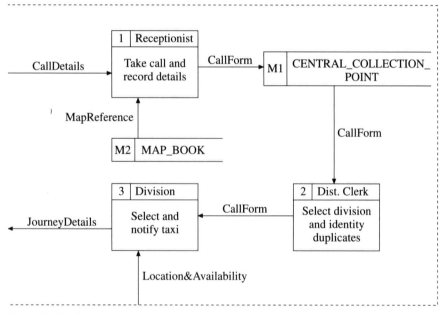

Figure E4.4(b) Taxi system: level 1 current physical data flow diagram

Exercise 4.5

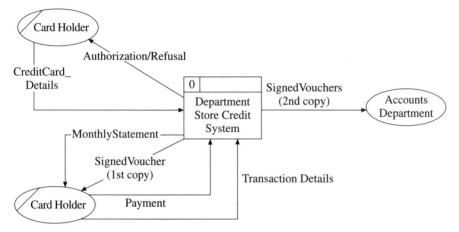

Figure E4.5(a) Credit system: context diagram

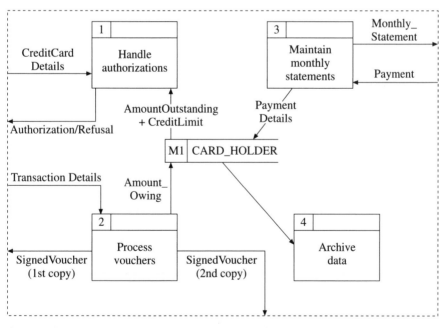

Figure E4.5(b) Credit system: level 1 current physical data flow diagram

Exercise 4.6

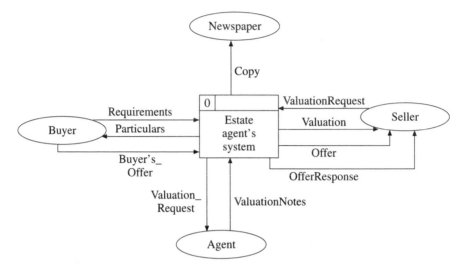

Figure E4.6(a) Estate agent's system: context diagram

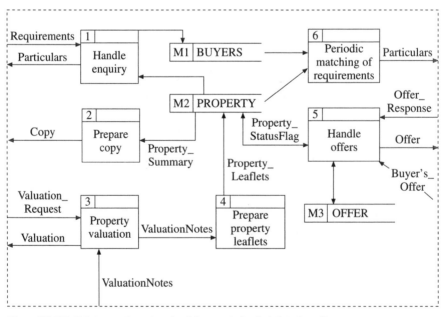

Figure E4.6(b) Estate agent's system: level 1 current physical data flow diagram

Note:

- The data flow **Particulars** appears twice on the diagram.
- Agent is shown as an external entity—this is an artificial contrivance to get **ValuationNotes** into the system. Another approach would be to have the **ValuationNotes** coming directly from the external entity **Seller**, but this seems slightly unsatisfactory.
- Two-way arrows are used to indicate data is both retrieved and updated.

Exercise 4.7

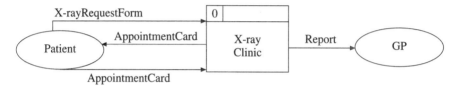

Figure E4.7(a) X-ray clinic: context diagram

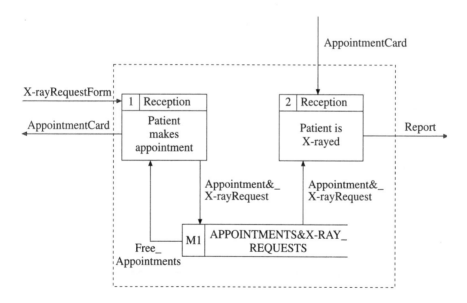

Figure E4.7(b) X-ray clinic: level 1 current physical data flow diagram

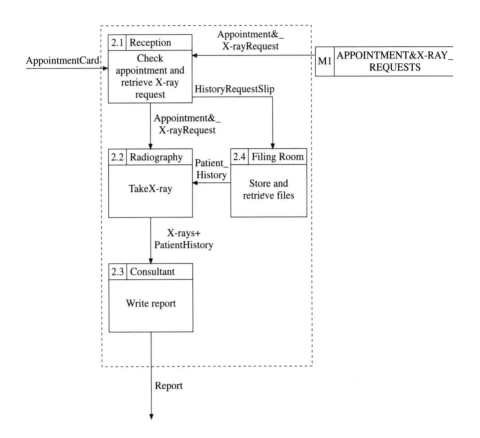

Figure E4.7(c) X-ray clinic: level 2 current physical data flow diagram

Note. The data store **M1 APPOINTMENTS&X-RAYREQUESTS** is shown outside the boundary. This indicates that the data store has already appeared in a higher-level diagram.

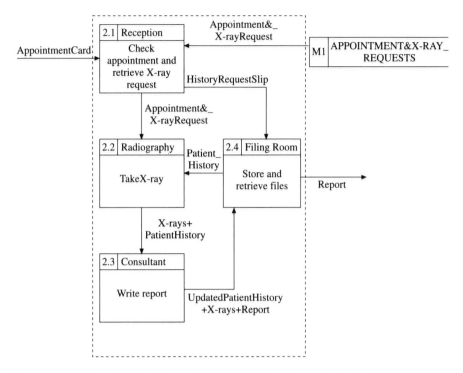

Figure E4.7(d) X-ray clinic: level 2 current physical data flow diagram (revised version)

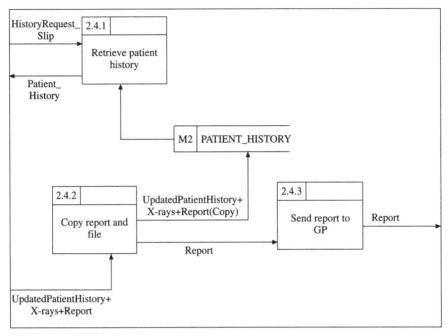

Figure E4.7(e) X-ray clinic: level 3 current physical data flow diagram

Exercise 4.8

1. The data flow between process 1.3 and the external entity **H.O.** should be labelled.
2. The flow between processes 1.2 and 1.3 has no label—it seems to be modelling flow of control, which is not allowed.
3. One of the flows from process 1.2 is labelled **SendOutBill**. This contains an active verb, indicating that the flow is being used to model an activity.
4. The diagram has no boundary.
5. The data flow between data stores D1 and D2 is not allowed—it must go via a process.
6. The process **Handle stock requirements** has no reference number.
7. The duplication indicator should appear on both occurrences of the data store **ROUNDSMAN'S BOOK**.
8. The flow NewPrices from the external entity **H.O.** to the data store **ROUNDSMAN'S BOOK** should go via a process.
9. The data stores should have a reference number prefix **M...** not **D....**

Exercise 4.9

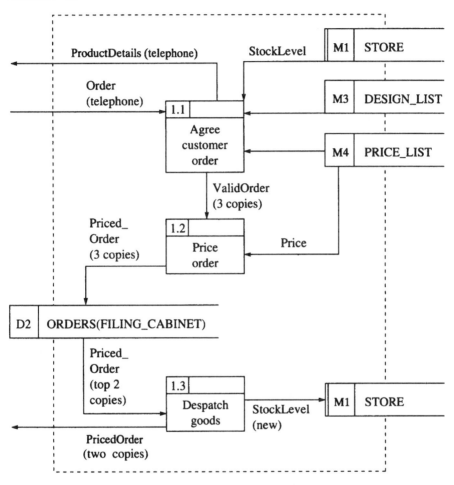

Figure E4.9 Just a Line CPDFD level 2 expansion of process 1

Exercise 4.10

Questions might include:

- When and how is the Design list updated?
- When and how is the price list updated?
- Are the petty cash and banking transactions to be excluded from the project?
- Exactly what information is recorded in the cash book?
- Exactly what information is recorded in the design list and price list?
- Are customers charged for delivery or postage?
- Do the designs have code numbers or are they identified by description only?

Exercise 4.13

Points include:

- CPDFDs are useful if the system seems very complicated and users give conflicting accounts.
- CPDFDs see the system in the user's terms (forms in triplicate, pink cards, filing cabinets, telephone calls, etc.). Less sophisticated users may find this easier to follow than the more abstract CLDFD.
- Drawing a CPDFD may influence the system developer's design of the new system; it may prove hard to break away from the old design.
- Drawing both a CPDFD and a CLDFD is time-consuming.
- Experienced developers may draw data flow diagrams *while* the user is describing the system. This helps the user to understand the notation and helps the developer to realize where there are gaps in his or her understanding of the system and ask appropriate questions.

Exercise 4.14

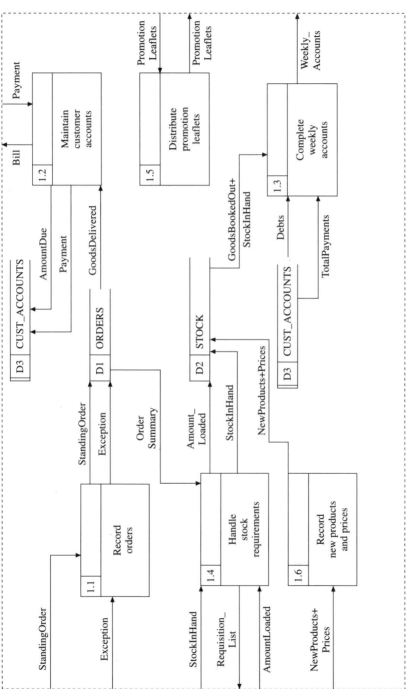

Figure E4.14 Milk delivery: level 2 current logical data flow diagram

Note:

- Notice that the level 1 diagram partitions the system into the jobs done by different people at Buttercup Dairies. This is often how users view the system and therefore it is helpful to model it in this way.
- On the level 2 CPDFD the jobs are clearly seen as those done at home, those done on the round and those done at the depot; i.e. jobs are grouped according to where they are done. Partitioning the system according to location is another typical feature of modelling done of the current physical stage. Both types of partitioning are abandoned at the current logical stage as it becomes irrelevant who does a particular job, or where it is done.

Exercise 4.18

Change	= *amount of money returned if Money > Price*
Money	= *amount input by User*
Price	= *price of ticket*
Ticket	= Date + IssuingStation + Destination + Price + TicketType
TicketDetail	= Destination + TicketType + Price
TICKET_PRICES	= Destination + {TicketType + Price}
TicketRequest	= Destination + TicketType
TicketStatistics	= TicketRequest
TRAVEL_STATISTICS	= {WeeklyStatistics}
WeeklyStatistics	= Date + {Destination + {TicketType + No.Sold}}

Exercise 4.19

Statement	= StmtNo + CardNo + StmtDate + CustName + CustAddr + {TransactionDate + Code + (DebitAmt) + (CreditAmt)} + PaymentDue + CreditBalance
Code	= [Department	Reference]

Alternatively, the document can be described more elegantly using data structures:

Statement	= StmtHeader + {StmtLines} + PaymentDue + CreditBalance
StmtHeader	= StmtNo + CardNo + StmtDate + CustName + CustAddr
StmtLines	= TransactionDate + Code + (DebitAmt) + (CreditAmt)
Code	= [Department	Reference]

Exercise 4.20

StandingOrder	= CustomerDetails + StandingOrderDetails
CustomerDetails	= CustomerAddress + CustomerName + DeliveryPoint
StandingOrderDetails	= {Day + {Product + Quantity}}
Exception	= CustomerAddress *used as identifier* + {Date + {Product + Quantity *may be positive or negative*}}
ROUNDMAN'S_BOOK	= RoundNumber + {CustomerPage}
CustomerPage	= CustomerDetails + StandingOrderDetails + {WeeklyAccountDetails}
WeeklyAccountDetails	= {Week'sException} + AmountDue + (Payment)
Week'sException	= Date + {Product + Quantity}

Exercise 4.22

Red	Y	Y	N	N	
Amber	N	Y	N	Y	
Green	N	N	Y	N	
Go			X		
Stop	X				
Prepare to stop				X	
Prepare to go		X			

Figure E4.22 Decision table

Exercise 4.23(a)

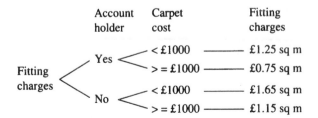

Figure E4.23(a) Decision tree

Exercise 4.23(b)

```
IF Customer is AccountHolder THEN
        IF CarpetCost < £1000 THEN
                FittingCharge = £1.25 per sq m
        ELSE (* CarpetCost > = £1000 *)
                FittingCharge = £0.75 per sq m
ELSE (* Customer not AccountHolder *)
        IF CarpetCost < £1000 THEN
                FittingCharge = £1.65 per sq m
        ELSE (* CarpetCost > = £1000 *)
                FittingCharge = £1.15 per sq m
```

Exercise 4.25(a)

Process 1: Calculate ticket price

Get **TicketRequest** from **User**
Get **Price** of **Destination** from **D1 TICKET_PRICES**
Display **Price** to **User**
Send **TicketDetail** to process 2: Issue ticket

Exercise 4.25(b)

Process 2: Issue ticket

Get **TicketDetail** from process 1: Calculate ticket price
Get **Money** from **User**
IF **Money** > **Price** THEN
        Give **Change** to **User**
Issue **Ticket** to **User**
Send **TravelStatistics** to process 3: Record travel statistics

CHAPTER 5

Exercise 5.1

(a) Candidate keys are EmpNo, Name and StartDate. Scale, DeptNo and OfficeNo are not candidate keys because none of them is unique to each employee. ExtNo is not a candidate key because I.Oxford does not have an extension number—this attribute, therefore, can have null values.
(b) EmpNo will make the best primary key because it uniquely identifies each

employee, its allocation is under the control of the system users, it never has a null value and it is not liable to change. Name would not make a good primary key as an employee's name can change and it is quite possible, over a period of time, that the company might employ two people with the same name, although that is not the case at the moment. StartDate would not make a good primary key because it is quite possible for two employees to start work on the same day.

Exercise 5.4(a)

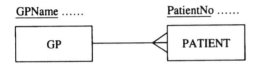

Figure E5.4(a) A GP has many patients, a patient has one GP

Exercise 5.4(b)

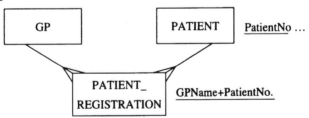

Figure E5.4(b) A GP has many patients, a patient may be registered with many GPs

Exercise 5.5

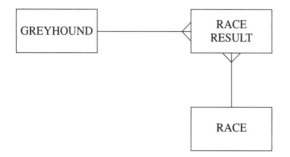

RACE_RESULT=DogNo+RaceNo+FinishingPosition...

Figure E5.5 Introduction of intersection entity

Exercise 5.6

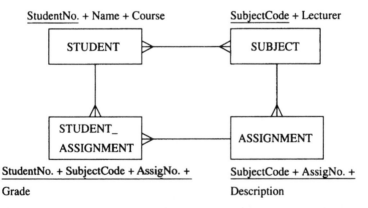

Figure E5.6 E–R model showing relationships of STUDENTS, ASSIGNMENTS and SUBJECTS

Exercise 5.7

UNF TREATMENT_CARD = AnimalNo. + Name + Breed + BlockNo. + Type + BlockName + {StartDate + DrugCode + DrugName + Dosage + Condition + Length}

1NF AnimalNo. + Name + Breed + BlockNo. + Type + BlockName
AnimalNo. + StartDate + DrugCode + DrugName + Dosage + Condition + Length

2NF AnimalNo. + Name + Breed + BlockNo. + Type + BlockName
AnimalNo. + StartDate + DrugCode + Dosage + Condition + Length
DrugCode + DrugName

3NF AnimalNo. + Name + Breed + BlockNo.*
BlockNo. + Type + BlockName
AnimalNo. + StartDate + DrugCode + Dosage + Condition + Length
DrugCode + DrugName

Exercise 5.9

1NF DrNo + DrName + DrAddr + DrPhone
DrNo + Day + Dept
DrNo + Day + Time + PatientNo + PatientName + PatientAddr + GPNo + GPName + GPAddr + GPPhone

2NF All of the 1NF entities are also in 2NF

3NF DrNo + DrName + DrAddr + DrPhone
DrNo + Day + Dept
DrNo + Day + Time + PatientNo*
PatientNo + PatientName + PatientAddr + GPNo*
GPNo + GPName + GPAddr + GPPhone

CHAPTER 6

Exercise 6.1

(a) Customer places order. (b) No, it must go through the validation process first. (c) Any number of times, including zero. (d) No. (e) The order must either have been delivered or cancelled.

Exercise 6.2

Figure 6.11(b) is correct.

Exercise 6.3

It is not correct to draw a repeat node and an event node at the same level from the same box.

Exercise 6.4

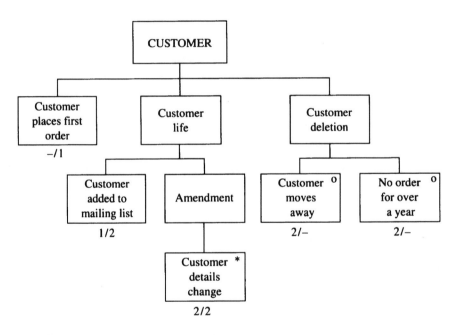

Figure E6.4 CUSTOMER entity life history for the Just a Line required system

Exercise 6.5

When an order is filled an occurrence of the INVOICE entity is created. During the life of the invoice one of two things will happen, either the invoice is paid or the goods are returned. Finally, the details of the invoice are deleted.

CHAPTER 7

Exercise 7.4

Points to be discussed could include:

- Symptoms. Systems are often late, over budget or not what was required.
- Possible causes. Today's systems are increasingly complex: we do not have enough properly trained software developers to satisfy demand.
- CASE tools solve many of the software developer's problems in using structured techniques—consistency checking, getting bogged down in detail, difficulty in modifying complex diagrams.
- CASE tools can help with documentation, version control and management of large projects.
- CASE tools support traditional methodologies. Is this the best way to develop the sort of system which are required today?

Exercise 7.5

Points to include:

- Formal notations are not designed for user communication, but are excellent for communication between trained software developers.
- They help the designer to gain a better understanding of the problem area.
- They force rigour and precision in the early stages of development.
- Some formal languages (e.g. Z) include extensive comments in natural English which can be understood by the average user.
- Possible tools for communication with the client include prototyping, diagrams and natural language.

Exercise 7.6

Points to include:

- The rigour and precision of introducing formality at an early stage in development raise many questions about the nature and problems of the system (e.g. error cases).
- A formal language is of particular use in safety-critical systems.
- It can be helpful in dealing with complex parts of any system.
- It takes time and effort to learn a formal notation.
- It is very difficult to use a formal notation when communicating with users.
- Formal notations have no underlying methodology to act as a framework for the development process.

Exercise 7.7

The schema in Fig. 7.14 does not include the pre-condition:

$$dom(CustomerDetails?) \cap dom(CustomerFile) = \{\}$$

This means that when the user tries to enter details for a new customer there is no check to see whether that customer is already on the Just a Line customer file. Failure to check for duplicate customers may result in a file with entries such as:

Blake	Mrs	Helen	14,	High Street, Oldham	OD1 8PL
Blake	Mrs	Helen	14,	High Street, Oldham	OD1 8PL
Blake	Mrs	Helen	74,	Hill Road, Oldham	OD4 6HJ

It is impossible to tell from this whether there are two Mrs Blakes or one Mrs Blake who has changed her address. There would be further confusion in the latter case, since we cannot tell which address is the current one.

CHAPTER 8

Exercise 8.1

It is very difficult to think of a system that has no links with any others. An example that comes close to total independence is the system of a chicken growing inside an egg.

Exercise 8.3

Evaluation of the three topologies should raise the following points:

Star topology:

- While the central machine has spare ports, more computers can easily be added.
- Controlling will be handled by the central machine.
- The topology does not involve much cabling.
- The central machine is a possible bottle-neck.
- If the central machine breaks down the whole network is disabled.

Fully connected point-to-point topology:

- No obvious bottle-necks.
- If a machine breaks down the others are not affected.
- Lots of cabling—expensive.
- It is complicated and expensive to add more machines.

Multipoint ring:

- Not too much cabling.
- Easy to add more machines.
- The central ring could become a bottle-neck.
- If one computer breaks down the others are unaffected, but if the central ring breaks down the whole network is disabled.

CHAPTER 9

Exercise 9.2

Examples of valid data:

- 46 72 9 501.   (random whole numbers)
- 34 34 34 8 33.   (more than one instance of largest number)
- 34 5 34 26 13.   (largest number appears more than once, but not consecutively)
- 0 123456 42 999.   (0 as instance of whole number)
- 5.   (only one number input)

Examples of invalid data:

- 4 8.7 32 1.   (real number included in series)
- 4 8 2F 22.   (hexadecimal number included in series)
- 4 8 M 22.   (letter included in series)
- 4 & 8 22.   (non-alphanumeric character included)
- 4 8 54 22   (no full stop to terminate series)

Exercise 9.3

School library system:

- Probably not large enough for phased implementation or pilot running, although could initially be introduced for one class only.
- Unlikely that there are enough staff to cope with the extra load of parallel running.

- If the system breaks down it is inconvenient, but not disastrous, so direct changeover is probably the most appropriate method.

GPs' system:

- Pilot running a possibility, using selected patients only.
- There must be a back-up for the system, so direct changeover is too risky.
- Parallel running is probably the best method, as long as the surgery staff can cope with the increased work load.

Dairy system:

- Probably not worth the extra effort of parallel running.
- Phased implementation possible.
- Direct implementation a possibility as long as the client understands the risks involved.
- Pilot running, using one round only, probably the most suitable option.

CHAPTER 10

Exercise 10.1

The following points should be included:

- A team of developers will be needed (potential problems of group work).
- Must have a project leader/manager.
- Organization and communication among team members take up time.
- Probably more than one user.
- More partitioning of the problem required.
- Many tasks to be scheduled.
- Task dependencies and the critical path become more important.
- More resources to be organized and allocated.

Exercise 10.2

Some project management will be needed, but too much could be overkill on a small project. Points raised could include:

- Optimum team size (small).
- Is a separate project manager necessary?

- Tasks need to be defined and scheduled.
- Resources need to be organized.
- Milestones should be set.
- The progress of the project needs to be monitored and controlled.

INDEX